W9-BZO-537

day trips® from
washington, dc

help us keep this guide up to date

We would love to hear from you concerning your experiences with this guide and how you feel it could be improved and kept up to date. Please send your comments and suggestions to:

editorial@GlobePequot.com

Thanks for your input, and happy travels!

day trips® series

day trips® from washington, dc

second edition

getaway ideas for the local traveler

beth kanter

travel

Guilford, Connecticut

Copyright © 2014 Rowman & Littlefield.

Day Trips is a registered trademark of Rowman & Littlefield.

Distributed by NATIONAL BOOK NETWORK

Maps: Ryan Mitchell © Rowman & Littlefield.
Spot photography throughout licensed by Shutterstock.com

ISBN 978-0-7627-9671-7
ISSN 2155-5508

Printed in the United States of America

contents

about the author

Beth Kanter's books and articles help visitors and locals alike experience the tastes, sights, and unique feel of the nation's capital. In addition to *Day Trips from Washington DC*, Beth has written two other books about her favorite city and the region surrounding it: *Food Lovers' Guide to Washington DC* and the critically acclaimed *Washington DC Chef's Table*. Beth's essays and articles have appeared in national newspapers, magazines, and online. Beth has an MSJ from Northwestern's Medill School of Journalism and, when not writing about her favorite city, teaches writing workshops and speaks about local food and travel trends.

acknowledgments

I am very lucky to have so many people to thank who helped me along the way with the creation of this guide. Many thanks to Amy Lyons and her team at Globe Pequot Press. Representatives at many of the visitor bureaus in the region were generous with their time and insights during the writing of both editions, including Tiffany Ahalt at the Tourism Council of Frederick County, Rocell Viniard at National Harbor, Jeanne Mozier at Travel Berkeley Springs, Erin Ebagnell at Richmond Metropolitan Convention and Visitors Bureau, and Susan Steckman at the Annapolis and Anne Arundel County Conference and Visitors Bureau.

Jennifer Buske-Sigal of Visit Loudoun, Barbara Curtis of Ladew Topiary Gardens, Monee Cottman at Visit Baltimore, Michelle Kershner with the Tourism Council of Frederick County and Frederick Visitor Center, Lori Sorrentino with the Culpeper Department of Tourism, Julie Smith with the Annapolis and Anne Arundel County Conference and Visitors Bureau, Sue-Jean Chun for Volt and Family Meal.

A shout-out to Gayle Neufeld, Steve Neufeld, Ethan Neufeld, Shira Neufeld, and Zoe Neufeld for their expert Eastern Shore tips as well as for their special brand of Shore hospitality.

My very own personal day trip entourage of Jeff, Gabriel, and Miriam always make the journey as much fun as the destination, and for that and so much more I am grateful. I can't imagine three better travel partners. And finally, to Jeff, thanks for being my ultimate travel companion, navigator, mapmaker, and copilot all these many years—past, present, and future.

introduction

For a time when I was growing up, Sunday mornings meant climbing into the backseat of my parents' beige Chevy Nova for a destination unknown. Unknown, at least, to my brother and me. While we always begged, pleaded, and hoped that the car would stop at Great Adventure, it never did. But even without Tilt-A-Whirls and log flumes, more often than not the places we wound up at turned out to be great adventures, or at the very least pretty good ones. Our Sunday morning mystery voyages helped me develop an affinity for the day trip, that wonderfully accessible act of hopping into a car (owned, borrowed, or rented) and driving somewhere pretty, fun, historic, or wacky without having to print out a boarding pass or fit your favorite pair of boots into a carry-on bag.

When I moved to Washington, DC, more than twenty years ago I brought with me my love of the road trip. And, as luck would have it, I landed in one of the best day-tripping starting points in the country. In addition to being a city packed with its own collection of places to explore, Washington neighbors states with an unbelievable number of parks, historic homes, waterfalls, monuments, farms, beaches, lakes, archaeological excavations, mountains, Civil War battlefields, campgrounds, trails, horse stables, wineries, museums, and even an amusement park or two that rivals the one I begged to go to as a kid. Along the way there are also world-class inns, restaurants, and performance venues as well as plenty of lesser-known but equally appealing greasy spoons, farm stands, coffeehouses, regional theaters, and artisan cooperatives. The diversity of the sites within driving distance from the city means most everyone can find something to make them happy. My favorites fill these pages.

The best part of being a local travel writer and the experience of researching this guide is that there always is a new favorite to be found. (Readers, feel free to insert your favorite life metaphor here.) Although I have been berry picking dozens of times in Gaithersburg, it wasn't until I started this book that I discovered an amazing farm where developmentally disabled adults harvest vegetables for local food banks and staff members live in a cutting-edge solar-powered farmhouse. In Poolesville a Buddhist temple with an aviary for abused and abandoned parrots somehow managed to escape my radar. The same holds true for the mother and daughter–run Seven Oaks Lavender Farm, the Annapolis Ice Cream Company (where the plastic spoon I decorated now joins a collection of many thousands), and the Stoltz Listening Room upstairs at the Avalon Theater. And I am not sure how I survived this long without Ladew Topiary Gardens, the Waterford Fair, the North Market Pop Shop, Gina's, and Comus Market in my life.

If you share my obsession for small picturesque towns you will be hard pressed to find ones more charming—or smaller than—Waterford, The Plains, Washington, Warrenton, or Paris, Virginia. Although each has its own distinct personality, all offer that back-in-time feeling so many of us crave when we place the city in the rearview mirror. The woman who runs Waterford's authentic (and only) general store often greets guests from behind her spinning wheel and can sometimes be seen out back tending to her sheep. Although Paris and The Plains claim about as many residents as a full transatlantic flight, they still play a huge part in creating the allure of Virginia's horse and hunt country. And the beauty of Little Washington and surrounding Rappahannock County make anything but a small impression. Berkeley Springs, known for its naturally occurring hot springs and the only place I know with the tagline "George Washington bathed here," often gets voted America's best small town and gets props from me, too. You'll likely be similarly persuaded after a soak in the Roman baths or a showing at a 1928 movie theater with a box of popcorn made in a vintage Manley hot-oil machine. Just a few miles from downtown Berkeley Springs is Cacapon Resort State Park. The park's rustic cabins, lake, and hiking trails might as well be the French Riviera to some kids I know, including my own, who weeks before we go literally start counting down the days until our annual trip.

Hiking trails near DC are by no means limited to Cacapon. The inns and campgrounds in and near the trail-filled Shenandoah National Park fill up during peak fall foliage long before the leaves start changing colors. The not-as-well-known Sugarloaf Mountain also has something of a cult following around these parts, probably because it embodies the day-tripping trifecta—close, easy, and beautiful. Ditto for Oxon Hill Farm and Brookside Gardens. Creatures big and small can be spied at both sites, throughout the region, and occasionally when you least expect it, so drive accordingly on those country roads. The Luray Zoo provides a home for abused animals, and the once endangered bald eagle soars again at Blackwater National Wildlife Refuge and the Pickering Creek Audubon Center.

You also can take a boat ride from one of the nearby Eastern Shore towns to get a better look at the sea life in the bay or collect sea breezes and charm in Talbot County, Maryland. Nearby, the Annmarie Garden Sculpture Park presents a whimsical take on life near the bay, life in general, and the human form.

Worry not if you break out in hives when you stray too far from the big city. Richmond has been perfecting its urban vibe in recent years with great results, and Baltimore, with all its John Waters–brand grit, is an urban adventure unto itself complete with quirky cafes, galleries, and even an anarchist bookstore. Alternatively, if you're not in the mood to dance at the revolution, you can spend a perfectly conventional but perfectly pleasant day at the ballpark watching a game.

Unlike when I first moved to the area years ago, you no longer have to stay within a city's limits to find a great meal, although Richmond and Baltimore certainly have many. (Baltimore's Woodberry Kitchen is worth every minute and every cent of gas it takes to get there.) Frederick's Volt and The Inn at Little Washington are shining stars of the destination-dining revolution and rival any downtown restaurant. Authentic, delicious, and affordable ethnic dishes are, along with Brookside Gardens, hidden treasures of Wheaton. If you crave retail therapy along with your meal then plan on spending some time in the many indie boutiques and shops outside of Washington, with the ones in Leesburg, Richmond, Baltimore, Culpeper, and Annapolis leading the pack. For something actually out of the box, check out on of the pop-up barn sales outside Frederick. These expertly curated sales will get up the heart rate of vintage shoppers and lovers of all things repurposed and pretty.

Whether you prefer urban streets, cobblestone sidewalks, sandy beaches, dirt roads, or historic pathways, the region surrounding the nation's capital holds many destinations where you'll want to leave your footprints over and over again. Even without the old Nova, I have a very good feeling that a great adventure awaits you.

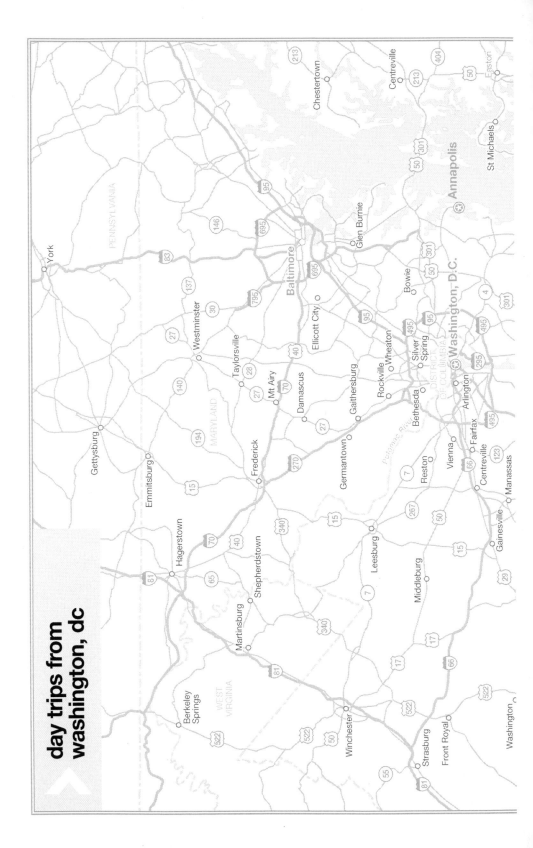

day trips from
washington, dc

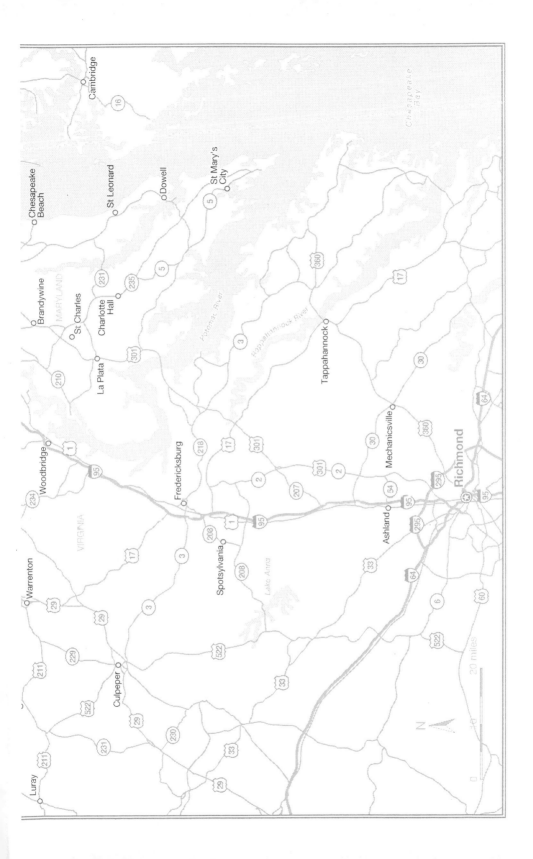

 **using this guide**

hours of operation, prices & credit cards

This book is organized by geographical direction—north, northeast, east, southeast, south, southwest, west, and northwest. I've recommended several trips, all within two hours of DC, in each direction with the hope that you will enjoy my discoveries in addition to finding some of your own. A good map or app can help supplement the directions given here and are both good traveling tools to always have on hand. Like most things in life, hours of operation and admission fees can and do change, so always remember to call ahead. Most establishments listed in the book accept major credit cards unless otherwise noted. Since you never know when you're going to find a roadside peach sale—or even a lemonade stand—having some cash on hand ranks up there with packing snacks as good road-trip practice.

pricing key

accommodations

Most room rates are based on double occupancy in a standard room before taxes. Many inns, hotels, and B&Bs offer off-season, online, and other special rates. During the height of the season and on weekends, many smaller places require a minimum stay of two nights or more and sometimes charge cancellation fees. It's always a good idea to inquire about these points before you book a room. Also, if you are traveling with children or pets, find out what the establishment's policy is prior to check-in.

$ inexpensive, less than $125

$$ moderate, $125 to $200

$$$ expensive, more than $200

restaurants

Restaurant prices are based on dinner entrees for two before tax. Some restaurants in smaller towns are closed Monday and Tuesday and for longer stretches during the off-season.

$ inexpensive, $20 or less

$$ moderate, $20 to $40

$$$ expensive, more than $40

driving tips

Talking on a cell phone and sending text messages while driving (collectively known as distracted driving) have become two of the biggest causes of traffic accidents in recent years. Texting while driving is banned in Maryland, DC, and Virginia and is always dangerous. Cell phone and texting laws seem to be moving in the direction of stricter regulation, so be safe and wait to send that message or return a call when you are *not* behind the wheel. In DC you can get a ticket for talking on a cell phone without using a hands-free device.

Moving violations aren't the only tickets written regularly throughout the region. Read signs very carefully when you park on the street, feed your meter often, and opt for parking structures when possible. (Trust me, I speak from experience . . .) City drivers often take the opportunity to fill up their gas tanks in Virginia, as the prices tend to be cheaper.

Many of the roads that take you to the places listed on these pages see the occasional deer and other animals. Be careful when driving, especially at night.

The regions surrounding Washington are not without their quirks and idiosyncrasies. Enough accents to make Henry Higgins's head spin can be heard in the area, so get ready to hear everything from "Bawlmer" to "y'all." No matter which direction you choose, crab is pretty much king when it comes to food. Expect to find numerous establishments claiming "the best" crab cakes around. I'll let you be the judge. As you head over the border into Virginia, the Southern influence can be seen in everything from the cuisine to the accent. Expect to see dishes like grits and scrapple popping up on menus. Sweet tea also is a favorite in these parts. If you order iced tea in Southern towns like Culpeper, you will likely get sweetened tea unless you specify otherwise.

Many restaurants and attractions, particularly those in smaller towns, are closed Monday and sometimes Tuesday, too. If you are planning a beginning-of-the-week trip, check before you go. Many sites also keep off-season winter hours, especially along the Eastern Shore. Some places even close in the dead of winter for weeks or months at a time.

where to get more information

general information

Maryland Office of Tourism Development
401 E. Pratt St., 14th Fl.
Baltimore, MD 21202
(866) 639-3526
visitmaryland.org

Virginia Tourism Corporation
901 E. Byrd St.
Richmond, VA 23219
(800) 847-4882
virginia.org

West Virginia Division of Tourism
West Virginia Department of Commerce
Capitol Complex, Bldg. 6, Rm. 525
Charleston, WV 25305-0311
(304) 558-2200
wvcommerce.org

lodging

American Historic Inns Inc.
PO Box 669
Dana Point, CA 92629
(949) 481-6256
iloveinns.com

BedandBreakfast.com
1011 W. 5th St., Ste. 300
Austin, TX 78703
(512) 322-2710

Bed and Breakfast Association of Virginia
(888) 660-2228
innvirginia.com

Maryland Bed and Breakfast Association
marylandbb.com

Mountainstate Association Bed and Breakfast
wvbedandbreakfasts.com

national park service

Department of the Interior
1849 C St. NW
Washington, DC 20240
(202) 208-3100
nps.gov

Maryland Park Service
Maryland Department of Natural Resources
580 Taylor Ave.
Tawes State Office Bldg.
Annapolis, MD 21401
(800) 830-3974
dnr.state.md.us/publiclands

Virginia Department of Conservation and Recreation
203 Governor St.
Richmond, VA 23219
(804) 786-1712
dcr.virginia.gov

West Virginia State Parks and Forests
324 4th Ave.
South Charleston, WV 25303
(304) 558-2764
wvstateparks.com

history

The Civil War Preservation Trust
1156 15th Street NW, Ste. 900
Washington, DC 20005
(202) 367-1861
civilwardiscoverytrail.org

Maryland Historical Society
201 W. Monument St.
Baltimore, MD 21201
(410) 685-3750
mdhs.org

Virginia Historical Society
428 North Blvd.
Richmond, VA 23220
(804) 358-4901
vahistorical.org

West Virginia Division of Culture and History
The Culture Center
Capitol Complex
1900 Kanawha Blvd.
East Charleston, WV 25305
(304) 558-0220
wvculture.org

wine & spirits

Maryland Wineries Association
22 W. Padonia Rd., Ste. C-236
Timonium, MD 21093
(410) 252-9463
marylandwine.com

Virginia Wine
1001 E. Broad St., Ste. 140
Richmond, Virginia 23219
(804) 344-8200
virginiawine.org

north

>>>

day trip 01

north

>>> **madame butterfly's magical gardens:**
wheaton, md

wheaton

At first glance Wheaton may seem like one of those places that you drive past, not drive to. But if you look beyond the box stores and the aging strip malls you will find gems hiding in this suburban Maryland town.

Wheaton Regional Park is that treasure. The massive park has many components to it that offer places to hike, picnic, play, and fish. Brookside Garden is the park's most beautiful section. The more than 50 acres of public gardens bloom year-round and offer many peaceful spots to walk, read, or wander. Brookside also runs a wide range of lectures, classes, and special events such as its wildly popular "Garden of Lights," where close to a million twinkling lights are turned into illuminated scenes for the winter holidays. The antique carousel and mini steam train nearby in Wheaton Regional Park proper will delight children, to say nothing of the child in you. The park also offers picnic spots, a lake, nature center, tennis bubble, ball fields, an indoor ice rink, and hiking trails. After a few spins on the merry-go-round, you might even feel ready to graduate to a real live horse at Wheaton Park Stables. So pack a picnic, charge your camera battery, and plan to stay awhile.

getting there

Brookside Gardens is about a twenty-minute drive from DC. Get on I-495 (Capital Beltway) and take exit 31A, Wheaton. Drive 3 miles north on Georgia Avenue to Randolph Road and

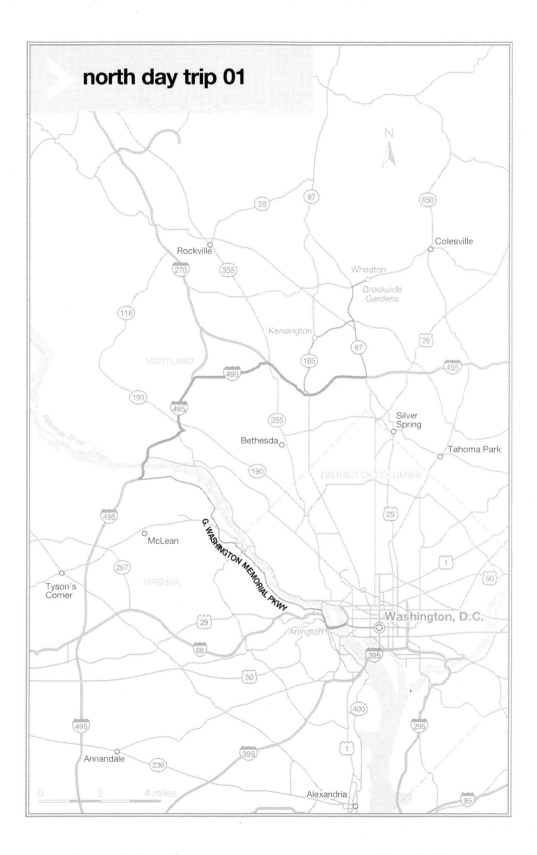

north day trip 01

turn right. At the second traffic light, turn right onto Glenallan Avenue. Make a right into the gardens.

Brookside Gardens technically is part of the Wheaton Regional Park. Follow the signs to drive to the adjacent park.

where to go

Brookside Gardens. 1800 Glenallan Ave., Wheaton, MD; (301) 962-1400; brookside gardens.org. Every time I drive through the gates to Brookside Garden I can almost feel my blood pressure drop a few points. And once I walk through the visitor center and into the gardens, I always wonder why I don't come to this botanical oasis more often.

The beautifully kept public gardens, which first opened in 1969, have many different faces and seasons. From June to September the rose garden draws in visitors with its pink, yellow, peach, and red blooms. Wooded paths, shaded benches, and fountains dot the garden, enticing visitors to stay awhile and admire the more than one hundred rose varieties, including the Julia Child Rose, a lovely variety that has a (what else?) buttery yellow flower.

The sweet-smelling blooms in this section act as perfumed reminder of the garden's original goal when it was first planted in 1972. This area originally was conceived as way to allow blind visitors to share in the garden experience through the scent of the flowers and the trickling sounds of the water features. The signs in this part of the garden have been translated into braille and still remain part of the garden. Today all visitors continue to have their sense tickled here. Elsewhere at Brookside, the semi-wooded azalea garden in early spring is saturated with color, while the Japanese-style garden, with its rolling hills and ponds, remains peaceful and understated in every season. A small children's section near the visitor center is the right size for preschoolers, who will likely love the whimsical tree houses and the chance to collect and examine leaves, pinecones, and sticks at the sorting display. A new theme graces the children's garden each year, but the cute factor and appeal always carry over to the new design.

In the fall, the foliage blazes with yellows, oranges, and reds of the season and the autumnal colors pop against the majesty of the bright blue fall sky and can be admired from all points in this enchanted garden.

While you are here please remember that food and drink are not permitted in the gardens; however, picnic facilities can be found nearby at the Shorefield Area of Wheaton Regional Park. Pets are not allowed in Brookside Gardens and permits are required for professional photography.

Brookside is perhaps best known for two of its annual events, the "Wings of Fancy" live butterfly exhibit and the "Garden of Lights" holiday display. Hundreds of butterflies from around the world flutter about from May to September in the Wings of Fancy greenhouses. It's somewhat magical to experience the winged creatures fluttering about en masse and to see up close why they have been given such descriptive monikers as Blue Tiger, Zebra Longwing, or Mournful Owl. Be prepared for the chance of a butterfly landing on your shoulder or camera lens. You also will get to see the entire life cycle of the colorful insects, from eggs to fully formed flying butterflies. Peak hours are from 10 a.m. to 1 p.m. Tickets, which cost $6 for adults and $4 for children, are required and your stamped stub allows you to reenter the exhibit at any point during the day.

The butterflies will stay away during the summer of 2014 while some scheduled renovations take place, but they will fly back for the 2015 season.

Garden of Lights brightens up dark December nights with its creative displays, crafted from small twinkling bulbs in a rainbow of colors. Lights are fashioned into everything from the Loch Ness Monster to swans that float upon the water. Twinkling snowflakes hang from trees and some years you may even spot a glowing giraffe or tiger poking out among the trees. Unlike many local light displays, this one allows you to get up close to it. Live music often accompanies the display and a hot chocolate run is a ritual for many a visitor. Tickets are needed, tend to sell out quickly, and cost about $15 per car Mon through Thurs and $20 per car on the weekend. You must enter in a car—pedestrians are not allowed through the gate. Brookside Gardens is open from sunrise to sunset year-round and visitor center hours are from 9 a.m. to 5 p.m. Admission is free except for special events, classes, and exhibits.

Brookside Nature Center, Wheaton Regional Park. 1400 Glenallen Ave., Wheaton, MD; (301) 962-1480; montgomeryparks.org. Just beyond the gardens you will find Brookside Nature Center. The center runs a full calendar of eco-centered, hands-on programs, classes, hikes, and lectures for children, families, and adults. Offerings include everything from mushroom identification walks to campfires with marshmallow roasts. Inside the center find a children's discovery room, exhibits, and observation stations. Glass tanks line a wall inside and contain the same kinds of small animals that inhabit the park, like snakes, tree frogs, and salamanders. Outside the center there are miles of hiking trails, a wildlife pond, and a wooded nature exploration area that is especially popular with kids. Three seasonal festivals anchor the center's year and all are worthy of adding to your calendars—a maple sugar festival in February, the "Forest Friends" festival in April, and the apple festival in October. If you can't get enough of this kind of stuff contact the Center for volunteer opportunities and you might just find yourself refilling the flying-squirrel feeders.

McCrillis Gardens & Gallery. 6910 Greentree Rd., Bethesda, MD; (301) 962-1455; montgomeryparks.org/brookside/mccrillis_gardens.shtm. The horticultural team of Brookside also works its magic at the McCrillis Gardens and Gallery in Bethesda. Managed by Brookside, the wooded Bethesda garden also serves as home to the Brookside School of Botanical Art and Illustration, which sponsors a range of classes and programs that link art with nature.

Wheaton Carousel & Miniature Train at Wheaton Regional Park. 2002 Shorefield Rd., Wheaton, MD; (301) 942-6703; montgomeryparks.org/enterprise/park_facilities/trains/wheaton.shtm. Hop on one of the thirty-three horses, three zebras, or two chariots and get ready for a magical ride on an early twentieth-century hand-carved, hand-painted carousel.

This beautiful Ovid Hazen Wells carousel once sat on the National Mall before moving to Wheaton Park in 1981. When you're done going around in circles, hop aboard a miniature replica of a Huntington steam locomotive for a ten-minute ride that winds through the park, past Pine Lake, and over a trestle bridge. In the rest of the expansive park you'll find grills, 11 miles of hiking trails, walking paths, playgrounds, picnic shelters, sports fields, and lake fishing. There is also an ice-skating rink and indoor and outdoor tennis courts on the south side of the park.

Wheaton Park Stables. 1101 Glenallan Ave., Wheaton, MD; (301) 622-2424; wheaton parkstables.com. Nestled in the north corner of the park is Wheaton Park Stables, which offers the opportunity to appreciate the park on horseback. On most Sundays at 1, 2, and 3 p.m. guided trail rides take riders—even those with no experience at all—along the park's 1.5 miles of bridle paths. Children must be at least eight years old to participate. The cost is $40 per person and reservations must be made in advance Check the website for current information and suggestions of best times to call to reserve your ride—to do so you must actually speak to someone at the stables. Riders must be at least eight years old. Private and group lessons are also available, as well, as is a summer camp for kids.

where to shop

Chuck Levin's Music Center, 11151 Veirs Mill Rd., Wheaton, MD; (301) 946-8808; chuck levins.com. This independent music store first opened in 1958 at 12th and H Streets in downtown Washington, DC. The store burned down during the 1968 riots following the assassination of Dr. Martin Luther King Jr. Soon after, Chuck Levin's Music Center reopened at its current Wheaton location and has been there ever since. Something of a local institution, the store still is run by members of the Levin family and is known for its expert sales staff.

Marylandica Gift Shops. 1800 Glenallan Ave., Wheaton, MD; (301) 962-1448; montgomery parks.org/brookside/visit_contact.shtm. There are two small but fun gift shops at Brookside Gardens. One located in the Brookside Gardens visitor center and the other in the conservatory. Both carry an eclectic range of items related to horticulture that include everything from ceramic boot planters, to flower-adorned teapots, to kids' gardening gloves. The main shop also carries a nice selection of gardening books for adults and children. Local artisans create many of the items found in the shops, and some of the treasures here are crafted from sustainable or recycled materials.

The Toy Exchange, 11265-1126 Triangle Ln., Wheaton, MD; (301) 929-0690; thetoy exchange.com. In the market for an original 1937 Lionel Blue Streak engine to complete your set, a vintage Luke Skywalker action figure like the one you had as a kid, or maybe some old-school Matchbox cars? If so there is a good chance The Toy Exchange can help you. Whether you are buying, selling, or browsing down memory lane, The Toy Exchange, which has been a local fixture in the collecting world for twenty-plus years, is a must for anyone interested in hard-to-find toys, collectables, or model trains. They also carry a range of video games, action figures, die-cast cars, and lots of other items to file under "they don't make 'em like that anymore."

The Yarn Spot, 11425 Grandview Ave., Silver Spring, MD; (301) 933-9550; theyarnspot .com. The Yarn Spot is a popular haunt with anyone who loves knitting, crocheting, felting, spinning, or weaving. The knowledgeable staff teaches a host of creative workshops, including a popular sock-knitting class. Private lessons may also be arranged here.

where to eat

Inexpensive ethnic eateries dot the strip malls of Wheaton and nearby Silver Spring, offering a range of authentic cuisine from Asian to Peruvian. Here are few noteworthy suggestions:

El Pollo Rico. 2517 University Blvd., Wheaton, MD; (301) 942-4419. Known for its well-spiced Peruvian chicken, El Pollo Rico packs in a crowd of loyal followers. Order at the counter and enjoy at one of the tables or take your chicken to go. $.

Hollywood East Cafe. 11160 Viers Mill Rd., Wheaton, MD; (240) 290-9988 hollywood eastcafe.com. Although it's changed locations several times over the past few years, those who know this Chinese restaurant make a point of finding it every time. $.

Kantutas Restaurant. 2462 Ennalls Ave., Wheaton, MD, (301) 929-2865. Locals come here time and time again for authentic Bolivian food. Kantutas is especially known for its *silpancho* and *anticuchos,* two meat dishes signature to the region. Sometimes there is such a high demand for these dishes that the kitchen runs out. $.

The Limerick Pub. 11301 Elkin St., Wheaton, MD; (301) 946-3232 or (301) 942-8282; thelimerickpub.net. Limerick is an old-school Irish pub. Locals swear by the Reuben and the fish-and-chips. The pub's dart league, trivia nights, whiskey tastings, and Irish author nights make it more than just a place to enjoy a pint. $.

Max's Kosher Cafe. 2319 University Blvd. West, Wheaton, MD; (301) 949-6297. During the weekday lunch rush people from seemingly all walks of life line up for the falafel here, some of the best in town. Choose from half or whole sandwiches and select toppings like pickled eggplant, tahini, and garlic sauce. Closed on Sat. $.

Oriental East. 1312 East-West Highway, Silver Spring, MD; (301) 608-0030; orientaleast .com. People line up and endure long waits to feast on the dim sum brunch served here every day from 11 a.m. to 3 p.m. During the week you can order the Chinese dumplings from a menu and on weekends you make your selection from rolling carts. A full menu is offered the rest of the day. $$.

Ren's Ramen. 11403 Amherst Ave., Wheaton-Glenmont, MD; (301) 693-0806; rens
-ramen.com. Many swear that this hole-in-the-wall shop with the limited menu serves the
best ramen in town. Open Mon to Sun. Closed every second and third Tues of the month. $.

worth more time

Historic Kensington, Maryland. explorekensington.com. Kensington is about 4 miles
from the gardens. Head back to Georgia Avenue and turn right onto University Boulevard,
which becomes Connecticut Avenue. Turn left onto Howard Avenue for about three blocks
until you see the antiques shops on the right.

Much like Brookside Gardens, nearby Kensington is a prize find hiding behind a nonde-
script main avenue. The tree-lined historic district started when the famed Baltimore & Ohio
Railroad began stopping there. In the early days Washingtonians retreated to Kensington
as a break from city life. As DC spread north, more and more people began residing in
Kensington's beautiful Victorian homes year-round.

Today Kensington's Antique Row is what draws people up from the city. Located on
Howard Avenue East, Antique Row has almost a hundred small shops and several places
to sit and have a sandwich, ice cream cone, or cup of coffee. Every Saturday a farmers'
market takes place near the train station from 8 a.m. to noon. The one-room Noyes Library
for Young Children, housed in a charming yellow Victorian, dates back more than one hundred years and is a favorite of the under-five set.

If you find yourself curious about the many historic homes and beautiful gardens here,
you might want to further explore the town with the Kensington Historical Society's self-
guided walking tour. You can pick up a pamphlet at the town hall or at one of the local
bookstores. But consider yourself warned. The flower-filled parks and gardens and the
historic homes might have you looking for the nearest real estate agent.

day trip 02

north

frederick for foodies:
frederick, md

frederick

For years the lure of treasures hidden in antiques shops brought visitors to Frederick's historic downtown. While the town is still a fabulous spot for antiquing, now food with a decidedly contemporary twist also tops the list of the city's biggest draws. Today Frederick counts several "destination restaurants" among its prized attractions, with Volt as the brightest star among them. The city now has its own annual restaurant week, food-themed walking tours of historic downtown (frederickrestaurantweek.com), and new culinary concepts continue to pop up in town all the time.

While you are in town indulging your palate, consider taking a turn on the Frederick Wine Trail, where you can travel historic roads to vintage, pun intended, destinations. If you want something more down-home, grab a pint of ale at one of the nearby brewpubs. And who knows, you might just find the perfect vintage stemware for your new favorite vintage while you're in town. Before you embark on your culinary adventure, do keep in mind that many of the local restaurants stay dark on Monday.

getting there

Frederick is an easy 45-minute ride up I-270 North. Get off at exit 31A and make a left onto Route 355. Follow the signs to the visitor center and park in one of the well-marked decks

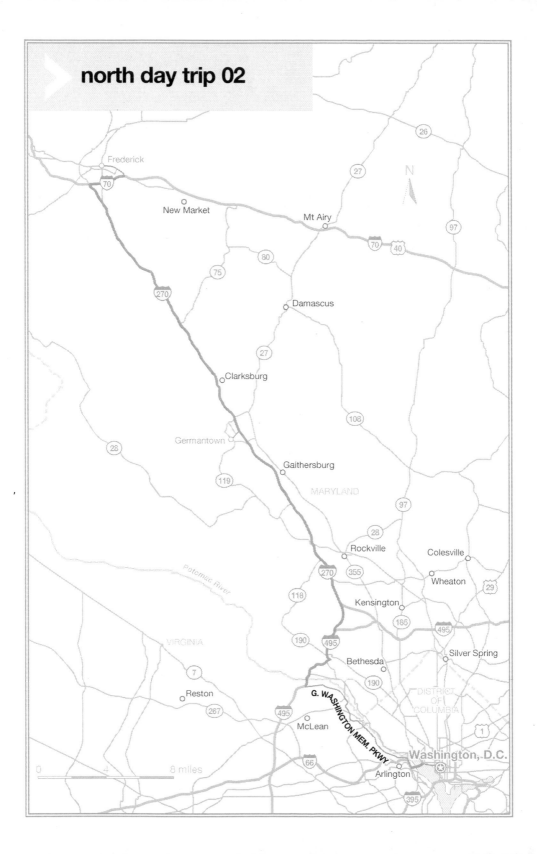

downtown. During the week MARC trains run between Washington and Frederick three times in the evening and come back to DC three times in the morning.

where to go

Community Bridge Mural and Carroll Creek Park Canal. Between East Patrick and East All Saints Streets. The trompe l'oeil mural of an old ivy-covered stone bridge painted on an unremarkable concrete bridge is so convincing that you might have to touch it to believe it. Frederick artist William Cochran's public art marvel stands as the centerpiece to this canal area and promenade, which is lined with restaurants, condo buildings, benches, and a walkway. Free concerts are given here during the summer

Delaplaine Visual Arts Education Center. 40 S. Carroll St., Frederick, MD; (301) 698-0656; delaplaine.org. Local art and artists are the focus of this large, three-level arts center housed in the renovated Mountain City Mill building downtown. Local art is sold in the shop and the center sponsors a popular local arts market. An array of programs and classes also are held here. Admission is free.

Flying Dog Brewery. 4607 Wedgewood Blvd., Frederick, MD; (301) 694-7899; flyingdog ales.com. Flying Dog's craft beers have developed something of a cult following around the country and you can see how the popular brew is made at the Frederick-based brewery. The tours cost $5 per person. Check the website for current schedules and some fantastically entertaining copy. You must be 21 or older to be part of the tour and, spoiler alert, to drink.

The Kitchen Studio. 5301 Buckeystown Pike, Ste. 125, Frederick, MD; (301) 663-6442; kitchenstudiofrederick.com. Sharpen your knife skills, learn to roll sushi, or figure out how to make fondant at a class at The Kitchen Studio, run by Frederick chef Christine Van Bloem. She also offers classes, camps, and birthday parties for kids and teenagers.

Monocacy National Battlefield. 5201 Urbana Pike, Frederick, MD, (301) 662-3515; nps .gov/mono/index.htm. American history buffs likely will be drawn to Monocacy Battlefield, site of what is known as the Civil War "Battle that Saved Washington." In 2010, National Park Service archaeologists uncovered the largest-known slave village in the mid-Atlantic region here on what once was a sprawling plantation known as L'Hermitage. Some ninety enslaved individuals, approximately ten times the number of slaves that would be expected for the size of the plantation, lived here. This was the second largest slave population in Frederick County at the time and among the largest in the state of Maryland.

Monocacy Brewing Company. 1781 N. Market St., Frederick, MD; (240) 457-4232; monocacybrewing.com. Monocacy Brewing produces its own line of craft beers, as well as craft beers sold at Brewer's Alley in downtown Frederick. Both the brewery and tasting room are open to the public. Tours are offered the third Saturday of the month.

National Museum of Civil War Medicine. 48 E. Patrick St., Frederick, MD; (301) 695-1864; civilwarmed.org. The museum tells the "medical story" of the Civil War.

South Mountain Creamery. 8305 Bolivar Rd., Middletown, MD 21769; (301) 371-8565; southmountaincreamery.com/home.php. Located in Frederick County, South Mountain Creamery is Maryland's first on-the-farm processing plant. Here they grow the crops, raise the animals, milk the cows, and even bottle the milk in glass bottles. Visitors are welcome at the farm and can watch cows being milked and the calves being fed—check the website for time and details. There also is a farm market and creamery on site.

Taste Frederick Food Tour. (800) 979-3370; tastefrederickfoodtours.com. If you don't know where to start your culinary journey of town then consider signing up for a Taste Frederick Food Tour. The three-hour walking tours offer healthy helpings of downtown Frederick history and food, with lots of tasting along the way.

frederick wine trail

The Frederick Wine Trail allows lovers of the grape to travel pretty, historic roads to vintage destinations. The Frederick Wine Trail is made up of several wineries that welcome visitors. Together these wineries are responsible for more than half of Maryland's wine production. Here are some of the wineries that dot the trail.

__Black Ankle Vineyard.__ blackankle.com. The tasting room at this boutique winery was created with the goal of using as many materials from the farm as possible. The building is framed with locally milled wood that was harvested from the property's forest, its walls are insulated with straw bales grown on site, and they are finished with handmade plasters that were made with the clay and water from the farm.

__Catoctin Breeze Vineyard.__ catoctinbreeze.com. A DC couple made their dream of moving to the country and making wine come true when they opened the Catoctin Breeze Vineyard, with its beautiful views of the Catoctin Mountains. The tasting room is open on Saturday and by appointment only during the rest of the week.

__Distillery Lane Ciderworks.__ distillerylaneciderworks.com. Small-batch hard cider ranks high on the foodie "it" list thanks in part to places like Distillery Lane Ciderworks, Maryland's first licensed cidery in Maryland. The family-owned and -operated farm also grows a variety of apples sold in the store here along with sweet cider and other apple goodies.

Weinberg Center for the Arts. 20 W. Patrick St., Frederick, MD; (301) 600-2828; weinberg center.org. Pair your perfect dinner with a showing at a perfectly stunning 1926 theater. The Weinberg Center for the Performing Arts—the grand Tivoli movie house from once upon a time—sponsors an array of live performances and sometimes screens old silent films while a musician plays the theater's original Wurlitzer organ.

where to shop

Candy Kitchen. 52 N. Market St., Frederick, MD; (301) 698-0442; the-candy-kitchen.com. The corner candy store once again proves that chocolate-covered pretzels, chocolate-covered cookies, and chocolate lollipops never go out of style. But you knew that. For more than a century the Candy Kitchen has been satisfying the county's sweet tooth with

Elk Run Vineyards. elkrun.com. Located on a historic property, this vineyard and winery once was a land grant to Lord Baltimore. Elk Run grows 25 acres of Vinifera grapes.

Linganore Winecellars. linganorewines.com/visit. Berrywine Plantations/Linganore Winecellars is a family operated vineyard and winery and the oldest family-owned winery in Maryland. Visitors can tour and taste here, and, once a month, participate in a tasting of food and wine pairings.

Loew Vineyards. loewvineyards.net. Visit on Friday, Saturday, or Sunday afternoon to sample wines and stroll in the vineyards. The Loew family's winemaking roots date back to mid-nineteenth-century Europe.

Orchid Cellar. orchidcellar.com. Meads and traditional Merlots are made at this picturesque winery located in the foothills of the Catoctin Mountains.

Springfield Manor Winery & Distillery. springfieldmanor.com/Winery_Distillery .html. Known for refined and dignified wines, Springfield Manor Winery & Distillery can be visited by appointment only. The winery's magnificent lavender field and market may also be visited at times by calling ahead.

Sugarloaf Mountain Vineyard. smvwinery.com. Nestled in the base of Sugar-loaf Mountain, this winery can be found just twenty-five minutes from the beltway. Sugarloaf Mountain Vineyard operates a popular tasting room and hosts events throughout the year.

its old-fashioned confections. If you have a favorite treat in mind, you can even call ahead and the folks at the Candy Kitchen will have it ready to go when you arrive.

Chartreuse & Co. 4007 Buckeystown Pike, Frederick, MD; (310) 874-1882; chartreuse andco.com. Once a month three barns and the outdoor areas surrounding them are transformed into a magical multi-vendor sale of all things vintage, repurposed, restored, reproduced, and salvaged.

Firestone's Market. 109 N. Market St., Frederick, MD; (301) 696-8586; firestonesmarket .com. A neighborhood gourmet market in the heart of Frederick's historic district with a great selection of sandwiches, fresh-baked breads, artisan cheeses, wine and beer, foodie gifts, and gourmet baskets.

Lebherz Oil & Vinegar Emporium (L.O.V.E.). 214 N. Market St., Frederick, MD; (301) 228-3996; loveoliveoilvinegar.com. Almost fifty different olive oils and vinegars (think blood orange–infused olive oil or jalapeño white balsamic vinegar, and you will start to the get the idea) are on tap here to browse, sample, and purchase.

McCutcheon's Factory Store. 13 S. Wisner St., Frederick, MD; (301) 662-326; mccutcheons .com. For generations McCutcheon's preserves, jams, jellies, and apple butter have been a favorite of locals, and over the years they have built up a loyal following well outside the city limits.

Molly's Meanderings. 17 N. Market St., Frederick, MD; (301) 668-8075; mollysmeanderings .com. Step into Molly's Meanderings for a dose of Victorian charm and a selection of clothing, jewelry, and accessories that take a cue from the store's ladylike theme. Molly's Meanderings is a good place to pop in if you want something new to wear for dinner out. Warning: You might suddenly get the urge to reread *Great Expectations* while perusing the old-fashioned hat racks.

The Muse. 19 N. Market St., Frederick, MD; (301) 663-3632; shopthemuse.com. The Muse remembers to keep the "fun" in "functional." The store sells funky jewelry, house-wares, baby goodies, kitchenware, and other assorted functional gift items all made by local artists. Embrace your inner Martha during one of the store's regular classes or the monthly Make and Take Sundays or Wednesday Craft Parties. Classes are BYOB and refreshments often are served. Check out the store's website for details and other fun tidbits.

North Market Pop Shop. 237 N. Market St., Frederick, MD; (240) 575-9070; northmarket popshop.com. The North Market Pop Shop will make you feel all fizzy inside. This Frederick foodie find specializes in glass-bottled, cane sugar, and vintage soda pops, many of which come from small bottling plants. The shop also stocks ice cream from nearby Trickling Springs Creamery and will artistically indulge your sweet tooth by mixing any flavor of soda with any flavor of ice cream to create a perfect float.

the covered bridges of frederick county

The image of Meryl Streep and Clint Eastwood falling in love on the big screen against the backdrop of Iowa's covered bridges made an already iconic symbol of the American countryside even more romantic. While the three covered bridges still standing in Frederick County never made it onto the screen during Bridges of Madison County or into the novel by Robert James Waller on which the movie is based, they still are enormously evocative and worth seeing. Covered bridges, like those in the Frederick area, often spanned rivers or streams and were covered to keep dry the wood used to construct them. Only a handful remain. Follow this route to take a little-covered diversion from urban life. It's about a 30-mile round trip to catch all three.

Begin the journey at the junction of Route 15 North and Route 26, which is just north of Frederick, and drive about 4 miles north to Old Frederick Road. Turn right and drive about 1.5 miles and make a left onto Utica Road to the Utica Mills Covered Bridge.

Utica Mills Covered Bridge. Old Frederick Road near Utica. The Utica bridge spans a fishing creek and dates back to about 1850. The reddish bridge was rebuilt and moved to its current location circa 1900.

Head back to Old Frederick Road, make a left, and drive for about 4 miles to a stop sign, where you will turn left onto Route 550. Drive a little less than a half-mile and make a right onto Old Frederick Road. Go about 2 miles and turn left into the Loy's Station Park parking lot.

Loy's Station Covered Bridge. 3600 Old Frederick Rd., Thurmont. Loy's is a favorite among locals not only because it is a scenic structure but also because it sits next to a park with picnic tables and a playground, Visitors, particularly young ones, get a kick out of wading in the calm creek.

From the parking lot of Loy's Station Park, turn left and drive through the bridge. Continue to a stop sign and make a left onto Rocky Ridge Road. Drive about 3 miles and turn right onto Apples Church Road, which turns into Roddy Road. Go straight on this road for about a mile and a half to the bridge. Drive through the Roddy Road Covered Bridge to the parking lot on the left.

Roddy Road Covered Bridge. 14760 Roddy Rd., Thurmont. At only 40 feet long, Roddy Road is the smallest of the county's covered bridges and dates back to the 1850s. The park next to it screams "picnic."

The Perfect Truffle. 16A N. East St., Frederick, MD; 301-620-2448; theperfecttruffle.com. Handcrafted chocolates are the star of the show here. Chef and owner of The Perfect Truffle, Randy Olmstead frequently teams up with Flying Dog Brewery to present beer and truffle pairings. The local brewery's ales are even used as ingredients in some of the truffles.

Sweet Clover Barn. 4051 Stanford Ct., Frederick, MD; sweetcloverbarn.com. Sweet Clover is a monthly tag sale of vintage home decor and handmade items held in a dairy barn on Frederick horse farm.

The Salt Pig. 115 N. East St., Frederick, MD; (301) 662-SALT (7258); salt-pig.com. The Salt Pig has the potential to be a black hole for foodies with its fabulous collection of gourmet edible salts from around the world—sea salts, mineral salts (fine and course ground), flakes, finishing salts, smoked salts, flavored salts, salt slabs, and salt stones are some of what you will find here. Also check out the collection of handcrafted "salt pigs" made by variety of local artisans.

Zoe's Chocolate Co. 121 N. Market St., Frederick, MD; (301) 694-5882; zoeschocolate .com. This little upscale chocolate shop is a piece of brown and pink candy heaven. The handmade chocolates blend modern style with good old-fashioned candy-making techniques. Signature chocolates reflect the chocolatier's Mediterranean heritage and include tahini, pomegranate, and baklava truffles.

where to eat

Brewer's Alley Restaurant.124 N. Market St., Frederick, MD; (301) 631-0089; brewers -alley.com. Many who come to Brewer's Alley wind up not only loving the house brews but also wind up pleasantly surprised by the food. Found in a lovely old building that once served as Frederick's city hall, the brewery has several dining areas including outdoor patio seating. $$.

Cafe Anglais. 238 N. Market St., Frederick, MD; (301) 698-1223. Cafe Anglais is a hidden-in-plain-sight find for traditional British tea. The unassuming storefront not far from the center of town won't necessarily call to you, but it's worth stepping inside and then stepping back out again to the lovely little tea garden in back. High tea offers the chance to nibble on finger sandwiches, sweets, and scones with clotted cream while sipping a pot of freshly brewed English tea. $$.

Family Meal. 880 N. East St., Frederick, MD; (301) 378-2895; voltfamilymeal.com. Family Meal is a modern take on comfort food from local son Bryan Voltaggio, the popular chef with the inked-up crossed arms pose. Breakfast, lunch, and dinner are served at Family Meal seven days a week, and the restaurant sponsors free old-school drive-in movies every week during the summer. $$.

Firestone's Culinary Tavern. 105 N. Market St., Frederick, MD; (301) 663-0330; firestones restaurant.com. Firestone's is Chef Jack Walker's take on a British gastropub with a decidedly American flair. Located in the historic section of downtown, this eatery with the tavern-like vibe boasts good food in a relaxed atmosphere. $$.

The Orchard. 45 Market St. N., Frederick, MD; (301) 663-4912; theorchardrestaurant .com. The Orchard's menu relies heavily on fresh produce to create its tasty stir-fries, salads, and soups and the restaurant always keeps its kitchen stocked with lots of local seasonal ingredients. All the dressings and sauces are made from scratch, and the tomato tamari dressing is a house favorite for good reason. There are many options here for vegans, vegetarians, and those who eat gluten-free. $$.

Tasting Room. 101 N. Market St., Frederick, MD; (240) 379-7772; tastetr.com. Frederick's first wine bar still packs in a crowd for its diverse, pages-long wine list and contemporary fare. The Tasting Room is also known for its seasonal cocktails, such as the lychee Bellini, agave nectar margarita, and blueberry martini. Situated in a light-filled location at the corner of Church and Market, the Tasting Room gives off a decidedly cosmopolitan vibe and is Zagat-rated. $$$.

The Wine Kitchen. 50 Carroll Creek Way, Frederick, MD; 301-663-6968; thewinekitchen .com. Set along Carroll Creek in downtown, The Wine Kitchen offers a seasonal American bistro menu focusing on local ingredients and is known for its wine flights and small plates. $$.

Volt. 228 N. Market St., Frederick, MD; (301) 696-8658; voltrestaurant.com. Owner Bryan Voltaggio of *Top Chef* fame crafts menus based on the seasonal flavors and local ingredients available in and around his hometown of Frederick. The restaurant is housed in a spectacular 1890s brick mansion. Saturday-night reservations book far in advance, as does "Table 21," the restaurant's kitchen seating, where patrons dine on a 21 course tasting menu while watching the culinary magic around them. An a la carte menu is also available at Table 21. Closed Mon and Tues. $$$.

where to stay

Hill House Bed & Breakfast. 12 W. 3rd St., Frederick, MD; (301) 682-4111; hillhouse frederick.com. Hill House is a nice choice if you don't want to (or shouldn't) drive back to DC after a day of food and drink. The three-story Victorian inn has four guest rooms and is in the historic district, putting it within walking distance of many popular restaurants and shops. $$.

The Inn at Stone Manor Bed & Breakfast. 5820 Carroll Boyer Rd., Frederick, MD; (301) 371-0099; stonemanorcountryclub.com. The B&B side of the Stone Manor Country Club offers a scenic retreat from the city. Lawns, gardens, and a pond surround the manor, adding to the feeling of privacy. The pretty suites have fireplaces, whirlpool tubs, and porches. Breakfast is served in the dining room at 8:30 a.m. and includes homemade muffins and rich casseroles. Stone Manor is a few minutes' drive from downtown. $$$.

10 Clarke Place. 10 Clarke Pl., Frederick, MD; (301) 660-6707; 10clarke.com. Just as the name suggests, this two-room B&B sits on Clarke Place, which means it's in downtown Frederick and within walking distance of many of its restaurants and sites. The B&B is housed in an old Victorian home with landmark status. $$.

day trip 03

north

because the mountains won't come to you:

sugarloaf mountain, catoctin mountain park, cunningham falls state park, md

When I lived in the Midwest I couldn't believe how far I had to drive to see a real live mountain. As a result, when I moved back to DC, I found myself craving all mountains all the time. Fortunately I didn't have to go very far to find some good ones. In less than an hour into Maryland stand several beautiful mountains, many complete with hiking trails, cabins, and picnic areas. And all come with varying degrees of wildlife, foliage, and blissful peace and quiet. Sugarloaf Mountain, Catoctin Mountain Park, and Cunningham Falls State Park are three great natural destinations in Maryland for anyone who is like me and sometimes wakes up needing a little mountain in her life.

sugarloaf mountain

getting there

Go north on I-270 to the Hyattstown exit, circle under I-270, and continue on Route 109 to Comus, then turn right on Comus Road to the Sugarloaf Mountain entrance. About a 45 minute drive from the city.

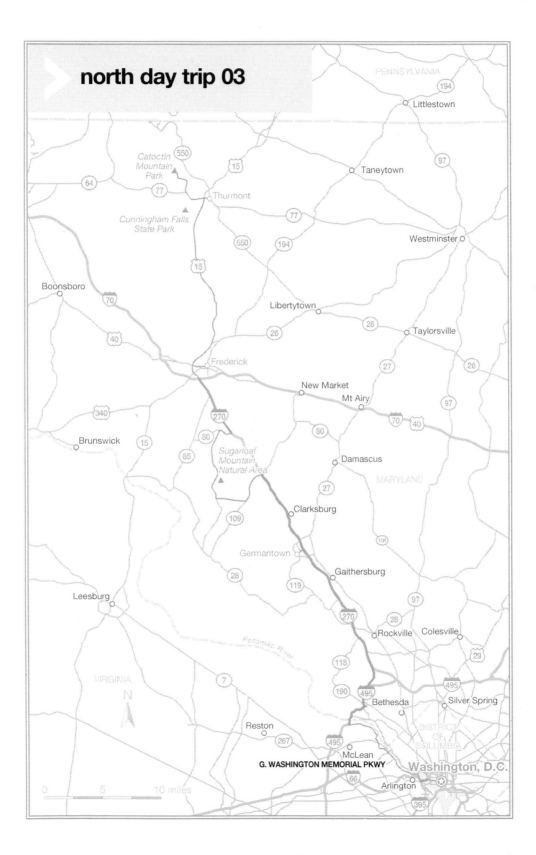

where to go

Sugarloaf Mountain. (301) 874-2024 or (301) 869-7846; sugarloafmd.com. Sugarloaf Mountain is one of those great finds that is free, requires little planning, and is less than an hour from DC. The pretty mountain got its sweet name from the early hunters and pioneers, who thought it looked like the cones with rounded tops that sugar was sold in before it was processed into granules or cubes. Pieces of sugar were broken off sugarloaves with a metal tool called a sugar nip. Fortunately the mountain has fared better than its namesake and the elements have not chipped away at it too much over the years, leaving a lovely spot with splendid views in all directions.

The mountain offers 13 miles of hiking trails, some of which are easy enough for little ones and those who are not seasoned climbers to conquer. It's a good destination if you want to spend some time in the great outdoors but don't necessarily want to spend all day out on a trail or an endless "are we there yet?" car ride. There are even a few spots at Sugarloaf where you can see nice views not very far from the parking areas. Hikers who want something more serious also can get their heart rates up as they explore this National Natural Landmark.

When you stand at the East View and West View points it becomes very easy to see why Sugarloaf was used as an observation point during the Civil War. In the spring the mountain blooms with wildflowers and in fall it's ablaze with autumn leaves. Picnic tables are scattered throughout the mountain, which rises 800 feet above the farmland below. Plenty of wildlife call Sugarloaf home, so get your camera ready to snap shots of red fox, owls, wild turkeys, woodpeckers, hawks, and flying squirrels.

Sugarloaf, a private park run by a nonprofit corporation, allows mountain biking but only on the yellow trails, and there are special paths to take on horseback. Trail maps are available at the mountain's base. Hunting, overnight camping, campfires, and off-leash dogs are never allowed and they mean it. As the sign at the bottom of the mountain says, our trees have eyes.

Historic White's Ferry. 24801 White's Ferry Rd., Dickerson, MD; (301) 349-5200. There once were some hundred ferries running on the Potomac. White's Ferry is the only one left. The historic ferry has been in operation since 1782 and continued to take pedestrians, cars, and other vehicles across the Potomac River between Maryland and Virginia for a small fee. On the Virginia side the ferry can be found north of Leesburg and in Dickerson near Sugarloaf on the Maryland side.

Even if you don't need a ride, the picnic area here is worth checking out, as is White's Ferry Store & Grill. Open during the spring and summer months. The store sells hot and cold food, snack items, wine, and beer. You can also rent canoes and grills for the day.

the great pumpkins

Comus Market. 23830 Old Hundred Rd., Dickerson, MD (near the intersection of Comus and Old Hundred Roads); (301) 349-5100; comusmd.com. Before I stopped at the Comus Market, I thought pumpkins came in two varieties: big and small. How wrong I was. Here at his picturesque roadside stand, farmer, bee-keeper, and local son David Heisler sells some of the more than thirty varieties of pumpkins and squashes he grows on his nearby farm. There are striped pump-kins, bumpy pumpkins, white pumpkins, green pumpkins, and blue-gray pump-kins. He even grows a flat, round pumpkin that looks remarkably like the "before" picture of Cinderella's coach.

In addition to the rainbow of heirloom and unusual pumpkins, Heisler also sells locally harvested apples, fresh cider, and honey from the beehives he keeps out back. (You can see some of his bees buzz by on the way to the hives while you shop.) The market is open only in the fall. The hours tend to be from 10 a.m. until dusk and the last day of the season is Dec 24.

where to eat

Comus Inn. 23900 Old Hundred Rd., Dickerson, MD; (301) 349-5100; thecomusinn.com. In 2002 a group of local investors pooled their resources to purchase Comus Inn so they could renovate and preserve the historic property at the mountain's base. Comus Inn has been back in business ever since and serves country cuisine and romantic views for lunch, dinner, and Sunday brunch. A special seven-course tasting menu is offered Wed through Fri and requires advance reservations. $$$.

where to stay

Pleasant Springs Farm Bed & Breakfast. 16112 Barnesville Rd., Boyds, MD; (301) 972-3452; pleasantspringsfarm.com. If the thought of returning to civilization after a day on the mountain is too painful to bear, then the secluded log cabin at Pleasant Springs Farm might be for you. The current owners restored the eighteenth-century cabin when they purchased it more than ten years ago and midway through the process decided to turn it into a B&B. Guests can curl up by the fire, sip tea on the porch, or explore the 30 acres of gardens, pastures, and woodlands that surround the charming old house. Innkeepers serve a full homemade breakfast at the time of your choosing between 7 and 10 a.m. They also will prepare brunch and afternoon tea with advance notice and reservations. The house sleeps up to 5 and has a two-night minimum on weekends. Hand-spun and hand-dyed yarn from the sheep grazing outside in the pasture often is on display and for sale. Some of the dyes used come from plants grown in the garden behind the log cabin. $$.

catoctin mountain park

If one mountain is good, two are better. If you're up for it, make Sugarloaf a warm-up for exploring other heights in the area. From Sugarloaf you can easily drive to Catoctin Mountain Park, where you can not only hike, picnic, and explore, but also spend the night at one of the park's on-site cabins.

getting there

From Washington, DC, take the George Washington Memorial Parkway north to I-495 (Capital Beltway) to I-270 North 27 miles to Frederick, Maryland. Take Route 15 north 17 miles to Thurmont, Maryland. Take Route 77 West; the exit sign is marked CATOCTIN MOUNTAIN PARK. Travel approximately 3 miles west on 77 and turn right onto Park Central Road. The visitor center is on the right.

where to go

Catoctin Mountain Park. 14707 Park Central Rd., Thurmont, MD; (301) 663-9330; nps .gov/cato. The most famous part of Catoctin Mountain Park is not open to the public and doesn't even show up on park maps: Camp David. The presidential retreat dates back to FDR, who called it Shangri-La and used it to escape the hot, humid Washington summers. During Roosevelt's presidency a camp in the park for federal employees was converted into a camp for the federal employee-in-chief. President Dwight Eisenhower renamed the site in honor of his grandson. Although you can't visit Camp David—or even get close to it unless you have friends in some very high places—you can enjoy the vast majority of this beautiful and historically significant national park.

So even if your return address is not 1600 Pennsylvania Avenue you can still fly-fish, picnic, bike, and cross-country ski at Catoctin. There are some 25 miles of trails that range from easy to expert. And unlike at Sugarloaf, you can camp here.

where to stay

There are three options for overnighting at Catoctin:

Camp Greentop. Camp Greentop also has its roots in the WPA. The site can be rented only by groups of sixty people or more. Go to nps.gov/cato/planyourvisit/greentop.htm for an application and other information. $.

Camp Misty Mountain. (301) 271-3140. The rustic wood cabins here started as a WPA project. The cabins are bare bones with cots and a single light on the ceiling. There are no electrical outlets, bathrooms, or running water in the cabins but you will find a grill, fire ring, and picnic table outside each bunk. Bathrooms and a dining hall with cooking ranges, sinks, and food prep areas are housed in communal locations.

Campers can cool off in the campsite's swimming pool, which is open from Memorial Day to Labor Day. The campsite itself stays open from April to November. You can call for reservations or visit nps.gov/cato/planyourvisit/mistymount.htm for a rental application and current prices. The campsite begins taking reservations on January 1 for that calendar year. $.

Camp Round Meadow. The four dorms here are designed for groups and are rented out as such. Each of the heated buildings sleeps thirty people and features shared bathroom and shower facilities. Don't forget to pack bedding, towels, and toilet paper—they are not provided. Groups with preapproval can use the kitchen facilities in the dining hall to cook meals. Log on to nps.gov/cato/planyourvisit/roundmeadow.htm for an application. $.

cunningham falls state park

Cunningham Falls serves as a kind of twin park to Catoctin and also has an array of activities to offer visitors.

getting there

Cunningham Falls is 18 miles north of Frederick and west of Thurmont.

where to go

Cunningham Falls State Park. 14039 Catoctin Hollow Rd., Thurmont, MD; (301) 271-7574 or (888) 432-2267; dnr.state.md.us/publiclands/western/cunningham.asp. Nestled among the Catoctin Mountains is Cunningham Falls State Park, a fun place to canoe, fish, hike, or hunt. The Maryland state park makes for a nice day trip or an overnight adventure, with several campsites and nine cabins available for rent. Campsites at Cunningham Falls have a reputation for being clean and well kept.

The 78-foot-high cascading falls are the main attraction here. You can hike near the falls, which can be accessed from the popular lake area. You can also swim, boat, and fish on the lake in designated areas and rent paddleboats from the park during the summer. The park borders north with Catoctin and the two share some trails, which range in difficulty from beginner to extreme. If you are traveling with kids, head for the recycled-tire playground in the Manor Area, which volunteers crafted from some 3,000 old tires.

where to shop

Catoctin Mountain Orchard. 15036 N. Franklinville Rd., Thurmont, MD; (301) 271-2737; catoctinmountainorchard.com. Spend some time at this pretty family-run orchard and farm. You can pick your own berries and sour cherries during the summer and also stock up on produce and baked goodies at the farm market.

where to eat

Thurmont Kountry Kitchen. 7 Water St., Thurmont, MD; (301) 271-4071. Home cooking in a small country restaurant known for its "broasted" chicken. A good place to fill up on old-school country cooking before heading back to the big, bad city. $.

where to stay

The park has two camping areas suitable for tents or RVs. Each campsite has a stone dust pad and a gravel driveway. A few have electric hookups. If you want to rough it but still have a roof over your head, reserve one of the nine camper cabins at the park. The very simple cabins sleep four and have two bunks, one double bed, two electrical outlets, an overhead light, a porch light, and a door that locks. The cabins are unheated and all cooking must be done outdoors. Call (888) 432-2267 to reserve both the camping sites and the cabins.

The Ole Mink Farm. 12806 Mink Farm Rd., Thurmont, MD; oleminkfarm.com. The same family has owned and run this rustic site that has both furnished log cabins and an RV campsite. Guests staying at either option can fish, use the pool, or walk the nature trails. $$.

northeast

day trip 04

northeast

baltimore's urban villages:

mt. vernon cultural district, fell's point, hampden, harbor east

Baltimore sometimes gets the cold shoulder from Washingtonians who forget that it's a culturally and architecturally rich city and a destination worth exploring—the fact that it's only about an hour's drive away is a bonus. Some also forget that Baltimore has a playful streak with its share of off-the-wall clubs, shops, and traditions, to say nothing of that most fabulous nasal accent, hon. Baltimore's diverse grouping of neighborhoods house many of the city's treasures, each with its own rhythm and feel, not to mention sound. Find your favorites and visit often.

mt. vernon cultural district

Mt. Vernon is a neighborhood of Baltimore firsts. Baltimore's first monument to George Washington. Baltimore's first public library. Baltimore's first Catholic cathedral. Baltimore's first music academy. But don't let its long list of historic firsts fool you into believing that one of the city's oldest neighborhoods is stuck in the past. If anything, quite the opposite is true.

Once home to Baltimore's wealthiest citizens, Mt. Vernon stands as one of the city's most vibrant and culturally rich sections. World-class museums, cutting-edge performance venues, and respected institutions of higher learning can be found here along with a diverse selection of restaurants and shops. Mt. Vernon Place, a perfectly preserved original town square, rivals any in the country. Most of the neighborhood's nineteenth-century buildings and architecture have been expertly preserved, keeping the neighborhood's historic feel

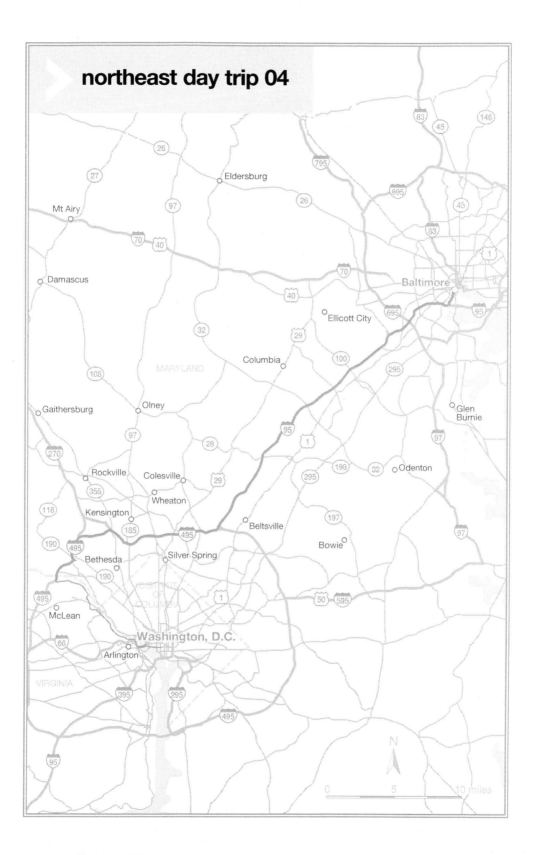

northeast day trip 04

while still embracing its decidedly modern urban vibe. About a half-mile from the Inner Harbor, Mt. Vernon also serves as a hub of Baltimore's gay community and is home to many diverse and proud citizens.

getting there

Avoid rush hour at all costs and drive north on I-95 to Baltimore, or depending on where you are within Washington, taking MD 295 North (Baltimore–Washington Parkway) might be a more direct route. You can also take the train from Union Station to downtown Baltimore.

where to go

Audrey Herman Spotlighters Theatre. 817 St. Paul St., Baltimore, MD; (410) 752-1225; spotlighters.org. The words "bold," "diverse," and "creative" top the list of adjectives used to describe the Audrey Herman Spotlighters Theatre, which has been part of the Baltimore theater community since 1962. The intimate space allows for a different kind of experience for both actor and audience than one finds in a more conventional venue. And a much less expensive one, too. The priciest ticket for nonmembers is $20 and anyone who contributes more than $25 to the theater, which has nonprofit status, is considered a member and thereby qualified for reduced ticket prices. Thursday performances always are $10.

Baltimore Basilica. 409 Cathedral St., Baltimore, MD; (410) 727-3565; baltimorebasilica .org. The stunning cathedral gracing Mt. Vernon's cityscape was the first great urban cathedral built in this country after the establishment of our nation. Designed by the architect of the US Capitol, the basilica took 15 years to construct and was completed in 1821. Tours are given Mon through Fri (and sometimes Sat) at 9 a.m., 11 a.m., and 1 p.m. and Sun at noon.

Centerstage. 700 N. Calvert St., Baltimore, MD; (410) 332-0033; centerstage.org. Centerstage is considered a pioneer of American regional theater and is known for its diverse range of performances. The beautiful old Baltimore façade welcomes theatergoers and the six floors of modern performance spaces, rehearsal studios, and multiple lobbies dazzle them. The Mezzanine Cafe serves prix-fixe menus before the curtain goes up.

Contemporary Museum. 100 W. Centre St., Baltimore, MD; (410) 783-5720; contemporary .org. The Contemporary Museum holds fast to its mission as a nomadic art museum that does not have and does not want a permanent collection. Instead the museum is based on the idea that audience is everywhere and its role is to operate as an incubator of talent by commissioning projects in different spaces and places. Visit the website to find out what and where the museum is exhibiting now.

Enoch Pratt Free Library. 400 Cathedral St., Baltimore, MD; (410) 396-5430; epfl.net. One of the country's first free public libraries can be found in Mt. Vernon. The city's central library continues to fulfill the dream of its founder and namesake, Enoch Pratt, who wanted to create a library "for all, rich and poor without distinction of race or color, who, when properly accredited, can take out the books if they will handle them carefully and return them."

Eubie Blake National Jazz Institute & Cultural Center. 847 N. Howard St., Baltimore, MD; (410) 225-3130; eubieblake.org. The Mt. Vernon center helps preserve and foster the art and culture of Baltimore's African-American community through a series of programs, exhibits, and classes. The center is open Wed through Sat and by appointment on Sun and charges $5 for admission.

Garrett-Jacobs Mansion. 11 W. Mt. Vernon Place, Baltimore, MD; (410) 539-6914; garrett jacobsmansion.org. In the late 1800s and early 1900s, the Garrett-Jacobs Mansion stood as the largest and most lavish home in the city, boasting forty rooms, one hundred windows, sixteen fireplaces, and its own theater. Much of the hand-carved oak as well as the spiral staircase and Tiffany glass dome remain intact. Today part of the mansion remains as a historic site and may sometimes be toured by the public by appointment.

Joseph Meyerhoff Symphony Hall. 1212 Cathedral St., Baltimore, MD; for tickets call (410) 783-8000 and for administrative issues call (410) 783-8100; bsomusic.org. The distinctive circular concert hall opened its doors in 1982 as the home to the Baltimore Symphony Orchestra. A wide range of performances and programs take place here at the concert hall, known for its superior acoustics. A limited number of discounted tickets for certain concerts are sold for $25 beginning one hour prior to the concert. Call the ticket office the Monday prior to performance day to find out about availability.

Peabody Institute and George Peabody Library. 1 E. Mt. Vernon Place, Baltimore, MD; (410) 659-8100; peabody.jhu.edu. Founded in 1857, the Peabody Institute was America's first music academy. Part of Johns Hopkins University, the institute still trains hundreds of musicians and dancers every year. The magnificent George Peabody Library is a breathtaking example of nineteenth-century architecture with the stack room standing as its pièce de résistance. In it, five tiers of ornate cast-iron balconies dramatically rise up around the atrium below and toward a massive 61-foot-high skylight.

Walters Art Museum. 600 N. Charles St., Baltimore, MD; (410) 547-9000; thewalters.org. The Mt. Vernon public art museum displays an impressive collection of paintings, sculpture, illuminated manuscripts, jewelry, and other artwork that represents thousands of years of world art. Some of the oldest pieces in the museum date back to ancient Egypt, such as the two 3,000-pound statues of the goddess Sekhmet. Newer but equally impressive pieces include Claude Monet's *Springtime* and ornate Fabergé eggs. William Walters and his son Henry Walters spent considerable time amassing the artwork that now makes up the core of the museum's permanent collection. The nineteenth-century Hackerman House displays the museum's extensive Asian art collection and is widely considered one of Mt. Vernon's most beautiful buildings. The museum is open from 10 a.m. to 5 p.m. Wed through Sun, and thanks to a grant, charges no admission fee. The museum offers a free guided tour most Sundays at 1 p.m. At 11 a.m. the third Saturday of every month, docents lead a forty-five-minute Walk, Wonder, and Explore program for families with young children. If you aren't at the museum when a docent is showing a group around, consider checking out a free audio tour. Among the options you can choose is a guide of Mt. Vernon Place, a nineteenth-century urban square. You can walk outside with the headset and listen to tales about the tony residents of days gone by who created much of this elegant neighborhood.

Washington Monument. 699 N. Charles St., Baltimore MD; (410) 396-0929 or (410) 396-1049. Although not nearly as tall as DC's version, Baltimore's Washington Monument holds the distinction of being the nation's first significant architectural monument to the father of our country. Visitors can climb the 228 steep steps to the marble column's top, which offers a nice view of the city. Mt. Vernon's residents ran a lottery to help raise funds for the monument, which was completed in 1829.

where to shop

Baltimore Farmers' Market & Bazaar. E. Saratoga St., Baltimore, MD; (410) 752-8632. Every Sunday starting at 8 a.m., vendors sell fresh produce, herbs, flowers, and other goodies at the Baltimore Farmers' Market, located underneath the Jones Falls Expressway at the corner of Holliday and Saratoga. The market runs from the beginning of May to the end of December. Stroll the bazaar section to browse a range of crafts and collectibles including jewelry, handbags, hair accessories, clothing, rugs, pottery and wooden items, stained glass, and photographs.

Charm City Cupcakes. 326 N. Charles St. #105, Baltimore, MD; (410) 244-8790; charm citycupcakes.com. Pretty bites of sweet little cakes are the name of the game here. Located near the Woman's Industrial Exchange, which was instrumental in helping the business get started, the shop will also make custom cupcakes.

Milk & Honey Market. 816 Cathedral St., Baltimore, MD; (410) 685-6455; milkandhoney baltimore.com. Milk & Honey Market carries a good variety of local and fresh items including produce, dairy, sustainably raised meats, specialty cheeses, and charcuterie. The shop also has a cafe that brews coffee drinks and makes all kinds of sandwiches.

Read Street Books & Coffee. 229 W. Read St., Baltimore, MD; (410) 669-4103; read streetbooks.com. Read Street is a great little indie bookstore find, the type that has become too far and between these days. New, used, and vintage volumes line the shelves of the space that has the feel of a well-loved home and also doubles as a coffee shop. It's great spot to sip, read, and forget about the outside world.

The Woman's Industrial Exchange. 333 N. Charles St., Baltimore, MD; (410) 685-4388; womansindustrialexchange.org. The exchange has been giving female artisans a chance

mt. vernon's rainbow connection

Mt. Vernon is known as a center of gay and lesbian life in Baltimore and has many clubs specifically for the GLBT community, including Leon's, the city's oldest gay bar at more than fifty years old. Here are some GLBT spots around the neighborhood:

Leon's. *870 Park Ave., Baltimore, MD; (410) 539-4850; leonsbaltimore.tripod.com.*

Club Bunns. *608 W Lexington St., Baltimore, MD; (410) 234-2866.*

Club Hippo. *1 W. Eager St., Baltimore, MD; (410) 547-0069; clubhippo.com.*

The Drinkery. *205 W. Read St., Baltimore, MD; (410) 225-3100.*

Grand Central Station Pub. *1001 N. Charles St., Baltimore, MD; (410) 752-7133; centralstationpub.com*

Coconuts' Cafe. *311 W. Madison, Baltimore, MD; (410) 383-6064.*

to sell their work and perfect their craft since it started in 1880. The shop sells handmade clothing, jewelry, ceramics, and other original items on behalf of the local women who created them. During the week take a break from shopping to grab lunch from The Women's Industrial Exchange Kitchen with its home-inspired comfort-food focus.

where to eat

Anastasia Italian Restaurant & Bar. 1636 Thames St., Baltimore, MD; (410) 534-6666; anastasiabaltimore.com. Anastasia serves Italian fare and offers a list of Italian wines. Italian beers are on tap. As the evening wares on, a DJ spins tunes as the crowd dances into the night. $$.

The Brewer's Art. 1106 N. Charles St., Baltimore, MD; (410) 547-6925; thebrewersart .com. The menu here changes to reflect the flavors of the season. The Brewer's Art offers many temptations for your palate along with an extensive selection of beer, wine, and scotch. $$$.

George's on Mt. Vernon Square. 101 W. Monument St., Baltimore, MD; (410) 727-1314; peabodycourthotel.com/dining.php. Located in the Peabody Court Hotel, George's serves New American cuisine with a French influence. The restaurant takes its name from three famous men with ties to Charm City—George Washington, George Peabody, and George Herman "Babe" Ruth. $$$.

Indigma Restaurant. 802 N. Charles St. Baltimore, MD; (410) 605-1212; indigmarestaurant .com. Indigma has won many an award and accolade for its upscale Indian menu and ambience. $$.

Minato Sushi Bar. 1013 N. Charles St., Baltimore, MD; (410) 332-0332; minatosushibar .com. A hip and fun sushi bar that is known for its creative and tasty rolls and pho. $$.

Nina's Espresso Bar. 600 N. Calvert St., Baltimore, MD; (410) 385-2800. A favorite Mt. Vernon spot for espresso and Asian food. And yes, you read that correctly. $.

Sotto Sopra Restaurant. 405 N. Charles St., Baltimore, MD; (410) 625-0534; sottosopra inc.com/. Housed in a nineteenth-century Mt. Vernon townhouse next to the basilica, Sotto Sopra serves a variety of Italian dishes created by a team of up-and-coming young chefs. But you haven't truly experienced all that is Sotto Sopra until you have eaten your way through one of its Opera Nights. Professional singers perform Italian operas while guests dine on a six-course gourmet dinner on select Sundays. Opera Nights fill up quickly, so reserve well in advance. $$.

Tio Pepe. 10 E. Franklin St., Baltimore, MD; (410) 539-4675; tiopepebaltimore.com. Tio Pepe is a Baltimore fixture and has long been considered a go-to special-occasion restaurant for Baltimorians. Tio Pepe been cooking up Spanish and Mediterranean food for more than forty years. $$$.

where to stay

4 East Madison Inn. 4 E. Madison St., Baltimore, MD; (410) 332-0880; 4eastmadisoninn .com. The 1845 home at—where else—4 East Madison offers travelers nine antiques-adorned guest rooms with private baths and free Internet access. The bed-and-breakfast also has two beautiful parlors for lounging and a striking nineteenth-century stained-glass skylight near the entrance. Breakfast is served every morning to overnight guests, and on Wed, Thurs, and Fri the general public can come and order from the inn's special lunch menu, served in the house's charming side garden. $$$.

Wyndham Baltimore Peabody Court. 612 Cathedral St., Baltimore, MD; (410) 727-7101; peabodycourthotel.com. This boutique hotel in a former 1928 apartment building welcomes guests who want to spend a little more time getting to know Baltimore and its neighborhoods. The Inner Harbor, the National Aquarium, and a slew of theaters are all within walking distance from the small hotel, which features marble bathrooms and free high-speed Internet access. $$.

fell's point

Bars, restaurants, and shops line the cobblestone streets of Baltimore's Fell's Point. Located to the east of National Harbor, although grittier and with more of a neighborhood feel than the harbor, Fell's Point is filled with historic buildings, pubs, and water views.

getting there

Fell's Point is only about a mile and a half from Mt. Vernon.

where to go

Baltimore Tattoo Museum. 1534 Eastern Ave., Baltimore, MD; (410) 522-5800; baltimore tattoomuseum.net. This small museum is devoted to the art of electric tattooing and has free admission. If you are so inspired, you can take home a permanent souvenir from the parlor attached to the museum.

Douglass-Myers Maritime Park & Museum. 1417 Thames St., Baltimore, MD; (410) 685-0295; douglassmyers.org. The Douglass-Myers Maritime Park and Museum celebrates African-American maritime history. Frederick Douglass worked on the Baltimore docks and purchased his first book not far from the spot where the museum stands. Docent-led tour included with the $8 admission fee.

Fells Point Food Tour. Charm City Food Tours, Baltimore, MD; (202) 683-8847; baltimore foodtours.com/fells.html. Walk the cobblestone streets of historic Fells Point as you sample local delicacies from some of the neighborhood's most beloved family-run restaurants. Your guide from the Charm City Food Tours will help marry history, culture, and food during this three-hour exploration. Tours cost about $58 per person and should be reserved online.

Green Rider, LLC. 714 S. Broadway St., Baltimore, MD; (410) 522-5857; greenriderusa .com. Zip around the point in a low-speed electric vehicle (LEV), which, unlike a gas scooter, doesn't leave a big carbon footprint. Green Rider both sells and rents the trendy vehicles and also carries amazingly cool-looking electric folding bikes.

Historic Ships in Baltimore. Piers 3 and 5 on Baltimore's Inner Harbor, 802 S. Caroline St., Baltimore, MD; (410) 539-1797; historicships.org. A collection of historic military ships is permanently docked at the Inner Harbor, and tours give visitors a chance to get a look at life aboard the vessels. The collection of ships also runs many educational programs, including an overnight adventure on the mid-nineteenth-century Navy warship *Constellation,* the World War II–era Navy submarine *Torsk,* or the Coast Guard cutter *Taney,* which witnessed the bombing of Pearl Harbor. Participants sleep in a hammock or bunk and eat two meals aboard the ship.

where to shop

Killer Trash. 602 S. Broadway, Baltimore, MD; (410) 675-2449. A secondhand store packed with vintage clothing, shoes, and accessories—much of it falling into the off-the-wall category that so many vintage shoppers seek.

Maja. 1744 Aliceanna St., Baltimore, MD; (410) 327-9499; majacollections.com. Maja is the place to go if you delight in artful jewelry with an ethnic or international flair. Many of the pieces are handcrafted and come from African artists. Clothing, music, and African art are also sold. The store began its life as a pushcart business on the Inner Harbor.

Red Emma's Bookstore Coffeehouse. 800 St. Paul St., Baltimore, MD; (410) 230-0450; redemmas.org. Just your friendly neighborhood anarchist bookstore. Named in honor of Emma Goldman, Red Emma's is a collectively run radical bookstore and vegetarian co-op kitchen–run cafe. All the coffee comes from free-trade sources and the Wi-Fi is free.

where to eat

Blue Moon Cafe. 1621 Aliceanna St., Baltimore, MD; (410) 522-3940; bluemoonbaltimore .com. Five words for you: Cap'n Crunch–Encrusted French Toast. You had me at Cap'n Crunch. Expect a wait. The cafe is small and popular. $$.

Louisiana Restaurant. 1708 Aliceanna St., Baltimore, MD; (410) 327-2610; louisianas restaurant.com. Creole and French dishes are served in the owner-designed space, which showcases many items he has salvaged from local historic sites. The banister on the staircase is from the Old Inner Harbor Power Plant and the pink marble on the walls once adorned a local department store. $$$.

Ostrowski's Famous Polish Sausage. 524 S. Washington St., Baltimore, MD; (410) 732-1118; ostrowskiofbankstreetsausage.com. The name pretty much says it all. Cash only. Open from 6 a.m. to 1 p.m. every day but Sun. $.

Pazo. 1425 Aliceanna St., Baltimore, MD; (410) 534-7296; pazorestaurant.com. Pazo serves tapas and other Mediterranean specialties in its stylish downtown digs. Pazo offers a nicely crafted wine list and many vegetarian options to go along with the meat and fish dishes. $$$.

where to stay

Hotel Monaco Baltimore. 2 N. Charles St., Baltimore, MD; (443) 692-6170; monaco -baltimore.com. Hotel Monaco set up shop in the former B&O Railroad headquarters, keeping many of the Beaux Arts details that define this 1906 landmark. The boutique hotel, Kimpton's first in Baltimore, weaves Charm City's strong railroad history into much of its funky decor. $$.

The Inn at 2920. 2920 Elliott St., Baltimore, MD; (410) 342-4450; theinnat2920.com. The Inn at 2920 is a bed-and-breakfast with a distinctly urban flair, from the exposed brick walls to the sleek color palette to the Jacuzzi tubs. Part of the nineteenth-century building once was a brothel but the inn has cleaned up its act since then—literally. 2920 prides itself on creating a low-allergen environment free of cigarette smoke, scented candles, pets, and aromatic flowers. The housekeeping staff uses fragrance-free, eco-friendly cleaning products and changes the air filters monthly. $$$.

hampden

In the 1990s Hampden joined the ranks of neighborhoods visited by the gentrification fairy. Artsy types began moving into row houses that once housed mill workers and helped change Hampden's status from up-and-coming to up. "The Avenue" (36th Street) serves as the neighborhood's main drag, lined with indie shops, restaurants, galleries, and a yoga studio. Hampden has the look and feel of its own little town while still having the benefits of being in a big city.

getting there

Hampden is about fifteen minutes north of Fell's Point and Mt. Vernon.

where to go

Walking around and soaking up the street scene is the best way to get a sense of Hampden. While there aren't really historical museums or sites, the neighborhood does sponsor two popular events, both of which fall into the "see it to believe it" category.

Christmas on 34th Street. christmasstreet.com. Every December the residents of Hampden's 34th Street start stringing up the lights and don't stop. Electric reindeer, light-up Santas, glowing angels, sparkly candy canes, and lots and lots of twinkly lights adorn the row houses up and down the street. Hubcap trees are also very popular in Hampden and make it into many of the displays. Just about every inch of every house on 34th Street is covered with something that lights up, blinks, or glows.

Honfest. honfest.net. For anyone who grew up in or near a blue-collar neighborhood in Baltimore, the greeting "hi, hon" is like mother's milk. The expression, said with the perfect nasal "o," has come to define a generation of women known for their high hair and circa-1962 jeweled cat glasses and clothing. Every June, Hampden honors the culture of the hon with its annual Honfest, where bouffant-wearing contestants compete to be crowned the winner of the hon pageant.

where to shop

Atomic Books. 3620 Falls Rd., Baltimore, MD; (410) 662-4444; atomicbooks.com. Atomic Books lets you embrace your inner geek. The shop is stocked with comics, graphic novels, local 'zines, and the long-forgotten but still adored vinyl record album. Film director and Baltimore native John Waters is a regular customer and the amusing collection of Christmas cards he sends to the store every year are up on the wall. Waters even gets his fan mail through Atomic Books. Mail a letter to him in care of the store and they promise to give it to him. They do not promise he will write back.

Avenue Antiques. 901 W. 36th St., Baltimore, MD; (410) 467-0329; avenueantiques.com. A favorite local antiques shop that stocks treasures from all eras, including a lower level filled with mid-twentieth-century finds. Several different vendors sell their wares in this packed space. Discounts are sometimes given if you pay in cash so ask before you hand over your greenbacks.

Double Dutch Boutique. 1021 W. 36th St., Baltimore, MD; (410) 554-0055; doubledutch boutique.com. Located on the top of The Avenue, Double Dutch Boutique sells fun, stylish women's clothing from independent designers. From 6 to 9 p.m. on the first Friday of each month, the store hosts a shoppers' social with food, drink, music, and a 10 percent discount.

reel life in baltimore

Charm City has appeared on the silver screen in many a movie. Here are some favorite films where Baltimore makes at least a cameo appearance:

The Accidental Tourist	He's Just Not That Into You
Cecil B. DeMented	Liberty Heights
Cry-Baby	Saved!
Diner	Silence of the Lambs
Hairspray	Sleepless in Seattle
Head of State	Twelve Monkeys
He Said, She Said	

Hanging On a Whim. 828 W. 36th St., Baltimore, MD; (410) 467-3233, hangingonawhim .com. Handpainted furniture and other items fill this shop.

The Pearl Gallery. 826 W. 36th St., Baltimore, MD; (410) 467-2260; thepearlgallery.com. Right on The Avenue, The Pearl Gallery specializes in Chinese antiques. At any given time you likely will find on display altars, tables, boxes and cabinets, and hand-carved figures.

Wild Yam Pottery. 863 W. 36th St., Baltimore, MD, (410) 662-1123; wildyampottery.com. Wild Yam is part gallery, part shop, and part ceramic arts studio. The items on display in the sunny, art-filled space are made in the studio housed behind Wild Yam. Many of the artists who create here will take custom orders.

where to eat

Artifact Coffee. 1500 Union Ave., Baltimore, MD; (410) 235-1881; artifactcoffee.com. From the geniuses behind Woodberry Kitchen comes this hip urban coffee shop with a relaxed vibe and superb pour-over coffee. The shop, housed in part of former sailcloth factory, serves breakfast and lunch and is especially known for its breakfast sandwiches on homemade English muffins. You can even order one topped with scrapple. The pies, donuts and other baked goods also boast a loyal following. Everything brewed, cooked, and served here adheres to the shop's fresh, local and handcrafted mantra. Artifact sometimes hosts burger nights and other events. Check the web site for the current calenderer. $$.

Cafe Hon. 1002 W. 36th St., Baltimore, MD; (410) 243-1230; cafehon.com. Food like someone's mom used to make, featuring lots of local favorites like the "Bawlmer" Omelet, filled with cheesy crab dip, provolone, and crabmeat. You can also order up crab cake sandwiches, cheese toast, and chili "hon" style with cheese and onions. Early-bird breakfast service starts at 7 a.m. during the week. $$.

The Charmery. 801 W. 36th St., Baltimore, MD; (410) 814-0493; thecharmery.com. Homemade ice cream in a rainbow of flavors including Old Bay, Fat Elvis, and Maryland Mud. $.

The Food Market. 1017 W. 36th St., Baltimore, MD; thefoodmarketbaltimore.com. The Food Market quickly became the "it" place to be on The Avenue. After eating here it's no wonder The menu is built around comfort foods and American flavors. Dinner is served every night and brunch on Fri, Sat, and Sun. Don't forget to check out the drink menu. $$.

Grano Pasta Bar. 1031 W. 36th St., Baltimore, MD; (443) 869-3429; granopastabar.com. Choose your pasta, choose your sauce, and then choose your post-meal workout. Gluten-free pasta available. $$.

Holy Frijoles. 908 W. 36th St., Baltimore, MD; (410) 235-2326; holyfrijoles.net. Mexican food on The Avenue, including build-your-own burritos. Portions are huge and the decor is eclectic and fun. Don't forget to check out the margarita menu. $$.

13.5% Wine Bar. 1117 W. 36th St., Baltimore, MD; (410) 889-1064; 13.5winebar.com. This hip urban wine bar takes its name from what is considered to be the ideal alcohol content in a bottle of wine. 13.5% is committed to keeping a large selection of affordable wines by the glass on its list. $$.

harbor east

During the past decade, Harbor East emerged as a trendy little part of town with shops, restaurants, and hotels dotting its 12 square blocks of harborside streets. Visitors and regulars alike are drawn to the popular neighborhood as a place to go out for the night.

getting there

Just as its name suggests, Harbor East sits east of Baltimore's harbor.

where to go

Harbor East Marina is 200-slip marina with a great skyline view.

where to stay

Four Seasons Hotel Baltimore. 200 International Dr., Baltimore, MD; (410) 576-5800; fourseasons.com/baltimore. Elegance and impeccable service define the Four Seasons Hotel Baltimore. That coupled with the hotel's magnificent city and harbor views have landed the luxury Harbor East hotel on many an impressive "top" lists. The hotel's high-end spa will help melt away any lingering stresses you've packed. $$$.

where to eat

Bond Street Social. 901 S. Bond St., Baltimore, MD; (443) 449-6234 bondstreetsocial .com. Small plates are called "social plates" at Bond Street Social and drive the menu that strives to fuse European, Latin, Asian, and Chesapeake Bay flavors. The ambience and decor here serve as a great backdrop to any meal.

Taco Fiesta. 618 S. Exeter St., Baltimore, MD; (410) 234-3782; tacofiesta.com. Locals flock to Taco Fiesta's weekly 5 p.m. to 7 p.m. Friday happy hour buffet for its impressive spread. Purchase two drinks and you are given a plate to load up with as much food as you can handle. During the rest of the week the kitchen serves up tacos, burritos, and other Mexican favorites.

Ten Ten. 1010 Fleet St., Baltimore, MD; (410) 244-6867; bagbys1010.com. Ten Ten makes it home in the courtyard of the historic Bagby Building and serves lunch, dinner and is popular destination for drinks on a night out. The restaurant's commitment to local food sustainability drives the kitchen here with most ingredients sourced from nearby Cunningham Farms or other nearby farms.

Wit & Wisdom. 200 International Dr., Baltimore, MD; (410) 576-5800; witandwisdom baltimore.com. Housed in the Four Seasons hotel, A Tavern by Michael Mina serves comfort food with a contemporary Eastern Seaboard flair. (Think steak and seafood.) A popular happy hour takes place every day in the lounge. In the warm weather the waterfront patio with its pretty urban views is a popular place to sip a cocktail or enjoy a glass of wine.

where to shop

Amaryllis Handcrafted Jewelry. 830 Aliceanna St., Baltimore, MD; (410) 576-7622; amaryllisjewelry.com. Stepping into Amaryllis is like a walking in to a whimsical jewelry box come alive. A locally owned jewelry store, Amaryllis has been selling baubles, bangles, and its other artistic creations since 1985.

Bin 604. 604 S. Exeter St., Baltimore, MD; (410) 576-0444; bin604.com. A neighborhood wine shop that specializes in lesser-known bargain wines, collectible wines, and low-yield vintners. Wine tastings and classes are held on Thursday from 6 p.m. to 8 p.m. and require advance registration. Bin 604 also hosts a variety of other classes and private tastings can be arranged.

Curiosity. 1000 Lancaster St.; Baltimore, MD; (410) 727-6262; katiedestefanodesign.com. You never know what you might pick up at this lovely shop but if it's a perfect gift or something to make a room pop, chances are it's here.

Loafers & Laces. 612 S. Exeter St., Baltimore, MD; (410) 244-5344; loafersandlaces.com. Loafers & Laces helps men step in style with its carefully curated selection of business and casual shoes for men. Impeccable service always is a goal here and has led to lots of customer loyalty. You can feel doubly good shopping here as Loafers & Laces donates $10 from each pair of shoes sold to an international nonprofit organization that helps people in need.

Su Casa. 901 S. Bond St., Baltimore, MD; (410) 522-7010; sucasa-furniture.com. Su Casa is a huge contemporary furniture and home accessories wonderland that comes from the people who brought this town the popular Big Iguana store in Fells Point.

day trip 05

northeast

triple-header day for baseball buffs:
bowie, baltimore, frederick, md

Washington is a great town for baseball lovers not just because the city once again has a major league franchise, but also because fans of the game can watch minor league play and another national ballclub without straying far from home. The Baltimore Orioles take the field at the charming Camden Yards in downtown Baltimore. The stadium stands just two blocks from Babe Ruth's birthplace, which is now a museum dedicated to the Bambino.

Not far from Camden Yards, contests, theme nights, and other minor league shenanigans keep fans happy who come out to cheer on the Bowie Baysox and the Frederick Keys. Minor league games are more affordable than the majors and, as a rule, are an easier get.

Choose Prince George's Stadium, home of the Bowie Baysox, for the first play in your quest for a shutout of a day trip devoted to our national pastime.

bowie

getting there

First base on this trip is Prince George's Stadium, home to the Bowie Baysox, a Class ZZ affiliate of the Baltimore Orioles. To get to the stadium take I-495 or New York Avenue to US 50 East (exit 19A off the Capital Beltway). Exit US 50 at MD 197 and follow it until it ends at US 301. Turn left onto 301 North, then right at the first light into Ballpark Drive. MARC

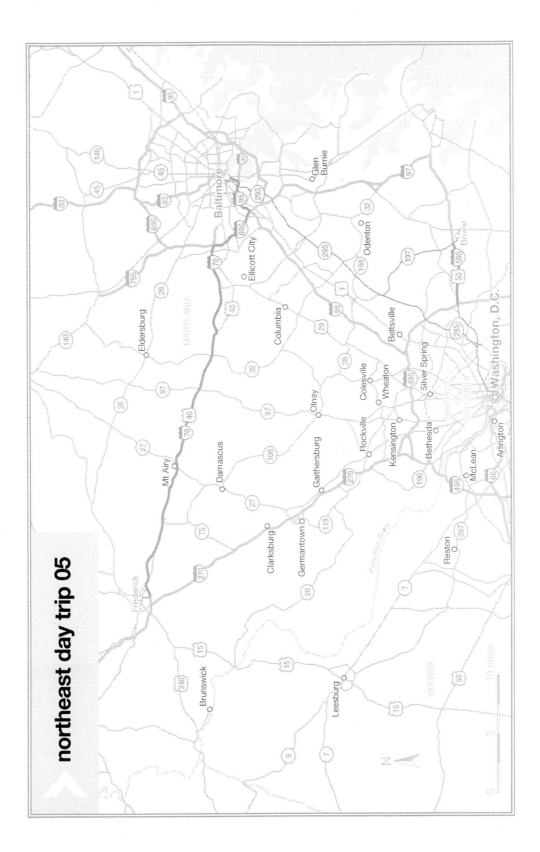

northeast day trip 05

train and subway service to Camden Yards runs daily. For the most current information, call (866) RIDE-MTA or visit mtamaryland.com.

where to go

Tickets cost between $9 and $14 and food will likely run you another $5 to $10, depending on what you get. Seniors and kids get discounts on tickets.

Bowie Baysox Prince George's Stadium. 4101 Crain Hwy., Bowie, MD; (301) 805-6000; baysox.com. The Bowie Baysox take the field here for home games and do a good job of keeping the crowd entertained. Fireworks go off after many night games and Louie, the team's green, furry mascot, rallies the crowd. The pink-haired (and proudly unidentifiable animal) Louie has a kids' club and the park has face painting and a rides area, complete with a merry-go-round for young fans. Food at the park is typical stadium fare, including hot dogs, peanuts, popcorn, nachos, ice cream, beer, and Pepsi.

The sky's the limit when it comes to campy theme nights and amusing antics at Prince George's Stadium. At a recent Country Night, willing ticketholders got to try their luck at a cornhole tournament, a sing-between-innings contest, and a hog-calling competition. The ballclub is also a wacky world-record chaser, so you never really know what you might be asked to do when you come to watch. So far the Baysox have attempted to make it into Guinness World Records for simultaneous toothbrushing, simultaneous yo-yoing, and simultaneous whoopee-cushion sitting. (Official results are still being certified by the Guinness officials, so the team is not listed in the book yet, but odds are they'll keep trying.)

Parking at the stadium is free and relatively easy, especially compared to most major league fields. But do yourself a favor and don't park in that enticing line of spots right next to the stadium. Regulars know it's not unheard of for a fly ball to make contact with a headlight or windshield.

baltimore

Some players spend their whole careers trying to get bumped up to the majors, but you can get from the minors to the majors in a little under an hour. To get from Prince George's Stadium to Camden Yards, get on the Baltimore–Washington Parkway/MD 295 North to Baltimore and drive about 20 miles until you see the signs for downtown Baltimore and Camden Yards.

Oriole Park at Camden Yards. 333 W. Camden St., Baltimore, MD; (888) 848-BIRD for tickets and (410) 547-6234 for stadium tour reservations and schedules; baltimore.orioles .mlb.com. Camden Yards opened in 1992 but embodies all of the old-time charm of such early twentieth-century ballparks as Ebbets Field, Shibe Park, and Fenway. The $110 million redbrick stadium sits right in downtown Baltimore on the site of the former B&O Railroad's

Camden Station rail yard. Camden Yards is considered the first retro urban stadium   one that helped start a trend among new ballparks throughout the country, including Nationals Park in DC. Camden Yards also practically sits in the shadow of the birthplace of George Herman "Babe" Ruth, making it something of a holy place for die-hard devotees of America's national pastime. As if that weren't enough, center field marks the location of the onetime Ruth's Cafe, operated by the Babe's father, who ran the business out of the ground floor of the family's residence—one of many reasons MLB stadium hoppers seem to love checking off Camden Yards on their national stadium tour scorecard.

The stadium has a relaxed, open feel, and it's fun to explore the different levels here on a pretty summer night. Tickets for the Orioles are far more expensive than those over in Bowie or Frederick. Premium seats go for as high as $80 and most cost between $30 and $50. If that's too steep for you, put on your most comfortable shoes and go for the $8 standing-room-only tickets, released for sold-out games. For about $12 you can also sit in some sections of the upper reserves at any home game.

A game without peanuts, beer, and hot dogs would be, well, un-American, so rest assured they all get sold here. But the food options here are hardly limited to those three stadium food groups. Oriole Park proudly holds the title of one of the top-ten vegetarian-friendly major league ballparks for offering choices such as vegan hot dogs, veggie burgers, and an array of salads at various concession stands. Noah's Pretzels sells gluten-free beer and pretzels at its stand on the first-base side of the main concourse and kosher dogs and burgers can be purchased inside the stadium. Camden Yards also offers a peanut-free suite during several games each season.

Kids who might need a seventh-inning stretch long before the seventh inning are the target audience for the Kids' Corner near Gate C, which features a playground, moon bounce, and speed-pitch throw. Children ten and younger receive free upper reserve seats when they come with a paying adult (maximum of two kids per adult). Kids' Night tickets can be purchased at the ticket window.

Stadium Tours. Enthusiastic baseball-loving guides give tours of Camden Yards about four times daily depending on game schedules. Groups start outside the park, include a stop at the scoreboard and JumboTron control room, and then head for the holy diamond—the field itself. Peppered throughout the tour are stories and trivia about the stadium and the area along with stops at luxury suites and a peek at the press level. Most tours end in the Orioles' dugout except on home game days. Tours cost $9 for adults, $7 for senior citizens and kids between four and fourteen (three and younger are free).

worth more time

Two museums right near Camden Yards rank as must-sees for sports fans who can't get enough of the game.

Babe Ruth Birthplace Museum. 216 Emory St., Baltimore, MD; baberuthmuseum.com. Follow the trail of 60 baseballs painted on the sidewalk between Camden Yards and the museum and you have arrived at the spot where the baseball legend came into the world. The Babe Ruth Birthplace Museum is dedicated to everything Babe. Learn about his humble beginnings and his record-setting baseball career, and catch a glimpse of some of his uniforms and home run–hitting bats. Tickets to the museum cost $6 for adults, $4 for seniors, and $3 for kids 3 through 12. You can purchase admission to both the Babe Ruth Birthplace and Sports Legends Museums for a discounted rate of $12 for adults, $8 for seniors, and $5 for ages 3 through 12.

Sports Legends Museum at Camden Yards. 301 W. Camden St., Baltimore, MD; (410) 727-1539; baberuthmuseum.com. If Maryland sports run through your veins, this is the place for you. The museum is dedicated to the history of sports in the state and features fun memorabilia and interactive exhibits. Kids and kids at heart will get a kick out of trying on professional uniforms, jerseys, hats, shin guards, cleats, and other equipment at the locker room in the Discovery Zone. Once you get suited up, you can even stand in the 2004 Orioles' on-deck circle. Admission is $8 for adults, $6 for seniors, and $4 for kids three through twelve.

where to eat

Looney's Pub. 2900 O'Donnell St., Baltimore, MD; (410) 675-9235; looneyspub.com. At Looney's there always seems to be a game on the TV (or games on the TVs) and lots of cold beer on tap. On the menu are burgers, cheesesteaks, and beloved bar food with the likes of wings, jalapeño poppers, potato skins, and something called a crab pretzel—a soft pretzel topped and baked with crab dip and cheddar cheese. Be warned: Notre Dame games trump all others here. $$.

where to stay

Harbor Magic. harbormagic.com. The Harbor Magic group owns three hotels in and near the Inner Harbor: the Pier 5 Hotel, the Admiral Fell Inn, and Brookshire Suites. Each allows guests to add special packages and "adventures" to their stay, including one adventure that features a sports walking tour of downtown. Check the website for availability and rates.

frederick

In the past few years Frederick has gone from a place to pass through to a destination all its own. A slew of highly rated new restaurants, a spruced-up canal area, and a baseball stadium bring more and more visitors to town every year. Frederick is an easy drive from both Baltimore and Washington. From DC take 270 to Route 70 East to exit 54. And from Baltimore take Route 70 West to exit 54.

Frederick Keys Harry Grove Stadium. 21 Stadium Dr., Frederick, MD; (301) 662-0013 or (877) 8GO-KEYS; frederickkeys.com. The Frederick Keys pack a lot into a season and in 2009 packed a lot of people into the stadium. The Advanced Class A affiliate of the Baltimore Orioles led its league and class in attendance. And for good reason. Harry Grove Stadium has gotten a makeover during the past few years, leaving it with a brand-new field, scoreboard, video board, sound system, some new seating, and spruced-up suites. The minor league team also works hard to make the games fun and affordable, with regular promotions almost every day of the week. In past seasons the ballclub has hosted Kids Eat Free Mondays, Guaranteed Win Tuesdays (where you get a free ticket if the team loses), Belly Buster Wednesdays with an all-you-can-eat picnic, Thirsty Thursdays with drink specials, and Sunday Fundays where you can bring your ball and glove and play catch in the outfield. Special one-time nights round out the team calendar and have at times included Bark in the Park, Faith Night, and Veterans' Night. On weekdays throughout the season, young fans dressed in their Little League jerseys and caps get in for free when they come to a game with a paying adult. Much like that in Bowie, the food sold here is classic bring-your-own-antacid fare, with pizza, hot dogs, cheeseburgers, grilled chicken, french fries, ice cream, and nachos topping the list.

day trip 06

northeast

gardens that fool the eye & tickle the senses:

ladew topiary gardens: monkton, md

ladew topiary gardens: monkton

Ladew Topiary Gardens seems to be one of those places that people drive past but never stop to see. When you do go ahead and take the turn into the 250-acre estate, you likely will be wondering why you didn't come here sooner. The well-manicured property is home to fifteen outdoor garden rooms designed by the property's onetime owner, colorful socialite millionaire Harvey S. Ladew. A self-taught gardener, Ladew set up a foundation so that his gardens would continue to grow long after his death. His foundation now runs and cares for his estate.

getting there

Ladew Topiary Gardens is about a half hour north of Baltimore. Take the Baltimore Beltway (I-695) toward Towson to exit 27B and head north on Route 146 (Dulaney Valley Road). Ladew Gardens is located on Route 146.

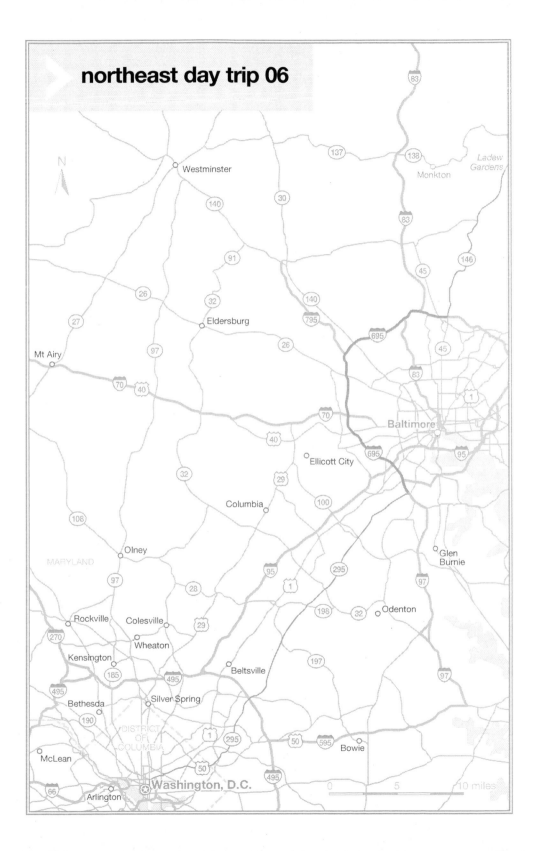

where to go

Ladew Topiary Gardens. 3535 Jarrettsville Pike, Monkton, MD; (410) 557-9466; ladew gardens.com. Harvey S. Ladew, the son of a wealthy factory-belt manufacturer, was born into the New York society scene. As a child, he received private drawing lessons from curators from the Metropolitan Museum of Art. Ladew grew up traveling the world, hosting parties, and riding horses. Early on he became taken with all things equestrian, especially foxhunting, and his passion for the hunt eventually led him to Maryland's horse country, where in 1929 he purchased the Pleasant Valley Farm, an old dairy farm adjacent to the Elkridge-Harford Hunt Club. Somewhat rundown when he bought it, without indoor plumbing or electricity, Ladew transformed the property into a magnificent estate, one visited by movie stars, intellectuals, and royalty. Lawrence of Arabia, Cole Porter, Charlie Chaplin, Clark Gable, and members of the English royal family were among those he counted as friends. The colorful millionaire redesigned and added to the house, turning an old smoke-house into a card room and one of the old barns into his studio. When trying to decide on the perfect spot in the house for a favorite oval desk, he wound up designing a room around it—a perfectly oval-shaped room known as the Oval Library. Ladew is open from April through October and has an admission fee ranging from $10 to $15 (and more if you plan on attending a concert while you are there). In the summer, outdoor concerts are held regularly. In May Ladew sponsors a popular Garden Festival, which includes a sale of hard-to-find, exotic, and unusual plants and flowers. Children's programs are also sponsored throughout the year, including story time, family nature walks, and a maple festival in February. Call or visit the website for the most current schedule.

> **Ladew Manor House.** Docents conduct regular guided tours of the grand manor house. English furniture, foxhunting memorabilia, and antique paintings fill the home and all belonged to Ladew, an avid collector who was known for having an eccentric streak. Complete with a secret door so he could sneak out when unwanted visitors showed up, the design marvel that is the Oval Library is probably the most popular stop on the house tour. Ladew's extensive book collection still lines the shelves of the library with many volumes dedicated to some of his favorite subjects: gardening, foxhunting, French literature, and art. A secret door hidden behind a secret panel leads straight out to the gardens.

> **The Gardens.** Ladew designed his gardens to be outdoor rooms inspired by the ones he fell in love with when he traveled across the pond to Europe. He assigned each room a theme, such as a common color or flower, to create a unified look. In his Garden of Eden room, a statue of Adam and Eve stands under an apple tree and is surrounded by crab apple blossoms. Carved into the steps leading up to Ladew's Garden of Eden is the quote, "If you would be happy for a week, take a wife. If you would be happy for a month, kill your pig. If you would be happy all your life, plant a garden."

Along with the help of local farmers, Ladow carved many of the topiaries, which stand as the focal point of many of the garden scenes. The ornamentally trimmed shrubs take the form of various objects and animals. He even designed a topiary scene of a foxhunt, complete with running dogs and a horse and rider. Ladew was one of the first people in the United States to practice the art of topiary design.

Topiaries cannot be trimmed constantly and survive, so the look and feel of the plant sculptures depends on when they have last been cut. Most of the topiaries at Ladew look the sharpest in the spring after they have been trimmed. The plants then are left to grow, giving them a fuller, fuzzier look during June, July and, August. They are cut again in the fall.

Nature Walk at Ladew. The 1.5-mile trail winds past a pond and through wooded grounds before leading walkers to a short boardwalk through a wetland forest and marsh. Ducks, geese, woodpeckers, butterflies, and bluebirds can often be seen from the path along with the occasional turtle or bullfrog. The trail fee is included with park admission, but you must pay to use the nature walk even if you don't tour the house and garden.

Maryland's Northern Central Railroad Trail. Maryland's Northern Central Railroad Trail, known more commonly as the NCR, is a hiking, biking, running, and horseback-riding trail that passes through Monkton around mile seven. The popular path was created out of part of the Northern Central Railroad right-of-way that ran through this area for many years and has a long, storied past. Union troops used it to transport soldiers southward during the Civil War, Abraham Lincoln rode it to Gettysburg to deliver his famous address, and following his assassination Lincoln's body was transported on the Northern Central Railroad.

You can pick up the trail in Monkton by taking York Road to Hereford and turning east on Monkton Road. Take Monkton Road for 3 miles until you come to a parking lot. Parking is limited and fills up very quickly, especially on sunny weekends.

Millstone Cellars. 2029 Monkton Rd., Monkton, MD; (443) 470-9818; millstonecellars .com. Housed in an old mill, Millstone Cellars produces some fine locally sourced, artisanal ciders and meads. Free tours and tastings are offered on Sat and Sun.

Monkton Bike Inc. 1900 Monkton Rd., Monkton, MD; (410) 771-4058; bikestuff.net. Feel like taking off on the NCR but didn't bring your bike? No worries. You can rent one here. The shop also does repairs and rents tubes, kayaks, tandem bikes, and children's bikes. About a fifteen-minute walk from the shop is a spot along the river that makes for a good start to a tubing trip. The folks at the shop will point you in the right direction. Active-duty military are entitled to free bike and tube rentals.

Tranquillity Manor Farms. 4101 Stansbury Mill Rd., Monkton, MD; (410) 628-6531; tranquillitymanorfarm.com. If the hunt-themed topiaries and English country antiques put

flower power: an overview to what blooms when at ladew topiary gardens

April: *tulips, daffodils, Virginia bluebells, early azaleas, pears, forget-me-nots, and crab apples*

May: *dogwoods, irisis, viburnums, lilacs, tradescantia, azaleas, irisis, cherries, peonies, coral bells, and foxgloves*

June: *roses, clematis, daylilies, dahlias, hosta, hydrangeas, irisis, weigelas, rhododendron, impatiens, and ageratum*

July: *roses, cimicifuga, buddleias, zinnias, phloxes, rudbeckia, clethras, and spireas*

August: *fall clematis, zinnias, phloxes, roses, and annuals*

September: *roses, asters, Mexican sages, Japanese anemones, and annuals*

images of riding in your head, then nearby Tranquillity Manor Farms would make a good next stop. The 200-acre horse farm offers group, semiprivate, and private riding lessons. Many of the horses at Tranquillity came to live on the farm through the owner's involvement in horse rescue efforts.

where to shop

Ladew Topiary Gardens Gift Shop. 3535 Jarrettsville Pike, Monkton, MD; (410) 557-9466; ladewgardens.com. Topiaries, gardening books, jewelry, ties, and decorative garden accessories are sold at the gift shop, which keeps roughly the same hours as the gardens and is closed during the off-season except around Christmas.

where to eat

Ladew Cafe. 3535 Jarrettsville Pike, Monkton, MD; (410) 557-9466; ladewgardens.com. Salads, sandwiches, soups, desserts, and cold and hot drinks can be purchased at the cafe located in the estate's former stables. The pretty outdoor patio is a nice spot to enjoy lunch or a snack after exploring the grounds. $.

The Manor Tavern. 15819 Old York Rd., Monkton, MD; (410) 771-8155; themanortavern .com. Housed in a lovely historic building that dates back to the 1750s, the Manor Tavern (known around town as The Tavern) serves Maryland cuisine, which seems to be code for "lots of crabmeat." The Tavern's lounge hosts music performances and offers its own menu and extensive beer, wine, and cocktail list. $$.

Milton Inn. 14833 York Rd., Sparks, MD; (410) 771-4366; miltoninn.com. The charming old country inn's ambience and classic cuisine make the Milton Inn a favorite among many locals celebrating a milestone or special occasion. Set in a 270-year-old fieldstone building once used as a coach stop for Quaker settlers, the Milton Inn serves many dishes that revolve around seafood, especially Maryland crabs. $$.

Monkton Village Market. 1900 Monkton Rd., Monkton, MD; (410) 472-9821. A great find for vegetarians or anyone in the area in search of yummy, healthy food and treats. Pick up a wrap or sandwich made from organic vegetables and ingredients, or try a smoothie. The store also sells ice cream made by a local creamery and sometimes carries vegan baked goods. $.

where to stay

Gramercy Mansion. 1400 Greenspring Valley Rd., Baltimore, MD; (410) 486-2405; gramercymansion.com. Don't let the Baltimore address fool you. This lavish bed-and-breakfast, about twenty minutes from downtown, sits on 45 acres of quiet, wooded land. The historic Tudor home once belonged to Alexander J. Cassatt, owner of the Pennsylvania Railroad and brother of famous painter Mary Cassatt. Each of the 11 rooms in the house has a private bath and has been carefully decorated with antiques. An Olympic-size swimming pool, a tennis court, an herb garden, walking trails, and croquet sets can all be found on the grounds, which bloom with color in the spring and summer. $$.

Jackson House Bed & Breakfast. 6 E. Main St., Railroad, PA; (717) 227-2022; jackson housebandb.com. The historic Jackson House Bed and Breakfast is located in Pennsylvania a mere 3 miles from the state line, putting it about twenty minutes from Ladew. Complete with stone walls and the restored original wood floors, Jackson House sits right along the NCR trail—the outdoor hot tub even overlooks the trail and a waterfall. All the rooms have private baths and the inn itself has terraced gardens and its own wine cellar, where guests can enjoy wine and cheese in the afternoon. $$.

east

>>>

day trip 07

east

>>> **seaside capital:**
annapolis, md

annapolis

The sailboat-dotted waters, carefully preserved historic homes, and easy pace make historic downtown Annapolis seem a million miles away from downtown Washington, DC, instead of the forty-five-minute drive east it takes to get here. Founded in 1649, the state capital is home to the US Naval Academy, Maryland's State House, and a charming brick-paved Main Street, as well as the requisite homemade ice cream and fudge shops.

Two separate circles serve as Annapolis's centerpiece—Church Circle and State Circle—a symbolic design gesture not lost on the early Americans who settled here. The State House lawn is a good place to start exploring the city, which sits where the Chesapeake Bay meets the Severn River. From this spot you can shape the rest of your visit, which you can happily fill with museum hopping, shopping, sailing, kayaking, or strolling. Taking it all in at one of the nearby watering holes with a plate of the local catch of the day works well, too. Whatever you choose, you almost always are guaranteed a healthy dose of charm and history when you spend the day in Annapolis.

getting there

Annapolis is an easy drive from Washington. The two cities are about 35 miles apart and the drive takes approximately 45 minutes. Leave the city via New York Avenue NW and take US 50 East for the majority of the trip. Weekday rush hour traffic can slow you down on

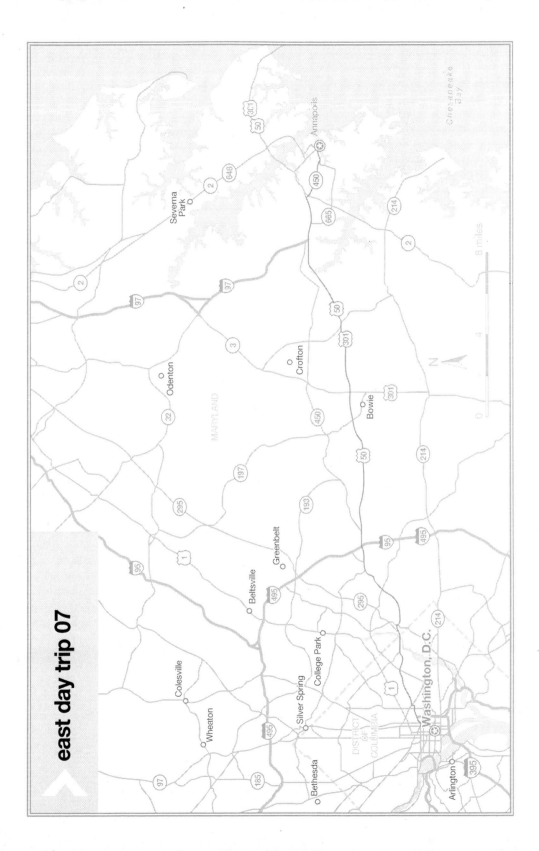

east day trip 07

either end, so your best bet is to leave before or after rush hour. You can also boat over to Annapolis and dock at one of the city's many marinas. Contact the harbormaster's office at (410) 263-7973 or (410) 263-7974 for details.

where to go

Annapolis City Dock. Bottom of Main Street, Annapolis, MD. Watch the boats come and go and eyeball the ones already docked. Lots of good people- and boat- (and sometimes duck-) watching here at the place locals sometimes refer to as "ego alley." The city dock gets very crowded during the summer. Public restrooms are nearby.

Annapolis Maritime Museum. 723 2nd St., Annapolis, MD; (410) 295-0104; amaritime .org. The Annapolis Maritime Museum is a free museum dedicated to engaging both children and adults with the ecology of the Chesapeake Bay and the maritime history of Annapolis. The museum makes it home in the old McNasby Oyster Co, the last oyster-packing plant in Annapolis, and uses its site to help visitors better understand the important role the oyster industry played in this part of the world. In addition to more traditional exhibits, the museum also boasts an "oyster view" aquarium, a locally made oyster boat, and one of the city's only public beaches where guests can wade, sit, or enjoy the city view. Boat trips to the Eastern Shore's fabled nineteenth-century Thomas Point Shoal Lighthouse run from the museum from June to early Oct, require reservations, and cost about $70 a person. During the summer, the museum holds its Tides and Tunes concert outdoor evening series and during the winter the museum takes its programming inside for its lecture series.

Annapolis Powerboat School and the Annapolis Sailing School. 7001 Bembe Beach Rd., Annapolis, MD; (800) 638-9192; annapolispowerboat.com or annapolissailing.com. Learn how to take a boat out on the open seas. One of the more popular offerings is "Become a Sailor in One Weekend." Call for prices and course offerings.

Banneker-Douglass Museum. 84 Franklin St., Annapolis, MD; (410) 216-6180; bd museum.com. Housed in the former Mt. Moriah AME Church, this museum helps tell the story of Maryland's black community from 1633 up to the present. Among the artifacts housed in the museum is the advertisement announcing the slave auction where Kunta Kinte, the hero of the epic book *Roots,* was sold against his will.

Compass Rose Theater. 49 Spa Rd., Annapolis, MD; (410) 980-6662; compassrose theater.org. The Compass Rose Theater is a professional teaching theater company with classes and workshops offered on-site and at other local venues. Compass Rose produces a full season of plays that include both professional actors and students.

Four Centuries Walking Tour. (410) 268-7600; annapolistours.com. Tour guides clad in colonial-era garb walk you through the historic highlights of Annapolis. The company also offers a ghost tour, an African-American history tour, and a slew of narrated boat cruises.

It's best to call or log on to the website for times, dates, starting locations, and prices before you hit town.

Hammond-Harwood House. 19 Maryland Ave., Annapolis, MD; (410) 263-4683; hammond harwoodhouse.org. This beautifully preserved colonial home houses an extensive collection of decorative objects and art from the late eighteenth and early nineteenth centuries. The landmark touts itself as having the "most beautiful doorway in America." Hours change during high and low season, so your best bet is to call ahead. A fee is charged for house admission but the boxwood garden and exhibit gallery are free.

Kunta Kinte–Alex Haley Memorial. Located at the head of City Dock across from the Market House. The life-size statue of author Alex Haley reading to three children helps pay tribute to the waves of enslaved Africans who arrived at this port in shackles and chains. Haley turned one of these individuals, his ancestor Kunta Kinte, into the protagonist in his Pulitzer Prize–winning novel, *Roots*. The outdoor memorial also contains a series of plaques and is always open.

Maryland State House. State Circle, Annapolis, MD; (410) 974-3400; msa.md.gov/msa/mdstatehouse/html/home.html. Perched atop the hill in State Circle, the Maryland State House stands as the focal point of the Annapolis skyline and possesses a rich history steeped in early American politics. Completed in 1779, the State House holds the distinction of being the oldest state capitol in continuous use and the only state capitol to have served as the US Capitol. George Washington resigned as commander-in-chief of the Continental Congress in the Old Senate Chamber and within these walls Congress ratified the Treaty of Paris, which ended the American Revolutionary War. The impressive wooden dome contains no nails (metal was in short supply after the war) and is instead held together with wooden pegs reinforced by iron straps.

Today the General Assembly meets in a newer section of the building, completed in 1905. When the assembly is in session you can watch the legislative process in action from the visitor galleries. Free self-guided tour information is available at the Office of Interpretation on the first floor, and several local companies offer guided tours for a fee. A current photo ID is required to enter the building.

United States Naval Academy. 52 King George St., Annapolis, MD; (410) 293-8687; usnabsd.com/for-visitors. Each year the best and the brightest high school graduates come to the US Naval Academy to begin officer training. Guided walking tours of the 338-acre waterfront college campus are given regularly for a fee and begin at the Armel-Leftwich Visitor Center. Highlights include a sample midshipman dorm room, the Main Chapel, adorned by Tiffany stained glass windows, and the Naval Academy Museum. If you are on campus at midday you can watch lunchtime formation, when the midshipmen line up for uniform inspection. The "Yard" conducts a special "Tour and Tea" Mon through Wed beginning at 1:30 p.m. and also runs a tour of the Commodore Uriah P. Levy Center and Jewish Chapel.

Military Reunion Tours and USNA Tour & Tea also are offered. Check the website for schedules. Everyone over sixteen must show a valid picture ID. Open daily.

William Paca House and Garden. 186 Prince George St., Annapolis, MD; (410) 990-4543; annapolis.org. The Historic Annapolis Foundation carefully restored this lovely historic home, which belonged to one of the four signers of the Declaration of Independence who called Annapolis home. The landmark house is considered a wonderful example of classic Georgian architecture and has been restored to portray colonial-era living, giving a glimpse into the lives of the family members and slaves who lived here. Tours of the property are given regularly and visitors are welcome to enjoy the 2 acres of manicured gardens when the house is open. Admission fee. The house has limited hours and sometimes closes during the winter.

where to shop

Annebeth's of Annapolis. 46 Maryland Ave., Annapolis, MD; annebeths.com. A favorite among locals for more than fifteen years, Annabeth's stocks specialty foods, beer, wine, gifts, and gift baskets of all shapes and sizes.

Capital Teas. 6 Cornhill St., Annapolis, MD; (410) 263-8327; capitalteas.com. The everything tea shop. More than sixty different loose-leaf teas can be found here. The shop also sells teapots, sandwiches, and drinks.

Lilac Bijoux. 145 Main St., Annapolis, MD; (410) 263-3309; lilacbijoux.com. Fun and funky jewelry, bags, and accessories are the name of the game in this little shop. The bead expert at the jewelry bar in the back of the store will help you create your own bauble.

Maine Cottage. 209 West St., Annapolis, MD; (866) 366-3505; mainecottage.com. A light and bright furniture store, Maine Cottage specializes in cottage furniture for coastal living in an array of happy colors and fabrics.

Re-Sails. 42 Randall St., Annapolis, MD; (410) 263-4982; resails.com. Just about everything here is crafted from repurposed boat sails. Pick out a one-of-a-kind duffle bag, jacket, or throw pillow. The items here have a distinct nautical look and feel and are no doubt great conversation starters.

Retropolitan Fine Antiques and Vintage. 14 Annapolis St., Annapolis, MD; (410) 263-0800; retropolitan.net. If words like retro, vintage, and midcentury modern get your heart rate going, then do not pass go and do not collect $200 before heading to Retropolitan Fine Antiques and Vintage. A treasure chest of upscale affordable finds, the shop has even outfitted several movie and TV sets with period sets and clothing.

Vivo. 6 Fleet St., Annapolis, MD; (410) 268-2258; vivoannapolis.com. Fair-trade and eco-friendly items fill the shelves here. A nice mix of clothing, accessories, housewares, and spa products. Many of the items—even the sari wrap skirts—are made from repurposed materials.

where to eat

Annapolis Ice Cream Company. 196 Main St., Annapolis, MD; (443) 482-3895; annapolis icecream.com. The ice cream here is made on site and very well might ruin you for the supermarket stuff forever. Flavors are displayed on flat-screen monitors and will let you know whether the seasonal choices like Cherry Pie or Gingerbread Cookie are available. You can even indulge your creative side while you indulge your sweet tooth by decorating a plastic spoon with the Sharpies kept on the counter. The store has tens of thousands (and counting) of art spoons from customers on display, which is as fun as the cold, creamy stuff that brought you here in the first place. Let me know if you spot mine. $.

Boatyard Bar & Grill. Severn Avenue and 4th Street, Annapolis, MD; (410) 216-6206; boatyardbarandgrill.com. The Eastport eatery ranks as a favorite with sailors, fishermen, and locals, not to mention anyone looking for a great weekend brunch. The crab cakes and raw bar here turn visitors into repeat customers and are often ordered with a cold pint. *Sail* magazine named the spot "one of the world's top sailing bars." Boatyard Bar & Grill is surprisingly child-friendly. $$.

Carrol's Creek Cafe. 410 Severn Ave., Annapolis, MD; (410) 263-8102; carrolscreek.com. Carrol's Creek has been around for some thirty years but its menu is brand new. In addition to the old favorites—like the scallop appetizer and cream of crab soup—the waterfront restaurant in the Eastport section of Annapolis has added many new items, including some gluten-free options. $$$.

Chick & Ruth's Delly. 165 Main St., Annapolis, MD; (410) 269-6737; chickandruths.com. An old-school deli with a personality as big as its multipage menu. Breakfast is served all day and features the house home fries. The family-run Annapolis institution claims "the largest shakes and sandwiches anywhere" and indeed they are big. Maryland memorabilia and photos of local personalities, politicians, and sports figures cover almost every inch of wall space and each morning at 8:30 a.m. (9:30 a.m. on the weekend) everyone stops, faces the flag over the counter, and recites the Pledge of Allegiance. $.

A Cook's Cafe. 911 Commerce Rd., Annapolis, MD; (410) 266-1511; acookscafe.com. A Cook's Cafe is a restaurant, cooking school, CSA program, market, and catering business rolled into one. $$.

Luna Blu. 35 West St., Annapolis, MD; (410) 267-9959; lunabluofannapolis.com. A charming and reasonable little restaurant serving classic Italian flavors. Fresh sauces are made daily and desserts are also made in house. A varied wine and martini list and a nice selection of antipastos, including such creations as a mozzarella and eggplant napoleon, round off the entree selection. $$$.

Mike's Crab House. 3030 Riva Rd., Riva, MD; (410) 956-2784; mikescrabhouse.com. Sure, Mike's serves things other than Maryland blue crabs, but many of the diners here simply aren't interested in anything else. Crab cakes, steamed crabs, crab soup, and crab quesadillas are some of the ways Mike's serves up the local delicacy. The large outdoor deck overlooking the South River can't be beat. The restaurant also has a tiki bar and karaoke nights. $$.

Miss Shirley's Cafe. 1 Park Place, Annapolis, MD; (410) 268-5171; missshirleys.com. Miss Shirley's menu blends southern dishes, local flavors, and favorites from the Bay. The menu changed with the seasons and can include such items as chicken-fried pork chops, Born on the Bay-O Eggs Benedict, and Old Bay waffles. $$.

Sofi's Crepes. 1 Craig St., Annapolis, MD; (410) 990-0929; sofiscrepes.com. Yummy sweet and savory crepes are made to order at this little eatery across from the Harbor Master and outside the pedestrian entrance to the Naval Academy. $$.

where to stay

The Annapolis Inn. 144 Prince George St., Annapolis, MD; (410) 295-5200; annapolisinn .com. Elegance is a permanent guest at the Annapolis Inn. The 3 suites in this restored eighteenth-century Georgian-style masterpiece exude warmth and charm and are impeccably furnished. The innkeepers pride themselves on personalized service and strive to honor most requests. Lounge over a three-course breakfast beneath the Austrian crystal chandeliers in the dining room, take your tea beside the marble fireplace in the parlor, or admire the koi pond in the enclosed garden patio. You may also want to ask about the inn's fabled past. A passageway below the property once served as part of the Underground Railroad, and Thomas Jefferson's doctor called 144 Prince George St. home at one time. $$$.

Royal Folly. 65 College Ave., Annapolis, MD; (410) 263-3999; royalfolly.com. The owners modernized this charming nineteenth-century home, adding a slew of upgrades including newly tiled bathrooms in its 14 guest rooms. The house boasts nine fireplaces, an outdoor Jacuzzi tub, and a deck overlooking St. John's College. Each of the royally named rooms and suites features a different decor and list of amenities. Gourmet breakfast is served every day except Sun, when a Champagne brunch is the order of the day. $$$.

Schooner *Woodwind*. On the docks of the Annapolis Marriott Waterfront Hotel, Annapolis, MD; (410) 263-7837; schoonerwoodwind.com. And now for something entirely different . . . a boat-and-breakfast. On Saturday from May to September you can spend the night aboard the Schooner *Woodwind*, a 74-foot sailing yacht that docks near downtown Annapolis. Arrive around 6 p.m. for a two-hour sunset cruise, then go get dinner in town and come back between 11 p.m. and midnight to bed down in one of the four double-occupancy rooms in the forward compartments. Rooms are spare but clean and there are two shared heads (bathrooms) for all guests. A continental breakfast is served on deck in the morning $$$,

State House Inn. 25 State Circle, Annapolis, MD; (410) 990-0024; statehouseinn.com. The cheery yellow facade and porch rockers draw guests into this bed-and-breakfast-style property located across from the State House. Rooms are individually appointed, a few have Jacuzzi tubs, and all have wireless Internet. A European-style continental breakfast is served daily. It's worth checking out the glass-bottom room on the main floor that gives a literal glimpse into the archaeological excavation below. Minimum stay required on some weekends and holidays. $$$.

Westin Annapolis. 100 Westgate Circle, Annapolis, MD; (410) 972-4300; westinannapolis .com. Done in a palette of earth tones and dark wood accents, the property gives off a Zen vibe from the minute you step inside. The chain's Heavenly Beds, Heavenly Cribs, and Heavenly Dog Beds help keep all travelers sleeping soundly. A heated indoor pool, Aveda spa, and Azure Restaurant complete the package. An hourly shuttle runs to downtown—it's otherwise a hike. $$$.

day trip 08

east

blue skies, blue waters, blue crabs:
chestertown & cambridge, md

Quaint historic towns dot Maryland's Eastern Shore, making it a peaceful antidote for the stresses of inside-the-beltway life. The towns range in size from small to tiny and, as a rule, are filled with colonial and Federal architecture, cozy B&Bs, and seaside pathways. And while all of that is wonderful, it's the allure of the Maryland blue crab that draws many shellfish devotees to this part of the state. The local delicacy is prepared every which way along the Eastern Shore and the business of crabbing stands is an important part of the area's identity. As a result, crabmeat dishes grace most of the menus here, be it in a gourmet restaurant or at a waterside shack.

chestertown

The Chester River not only gives Chestertown its name, but in many ways it also acts as the town's soul. The town's focus, color, and even history come from the water beside it.

In colonial times, Chestertown acted as a bustling port of entry for settlers coming into Maryland. Wealthy merchants who made their living on the waters built lavish homes here, and many of these eighteenth-century buildings have been restored or preserved and can still be viewed. Fast-forward to modern times, when Chestertown remains a beautiful town, rich with historic architecture, water views, and quaint B&Bs and shops.

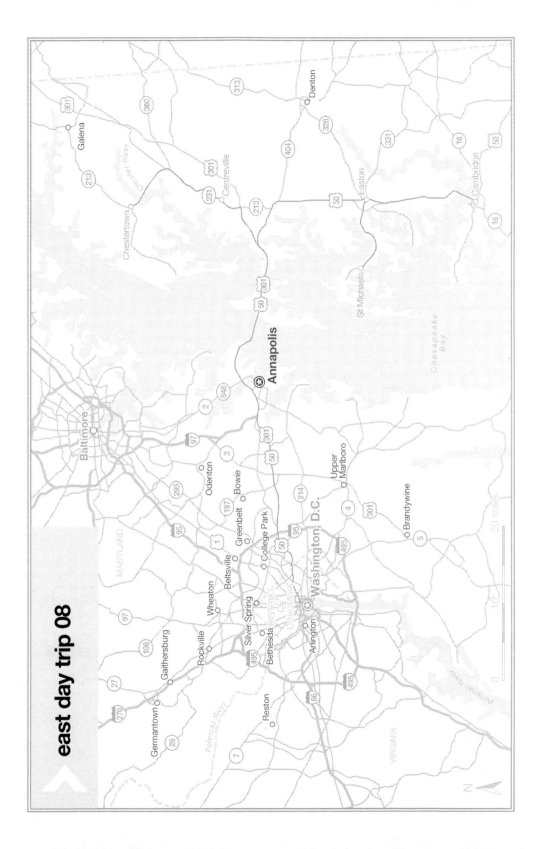

east day trip 08

getting there

Chestertown is about an hour and a half from the city, although beach traffic can add time, especially getting on and off the Bay Bridge. Take MD 50 East past Annapolis and then drive over the Bay Bridge. Continue on MD 50/301 through Kent Island. At the 50/301 split, take MD 301. Five miles north, turn right at the MD 213 North exit toward Centreville. Follow MD 213 North for approximately 20 miles to Chestertown.

where to go

Buckingham Wharf on Buckingham Road. Buckingham Wharf is a soft landing at the end of a country road on the upper Chester River and a good spot to launch a canoe or kayak. Bald eagles and osprey often are spotted here so be on the lookout as you paddle down the marsh-lined waters. Upstream from here is about 5 miles to the public boat ramp in Crumpton. And downstream, it is about a 3.5-mile paddle to Chestertown.

The Custom House. 101 S. Water St., Chestertown, MD; washcoll.edu/centers/starr/the-custom-house.php. Located on the campus of the historic Washington College, the Custom House is the home for the college's prestigious C. V. Starr Center for the Study of the American Experience. The center sponsors a wide variety of lectures and programs exploring American history. The building itself dates back to the 1700s. An audio guide of Chestertown can be picked up at the Custom House on Friday and Saturday afternoons. The campus of the liberal arts college is a beautiful place to explore and tour.

Fountain Park. Chestertown, MD. Right in the center of town sits Fountain Park, a popular hangout and site of many local events including a weekly farmers' and artisans' market, concerts, and the annual Art in the Park festival.

Geddes-Piper House. 101 Church Alley, Chestertown, MD; (410) 778-3499; kentcounty history.org. The Federal-era building houses the Historical Society of Kent County and a small museum, library, and gift shop. Among the objects on display here are a magnificent collection of Chinese export teapots, a colonial-era kitchen, and Native American artifacts. Closed Mon. From 4 to 6 p.m. on the first Friday of every month, the society sponsors History Happy Hours at the house. An informal historical program is paired with wine and cheese and is open to the public. You can also get information here about the society's ghost tours and other offerings.

Schooner *Sultana* and the Sultana Projects, Inc. 105 S. Cross St., Chestertown, MD; (410) 778-5954; sultanaprojects.org. The nonprofit Sultana Project offers the public hands-on opportunities to explore the Chesapeake and its past, present, and future significance. On regular two-hour sailing trips aboard the schooner *Sultana,* a replica of a vintage merchant vessel that served in the British Royal Navy, passengers get a glimpse of eighteenth-century seafaring life. The Sultana Project also offers longer, more involved educational sailing excursions for students.

where to shop

Chestertown RiverArts. 315 High St., Chestertown, MD; (410) 778-6300; chestertown riverarts.org. Part art gallery and part community art center, RiverArts hosts exhibits by local talent, as well as workshops and classes. The center's gift shop sells the items crafted by Eastern Shore artists and artisans.

Houston's Dockside Emporium. 315 High St., Chestertown, MD; (410) 778-9079; chestertown.com/houstons. Clothes, watches, housewares, and gift items with a regional flair can be purchased here. Think everything from drinking glasses decorated with dogs to tummy-tucking jeans and you get the picture of the mix of items sold here.

Robert Ortiz Studios. 207C S. Cross St., Chestertown, MD; (410) 810-1400; ortizstudios .com. The 2,000-square-foot multipurpose studio and shop is a must-see for anyone even remotely interested in the art of woodworking or furniture making. Artist Roberto Jorge Ortiz works in the Shaker and Japanese traditions creating stunning, impeccably designed original pieces. Visitors can often see him at work when they arrive at the store, which is housed in a restored mill.

Sophisticated Vintage. 204 High St., Chestertown, MD; (301) 642-5284; sophisticated vintage.com. Co-owners and friends of this treasure trove of vintage home furnishings search high and low for the items they spruce up, style, and sell in this shop. Hours are limited during the winter.

where to eat

Brook's Tavern. 860 High St., Chestertown, MD; (410) 810-0012; brookstavern.com. Local is always the special of the day at Brook's Tavern. The menu here is always crafted from locally sourced food and only in-season produce is used. The menu often features locally caught seafood and fish and grass-fed beef. The restaurant itself is housed in the historic Radcliffe Mill. Closed Sun, Mon, the last week in Feb, and the first week in Mar. $$.

fountain art

The colors and feel of the Eastern Shore have inspired many a talented local to create beautiful works of art. Each fall many of them flock to Chestertown's Fountain Park to show off and sell their creations to those who come out to celebrate local art and artists. Sponsored by the local arts league, Chestertown Art in the Park is held rain or shine, and it's not unusual to find such treasures as jewelry crafted from sea glass, wildlife watercolor paintings, and artful landscape photography.

Durding's Store. 5742 N. Main St., Rock Hall, MD; (410) 778-7957; Durding's takes you back in time to an old-fashioned ice cream parlor, with its authentic features and soda fountain. Enjoy a sundae at one of the counter stools or another treat at one of the old-fashioned booths. Durding's is located at the corner of Main and Sharp Streets. $.

Fish Whistle. 98 Cannon St., Chestertown, MD; (410) 778-3566; fishandwhistle.com. A small, casual eatery that cooks up all the seafood that helps define the region's cuisines, including catfish fingers, grilled mahimahi tacos, and, of course, Maryland crab cakes. Fish Whistle offers a different nightly specials every day of the week. $$.

Lemon Leaf Cafe. 337 High St., Chestertown, MD; (443) 282-0004; thellcafe.com. The Lemon Leaf Cafe is something of an Eastern Shore classic and a must visit for many who return to Chestertown. The crab soup is a customer favorite and has many awards to prove it. Miss Joanne, the Lemon Leaf's pastry chef, is a legend herself as is her lemon meringue pie. $$.

Play It Again Sam. 108 S. Cross St., Chestertown, MD; (410) 778-2688. Known around town as the best place to grab a cup of coffee. Take it to go or sit around and enjoy the board games and people-watching. $.

where to stay

Brampton Bed & Breakfast Inn. 25227 Chestertown Rd., Chestertown, MD; (410) 778-1860; bramptoninn.com. For anyone looking to spend a weekend curled up with a good book or curled up with a special someone, Brampton is just the place. Nestled on 20 acres of wooded rolling hills, the nineteenth-century plantation house meticulously maintains 12 guest cottages and rooms, each with a private bath, wood-burning fireplace, fluffy robes, flat-screen TVs, and DVD players—although anything on TV likely won't come close to the view outside. A rocker-filled porch overlooks the beautiful property and lawn, which also offers many places to sit and relax. The home-cooked breakfast at Brampton is the kind of stuff epicurean legends are made of and can feature anything from cheddar dill scones to rhubarb strawberry crisp to pumpkin chocolate chip muffins. Guests also can enjoy afternoon tea and the constant supply of homemade cookies. Guests in the cottages may request breakfast in bed. $$$.

Great Oak Manor. 10568 Cliff Rd., Chestertown, MD; (410) 778-5943; greatoakmd.com. A bald eagle makes a daily appearance high above the Great Oak Manor. Quiet, charm, and cozy touches also appear here daily. The historic waterfront manor has twelve guest rooms and offers such amenities as soaking tubs, working fireplaces, feather-top beds, and antique furnishings and artwork. The innkeepers keep a fleet of bicycles and kayaks for guests to use, and they pride themselves on the breakfast they prepare each morning that features the inn's signature dish, crab quiche. $$$.

Lauretum Bed & Breakfast Inn. 954 High St., Chestertown, MD; (800) 742-3236; lauretuminn.com. An 1881 Victorian guesthouse set on 6 acres, the pretty Lauretum Bed & Breakfast Inn, houses 5 rooms with private baths, cozy common rooms, and a porch filled with rocking chairs. During their stay guests can use the Chester River Yacht and Country Club, which is about 3 miles from the inn and has a golf course, pool, and restaurant. $$.

cambridge

One of the oldest in Maryland, Cambridge is a small Eastern Shore town with pretty views and places to explore. Cambridge sits on land once belonging to the Choptank Indian tribe. Colonists first settled here in 1684 and incorporated it as a town in 1793. Among the most famous Cambridge natives is Harriet Tubman, who was born here in the early 1800s. A historic marker alerts visitors to the spot.

getting there

Cambridge is about 40 miles past the Bay Bridge. Take US Route 50 to the bridge, cross over and continue eastbound to Cambridge.

where to go

Bill Burton Fishing Piers State Park. 29761 Bolingbroke Point Dr., Trappe, MD; (410) 820-1668; dnr.state.md.us/publiclands/eastern/choptankpier.asp. Not far from Cambridge, Fishing Piers State Park gives locals and visitors a place to fish year-round. Perch, striped bass, hardheads, sea trout, and catfish are a few of the catches to be had here. The pier is lighted for night fishing and is adjacent to MD 50 at the Frederick C. Malkus Bridge.

Harriet Tubman Museum and Education Center. 424 Race St., Cambridge, MD; (410) 228-0401. A small museum dedicated to the woman called Moses. The museum is small but does a nice job paying tribute with its collection of artifacts, letters, and photographs. Visit the-rock-newsmagazine.com/harriet.tubman.tours.html for information about tours.

Skipjack *Nathan*. Docked at the Long Wharf at the end of High Street; (410) 228-7141; skipjack-nathan.org. Visitors can sail back in time on the *Nathan of Dorchester,* a wooden boat built in the spirit of traditional Chesapeake Bay skipjacks. The boat takes passengers out on the Choptank River and also offers other educational programs. Check the website or call for current schedule and prices.

where to shop

Chesapeake Classics. 317 High St., Cambridge, MD; (410) 228-6509; chesapeake -classics.com. Ducks, ducks, and more ducks. Chesapeake Classics sells one of the largest collections of vintage and new waterfowling and fishing decoys, lures, and calls.

Heirloom Antiques Gallery. 19 Academy St., Cambridge, MD; (410) 228-8445. A cooperative shop selling the collections of many different antiques dealers. Everything from antique pottery to collectibles to jewelry to furniture can be found here.

where to eat

Bay Country Bakery. 2915 Ocean Gateway, Cambridge, MD; (410) 228-9111; baycountry bakery.com. Fresh baked cookies, cakes, pies, doughnuts, and Danish tempt anyone who walks through the doors at Bay Country Bakery. The bakery has an old-school feel to it with its large glass display cases for the baked goods and counter seating for a quick cup of coffee. Bay Country also specializes in wedding cakes. $.

Jimmie & Sook's Raw Bar and Grill. 421 Race St., Cambridge, MD; (443) 225-4115; jimmieandsooks.com. Oysters, clams, crabs, mussels, and more are the order of the day at this favorite local spot. Soups, salads, and burgers are also served. The restaurant hosts live music and other entertainment every Wed through Sat night. Check out the website for daily specials (for example, kids eat free after 3 on Mon). $$.

where to stay

Hyatt Regency Chesapeake Bay Golf Resort, Spa & Marina. 100 Heron Blvd., Cambridge, MD; (410) 901-1234; chesapeakebay.hyatt.com/en/hotel/home.html. When the beachfront Hyatt resort opened in 2002, it helped breathe new life into the small seaside town of Cambridge. Today the Hyatt continues to draw visitors and interest to the town. The hotel offers a pretty beach, indoor and outdoor pools, restaurants, spa, golf course, and marina. $$.

Lodgecliffe on the Choptank. 103 Choptank Ter., Cambridge, MD; (410) 228-1760; lodgecliffe.com/. Set on a bluff overlooking the Choptank River, the Lodgecliffe offers four pretty guest rooms and lovely waterfront views. Wake up to the smell of fresh coffee brewing and sample treats like cranberry sourdough french toast, puff pancakes, and phyllo dough egg blossoms. $$.

shore heart—
talbot county:

easton, md & st. michaels, md

Talbot County is located in the heart of Maryland's Eastern Shore. Charming historic towns, both Easton and St. Michaels are two gems of Talbot County. Both towns draw visitors throughout the year, particularly during the summer months.

easton

Easton has the feel of an old colonial town. It's known for its pretty architecture and friendly feel. You'll likely spot many cyclists pedaling around while you are here because a bicycle is a great way to experience this area. Easton's downtown has a good selection of restaurants, shops, and inns when you are ready to pull over for a spell. And, while you are here you should check out what's playing at the Avalon and upstairs at The Stoltz Listening Room.

where to go

The Talbot County Visitors Center. 11 S. Harrison St., Easton, MD; (410) 770-8000; tourtalbot.org. I love a good visitor's center to grab some information and to chat with the people at the desk about their favorite spots.

Academy of the Arts. 106 South St., Easton, MD; (410) 822-0345; academyartmuseum .org. This lovely little art museum began with a mere seven paintings. Today it counts more than a thousand works as part of its permanent collection, the majority of which are

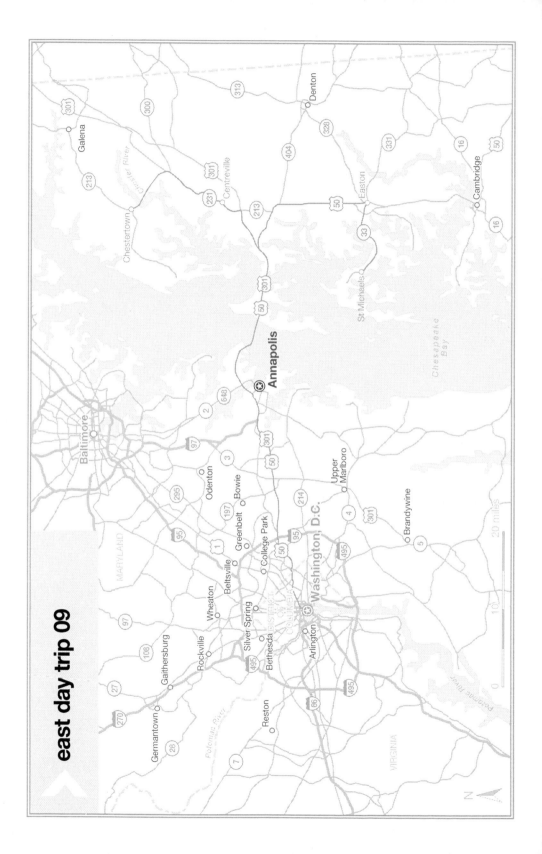

east day trip 09

European and American works on paper. The academy has a full calendar of interesting temporary exhibits and also sponsors lectures, workshops, and classes for adults and children.

The Amish Market. 101 Marlboro Ave., Easton, MD; (443) 239-2356; amishcountryfarmers market.com. Multiple vendors make the trip from Amish Country to Easton each week to sell their goods here on Thursday, Friday, and Saturday. Fresh meats, produce, cheese, pickles, and baked goods top the list of what can be found at this market, which also sells handcrafted furniture, clothing, and home decor. The hand-rolled soft pretzels rank as a fan favorite, as do the pies, fudge, and penny-style candy. Barbecued chicken, ribs, and other home-cooked items also can be purchased at the market and during the "Friday Night Social" between 5 and 7 pm., when participating vendors offer an all-you-can-eat platter along with other specials. The market is open from Thurs through Sat. Check the website for hours.

Avalon Theatre. 40 E. Dover St., Easton, MD; (410) 822-7299; avalontheatre.com. The Avalon Theatre is a standout of the Eastern Shore arts scene. The historic 1921 theater attracts all kinds of in-demand performing artists including up-and-coming acts and tried-and-true performers who are drawn back to the venue. Here you can experience everything from music to dance to film to plays and musical theater. The Avalon also is committed to showcasing local talent. The pretty theater spent many years as a movie house and even hosted the world premiere of the 1928 film The First Kiss, starring Gary Cooper and Fay Wray. The silent flick was filmed in Easton and St. Michaels.

> **The Stoltz Listening Room** upstairs at the Avalon offers an intimate and acousti-cally perfect club-like space to appreciate jazz, blues, and other live music while kicking back with something from the bar. The Stoltz Listening Room was built as a gift for Jack and Susan Stoltz for their fiftieth wedding anniversary from their son Keith. The Listening Room is favorite spot for music aficionados and performers alike who love the feel and sound of the space.

Easton Cycle and Sport. 723 Goldsborough St., Easton, MD; (410) 822-7433; easton cycleandsport.com. Bikes, kayaks, stand-up paddles, and even small Hobie Wave catamaran sailboats can be rented at Easton Cycle and Sport. It's also the place to pop in if the bike or equipment you brought with you runs into some trouble.

Pickering Creek Audubon Center. 11450 Audubon Ln., Easton, MD; (410) 822-4903; pickeringcreek.audubon.org. Pickering Creek Audubon Center sits on a 400-acre farm that is alive with a variety of habitats including old-growth forests, marshes, meadows, wetlands, and more than a mile of shoreline. Visitors can explore the walking trails, bird watch from the platforms, stroll through the gardens, or launch a canoe from the grounds. You can also check out the tool museum and the Watermen's Shanty here. And all for no charge. Pickering Creek is free and open to the public 365 days a year from sunrise to sunset.

where to shop

Dragonfly. 21 Goldsborough St., Easton, MD; (410) 763-9262; dragonflyboutique.biz. An upscale women's boutique that might entice you to expand your wardrobe before you leave town.

Easton Maryland Farmers' Market. Harrison Street, Easton, MD; no phone. Fill your basket with the bounty of the region and season every Saturday at the Easton's Farmers' Market, where growers sell local produce, flowers, plants, herbs, gourmet items, lotions, potions, and other items. The market is held from held from 8 a.m. to 1 p.m. every Sat from Apr through early Dec. Live music typically plays from 10:30 a.m. to 12:30 p.m.

easton events

Be it Independence Day, the great outdoors, or the start of a new year, Easton knows how to ring it in. The town plays host to a range of special events, festivals, and celebrations throughout the year. Here are a few:

__Chesapeake Chamber Music:__ Held in June, this two-week-long festival has been in play for more than a quarter century and includes a free young people's concert at the Avalon Theatre.

__Old Tyme Fourth of July:__ A daylong community Independence Day celebration capped off by a good ol' fireworks display.

__Plein Air-Easton:__ A carefully selected group of artists step out of their studios and into the great outdoors to paint what nature puts in front of them for this annual competition. These paintings and other works of art then are displayed in the Academy Art Museum and the winners are chosen. And during the last weekend of the festival, the paintings are for sale.

__Annual Waterfowl Festival:__ On the second full weekend in November, thousands of people from all around the country flock to Easton for this three-day celebration complete with wildlife art displays, duck-calling contests, and fly-fishing demonstrations, to name a few.

__First Night Talbot:__ One the very last night of the year, Easton celebrates the passing of the old year with First Night Talbot, a family-oriented, alcohol-free community festival. At midnight watch the crab drop. (Or, for those with kids or those who want to be asleep at midnight, come a few hours before the clock strikes twelve for the early drop.)

Luna Chic Boutique. 7 Goldsborough St., Easton, MD; (410) 822-4148; tholunachick .com. And now for something different. A shop filled with mosaics including a fantastical collection of adorned mannequins from the imagination of Christie Rottman, Luna Chic's owner and artist.

M. Randall & Company. 17 N. Harrison St., Easton, MD; (410) 820-4077; marcrandall .com. Stop in to this women's boutique for a new dress or outfit to wear out to dinner in Easton. Clothes and accessories here tend to be contemporary and easy to wear.

Piazza Italian Market. 218 N. Washington St. #54, Easton, MD; (410) 820-8281; piazza italianmarket.com. Piazza is a full-service Italian market selling groceries, cheeses, cured meats, and other Italian delicacies that don't often make it onto the shelves of other grocery stores. It's a good place to hit for sandwiches or other premade picnic provisions.

South Street Art Gallery. 5 South St., Easton, MD; (410) 770-8350; southstreetartgallery .com. A guild of professional artists share the business of running this art gallery housed in a welcoming white Victorian house with red trim. The group's main focus is representational paintings including Eastern Shore landscapes, plein-air studies, still lifes, portraits, wildlife, and figurative works. Additionally, inside find a selection of pottery and sculptures.

where to eat

Bartlett Pear Inn. 28 S. Harrison St., Easton, MD; (410) 770-3300; bartlettpearinn.com/ Home.html. The upscale restaurant attached to the Bartlett Pear Inn is considered one of the best on the shore—and for good reason. Foodies will want to add a meal at Bartlett Pear to their must lists when they come to town. $$$.

The BBQ Joint. 216 E. Dover St., Easton, MD; andrewevansbbqjoint.com. In a region of the country where people don't mess around when it comes to barbecue, The BBQ Joint manages to stand out. Spare ribs, pulled pork, and brisket are regulars on the menu here. You can dine in or take out. $.

El Dorado Restaurant. 4 S. Aurora St., Easton, MD; (410) 820-5155. The kitchen here cooks up Mexican and Latin American dishes. $$.

Joe's Bagel Cafe. Marlboro Ave. #63, Easton, MD; (410) 763-7410; joesbagelcafe.com. Joe's is your place in town for bagels, coffee, and shmears. You can pick up a dozen to go or eat your sandwich in the cafe while you take advantage of the free Wi-Fi. $.

Mabel's Bakery. 27 S. Harrison St., Easton, MD; (410) 443-9790; mabels-bakery.net. A pretty-in-pink little bakery in town filled with cupcakes, pies, and other sweet treats. $.

Mason's. 22 S. Harrison St., Easton, MD; (410) 822-3204; masonsgourmet.com. Mason's describes itself as "comfortably sophisticated." Classic cuisine infused with the flavors of the Eastern Shore is the order of day here. On gentle summer nights request a table in the garden courtyard. $$.

Olde Towne Creamery & Desserts. 9 Goldsborough St., Easton, MD; (410) 820-5223; otcreamery.com. Really, what's a small town without an ice cream shop? $.

Peacock Restaurant & Lounge. 202 E. Dover St., Easton, MD; (866) 450-7600; innat202 dover.com. Even if you are not checking in for the night, you can still dine at the popular restaurant found in the Inn at 202 Dover. Local influences and flavors can be found on the menu here. $$$.

Red Hen Coffee House & Cafe. 1 Goldsborough St., Easton, MD; (410) 690-3662; red hencoffee.com. Red Hen takes coffee very seriously. And, as a result, has a happy following of locals and visitors who like to start the day here with a cup in hand. The shop also sells baked goods, artisan breads, and other tasty menu items. If you can't get enough of the bread, inquire about Red Hen's CSB—like a CSA for really good loaves of bread. The shop also hosts music shows. $$.

where to stay

Bartlett Pear Inn. 28 S. Harrison St., Easton, MD; (410) 770-3300; bartlettpearinn.com/ Home.html. Since it opened its gracious doors, the Bartlett Pear Inn has collected quite an impressive collection of accolades and rave reviews. Equal parts perfect elegance, charm, and comfort, the Inn has seven guest rooms all named for a variety of pear. The location is just right for exploring town by foot, but it's also just as wonderful for staying put and forgetting about your big-city troubles. Be warned, the creative breakfasts here may spoil you for breakfasts for a while. $$$.

Bishop's House Bed & Breakfast. 214 Goldsborough St., Easton, MD; (410) 820-7290; An old Victorian house, this five-room B&B is known for its attention to service, comfy beds, and its big home-cooked breakfasts. Most of the guest room baths have whirlpool tubs and three have working fireplaces to cozy up to during the colder months. Guests can watch TV or a movie, borrow a book, or hang out in the third-floor sitting room, which the innkeeper stocks with complimentary coffee, teas, hot chocolate, sodas, and snacks. Outside on the wraparound porch, with its rockers and porch swing, is a favorite spot. The B&B also will lend guests bicycles (along with maps, helmets, locks, and chains) but bikes do need to be reserved before you arrive.

Inn at 202 Dover. 202 E. Dover St., Easton, MD; (866) 450-7600; innat202dover.com. A lovingly restored 1874 Colonial Revival mansion houses the Inn at 202 Dover, which is a member of the Historic Hotels of America. Guests can choose from four elegant suites, each with its own regional theme—France, Asia, England, and Africa. There is also one luxury en suite "Victorian" bedroom. A secret garden out back is a favorite spot among guests regardless of which room they choose.

st. michaels

Nestled between the Susquehanna River and the Chesapeake Bay, St. Michaels is bathed in small-town charm and sea breezes. Dotted with historic Federal, Colonial, and Victorian homes, cute shops, and charming inns, St. Michaels has a little something for most everyone.

getting there

St. Michaels sits beyond the Bay Bridge and its larger neighboring town of Easton. Take Route 50 to Route 322 to Route 33, which will bring you into town.

where to go

Chesapeake Bay Maritime Museum. 213 N. Talbot St., St. Michaels, MD; (410) 745-8010; cbmm.org. Spread out over an 18-acre waterfront campus, the Chesapeake Bay Maritime Museum stands as a living-history experience dedicated to preserving and furthering the Chesapeake Bay's heritage and culture. Rather than relying on display cases or costumed actors, the museum instead uses real people to tell the area's story. On any given day a master decoy carver could be at work, or restoration work on a traditional sea vessel might be happening in the boatyard. You can also take a break from the exhibits and just enjoy the lawn and the water view. There is an admission fee, and hours vary by season, so check before you go.

Linden Spa at The Inn at Perry Cabin. 308 Watkins Ln., St. Michaels, MD; (866) 278-9601; lindenspa.com. There is little that cannot be least temporarily forgotten while dressed in soft white robe and reclined in a comfy chair in the Linden Spa's aptly named relaxation room. Sunlight streams in through the large window in front of you and offers a pretty view of some of the inn's linden trees that inspired its name. Freshly brewed teas, berries, and other antioxidant-rich snacks are served on china plates and cups. And all of this before you even start your massage, facial, or other treatment.

St. Michaels Museum at St. Mary's Square. St. Mary's Square, St. Michaels, MD; (410) 745-9561; stmichaelsmuseum.org. The small-town museum runs two docent-led walking tours. One focuses on Frederick Douglass, who was a slave in St. Michaels when he was a teenager. The ninety-minute tour centers on sites important to his years here and also offers an overview of his extraordinary life and historic achievements. The museum's Historic St. Michaels Waterfront Tour gives visitors a sense of life long ago in the small waterfront village. Docents stop at sites of significance in the historic district, as well as point out some of the restored and original 1800s buildings and houses here. Tours cost $10 and are given at 10:30 a.m. Sat from May to Oct.

where to shop

American Holiday. 300 S. Talbot St., St. Michaels, MD; (410) 690-3150; iloveah.com. It's hard not to be pulled in to this light and bright boutique. It's even harder not to pull your wallet out as you explore its contemporary yet charmingly quirky inventory that ranges from super-soft mohair throws in delicious colors to melamine red Solo cups to darling pool cover-ups. The affordable store also carries a mix of women's clothes, jewelry, home accents, gift items, and lots more.

Coco & Company. 209 N. Talbot St., St Michaels, MD; (410) 745-3400; cocoandcompany .com. Vintage pieces artfully blend with new items at CoCo & Company, a beautifully eclectic shop that often graces the pages of national magazines for its special eye for style for the home.

Chesapeake Bay Outfitters. 100 N. Talbot St., St. Michaels, MD; (410) 745-3107. This shop has been around for more than thirty years and features clothing and shoes that reflect the Eastern Shore's historic, relaxed vibe. The store carries a range of boat shoes and many cute boots and sandals for the non-nautical set.

The Crab Claw. 304 Burns St., St. Michaels, MD; (410) 745-2900; thecrabclaw.com. Beer and crabs outside at The Crab Claw is something of rite of passage in this part of the world. You can boat up or drive up to the restaurant.

Sailor of St. Michaels. 214 N. Talbot St., St. Michaels, MD; (410) 745-2580. For more than twenty-five years, Sailor of St. Michaels has been outfitting locals and visitors with classic clothing and styles.

St. Michaels Candy & Gifts. 216 N. Talbot St., St. Michaels, MD; (410) 745-6060; candy isdandy.com. Handmade truffles, jelly beans, and even chocolate crabs fill the store's glass display cases. The cute shop also sells cards, candles, and other gift items.

where to eat

Big Al's. 302 N. Talbot St., St. Michaels, MD; (410) 745-3151. If you have crab on the brain then Big Al's is the place for you. Locals flock to Big Al's during the summer for its lump crab cakes as well as its soft shell crabs and crab deviled eggs. Big Al's offers eat-in or carry-out, featuring their famous crab cakes, as well as soft-shell crabs and pulled pork sandwiches. Big Al's also smokes turkeys and ribs, both of which are in big demand before Thanksgiving and Fourth of July. You take out or eat in, but seating is limited. During the height of fishing season you can also pick up live bait at Big Al's.

Blue Crab Coffee Co. 102 Freemont St., St. Michaels, MD; (410) 745-4155; bluecrabcoffee .com. The yellow house behind the supermarket brews fresh tea and coffee and other hot drinks. The shop has a general store feel about it. You can order a cup of joe to drink or take some beans home. $.

Carpenter Street Saloon. 113 S. Talbot St., St. Michaels, MD; (410) 745-5111. Tho kind of fabulous neighborhood dive bar where everyone knows your name. C-Street serves Lighthouse Ale, brewed on the Eastern Shore, and a host of other food and drinks. The popular upstairs game room has pool tables and video games. $$.

Gina's Cafe. 601 S. Talbot St., St. Michaels, MD; (410) 745-6400. This little place is fabulous every which way from its twinkly light-filled creative decor to its outrageously fresh Southwestern food. Gina is a genius of combining flavors to create her menu of tacos, burritos, and other inspired dishes. Don't forget to order a margarita and check out the fun bathroom. $$.

Justine's Ice Cream Parlour. 106 Talbot St., St. Michaels, MD; (410) 745-0404; justines icecream.com. For more than 25 years, Justine's has been the place in town for an ice cream fix. $.

Key Lime Cafe. 207 N. Talbot St., St. Michaels, MD; (410) 745-3158, keylime-cafe.com. Tucked into a cheery yellow cottage, the Key Lime Cafe serves a menu that changes weekly and includes many flavors from the sea. Special wine tasting events are held throughout the year and have featured everything from Italian wines to Chilean wines to ale tastings. $$.

Sherwood's Landing Restaurant. 308 Watkins Ln., St. Michaels, MD; (410) 745-2200; perrycabin.com. The restaurant at the famed Inn at Perry Cabin, Sherwood's Landing serves artfully prepared cuisine under the direction of master chef Mark Salter. Many of the dishes are inspired by regional flavors, and the dining room overlooks the Miles River. $$$.

208 Talbot. 208 Talbot St., St. Michaels, MD; (410) 745-3838; 208talbot.com. The family-run 208 Talbot quickly became the "it" restaurant in these parts, attracting diners from near and far. The team in the kitchen is committed to the farm-to-table philosophy, incorporating local and in-season ingredients into most every dish. Closed Mon. $$.

where to stay

The Inn at Perry Cabin. 308 Watkins Ln., St. Michaels, MD; (410) 745-2200; perrycabin .com. The picture-perfect Inn at Perry Cabin exudes understated luxury. Rooms in the beautiful seaside Victorian manor are done in a soothing palette and include a long list of amenities. The circa-1816 intimate resort sits on the water and has beautifully manicured gardens, including a historic one that boasts the state's oldest holly tree, dating back to the early 1800s. $$$.

Old Brick Inn. 401 S. Talbot St., St. Michaels, MD; (410) 745-3323; oldbrickinn.com. The Old Brick Inn actually is three separate buildings. The Kemp House, Main House, and Carriage House each have inviting, individually appointed rooms. All guests have access to the hot tub, open year-round, and the swimming pool, which is open only in the summer. $$.

day trip 10

east

wondrous wetlands:
blackwater national wildlife refuge, md

blackwater national wildlife refuge

Not far beyond the Eastern Shore's elegant architecture stands an example of nature's elegance. The Blackwater National Refuge and its thousands of acres provide a protected habitat for hundreds of species of waterfowl, birds, plant life, and animals. Often called the Everglades of the north, Blackwater offers visitors a place to hike, bike, and kayak among wildlife in its natural glory. Each season casts a new light on the refuge and brings with it a new species to admire, observe, and photograph.

getting there

The Wildlife Refuge is about 12 miles south of the town of Cambridge. After crossing the Chesapeake Bay Bridge, take Route 50 to Route 16 West (Church Creek Road) to Egypt Road. Continue on Egypt Road until you see signs for Wildlife Drive and the Refuge. The visitor center is the second building on the left.

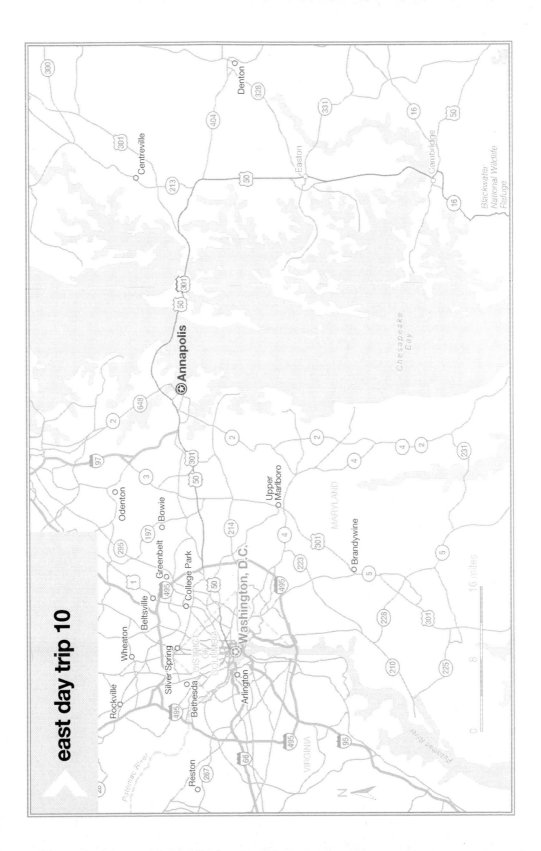

east day trip 10

where to go

Blackwater National Wildlife Refuge. 2145 Key Wallace Dr., Cambridge, MD; (410) 228-2677; fws.gov/blackwater. It's hard to imagine that this vast wildlife sanctuary where the bald eagle soars had a past life as a fur farm where muskrats were trapped and most of the trees were timbered. Today that same land now thrives as part of the Blackwater National Wildlife Refuge. Established in 1933, the 27,000-acre preserve serves as a safe haven for migratory birds and includes a rich tidal marsh, freshwater ponds, and dense forest areas.

If it's birds you want to see, birds are what you'll get here. Groups of Canada geese traveling on the Atlantic Flyway winter at Blackwater, and in the late fall the area plays host to tens of thousands of geese, swans, and ducks.

The conservationists at Blackwater take particular pride in the three "recovering" animal species that live here—the Delmarva fox squirrel, the migrant peregrine falcon, and the American bald eagle. Once classified as endangered species, these animals are beginning to thrive at Blackwater and appear to be emerging from their endangered status. Two types of deer, including the sika deer, also roam the refuge. Not everything that is alive at the refuge walks or flies. Approximately 165 endangered plant species grow at Blackwater. There is a small charge to enter the refuge.

Visitor center. Stop here on your way in, get the lay of the land, collect some information, and plan the rest of your day. Inside the two-story center you'll find lots of information, exhibits about wildlife, and an actual eagle's nest. The highlight of the center for many is the Osprey Cam, which streams live images from a 35-foot-high platform where the birds nest and near where they fish. The ospreys are migratory raptors and nest at Blackwater from March to September but the cam is kept on all year to capture images of the other birds attracted to the platform near the edge of the Blackwater River. The Osprey Cam was so popular that another cam was mounted over an active bald eagle nest, and viewers can't seem to get enough. The live Eagle Cam has proven even more popular than the Osprey

canoe and kayak rental and guide information

Blackwater Paddle & Pedal Adventures. 4303 Bucktown Rd., Cambridge, MD; (410) 901-9255; blackwaterpaddleandpedal.com.

Chesapeake Outdoor Adventures. PO Box 45, Sherwood, MD; (410) 745-9546; chesapeakeoutdooradventures.com.

Peake Paddle Tours. 30436 Belmont Dr., Trappe, MD; (410) 829-7342; paddletours.com.

a bird for all seasons

Different species can be seen at different times during the year. Here is a guide to what you can expect to see when:

January: *geese, swans, ducks, hawks, great blue herons, and a few species of shorebirds. Both bald and golden eagles can sometimes be spied, too.*

February: *killdeer, robins, and bluebirds. You might catch a peek at red-winged blackbirds passing through or the osprey returning from the winter.*

April: *blue-winged and green-winged teal. Many of the waterfowl and other species begin hatching, including the bald eaglets.*

May: *warblers and waterfowl.*

June: *ospreys, eaglets, and songbirds.*

July: *osprey, swallows, kingbirds, and flycatchers. Marsh hibiscus bloom.*

August: *wading birds and lots and lots of flies and mosquitoes.*

September: *egrets, herons, and toads. Sunflowers bloom.*

October, November, and December: *ducks, geese, swans, bald eagles, and golden eagles. Fall foliage peaks and many of the birds begin migrating.*

Cam, and numerous eaglets have hatched and fledged before the eyes of those tuning in. The camera is on most days during the summer and can also be viewed online through a link on the refuge's website.

Upstairs at the visitor center is the Birding and Natural History Library, a collection that focuses on local wildlife. The center stays open weekdays from 8 a.m. to 4 p.m. and weekends from 9 a.m. to 5 p.m.

Native Butterfly & Beneficial Insect Garden. Behind the visitor center hundreds of butterflies flit through the air in the Native Butterfly and Beneficial Insect Garden. You can catch a glimpse of the butterflies as you walk through the plant-filled area or watch them all day on one of the benches in the garden. Shutterbugs enjoy trying to capture the winged creatures through their lenses. Among the butterflies attracted by the plants and flowers in the garden are the Tiger Swallowtail, Eastern Tailed Blue, Question Mark, Painted Lady, Red Admiral, and Monarch. The butterfly garden also tends to be a good spot to catch a glimpse of a bald eagle soaring above.

Wildlife Drive. The paved Wildlife Drive takes visitors in cars, on bikes, or on foot through a 4-mile section of the refuge. The road goes past the Blackwater River and generally offers a chance to see waterfowl, shorebirds, turtles, bald eagles, ospreys, and the endangered Delmarva fox squirrel. The drive is open daily from dawn to dusk.

Hunting. Occasionally the refuge allows hunters with the proper credentials on the refuge to help control the deer population. Call for more information and to inquire about dates—hunting does not follow a set schedule. To participate in a sanctioned hunt you must have a valid Maryland hunting license and stamps, photo ID, and valid shotgun hunt permit.

Land Trails. Hikers can choose from four land trails at Blackwater National Wildlife Refuge: the Marsh Edge Trail, the Woods Trail, the Key Wallace Hiking Trail, and the Tubman Road Trail.

> **Marsh Edge Trail.** The only paved trail of the group, this trail runs along the Little Blackwater River and Blackwater River, offering pretty views along with access to picnic tables and an observation boardwalk. From the trail you can even get a peek at the osprey platform standing in the water and during nesting season have a good chance of seeing the birds fly.

> **Woods Trail.** If you want to spy one of the endangered Delmarva fox squirrels that make their home at the Blackwater Refuge, the Woods Trail is your best bet. The half-mile trail passes through part of the area maintained as an ideal habitat for the endangered squirrel.

> **Key Wallace Hiking Trail and Demonstration Forest.** Named for one of the early directors of the refuge, the Key Wallace Trail takes hikers through some of the forest that covers more than a third of Blackwater and serves as a haven for many of the species found here. The Key Wallace Trail is almost 3 miles long and takes most people about two hours to hike.

> **Tubman Road Trail.** Named in honor of Harriet Tubman, who was born not far from Blackwater, this trail is almost 2 miles long and winds through fields, forests, sloughs, and marshes.

Water Trails. On foot isn't the only way to explore Blackwater National Wildlife Refuge. Three water trails give visitors the opportunity to paddle through parts of the refuge—the Green Trail, the Purple Trail, and the Orange Trail. A water trail map is sold at the visitor center—or can be purchased online—and is a must for navigating the waters at the refuge.

> **Green Trail.** This trail is about 8 miles round trip, the easiest of the three trails, and the best place for beginners to dip in their paddles. During the summer months water lilies blanket much of the water and cattails pop up near the water's edge. The start is near the Route 335 bridge. If you are planning to attempt the

historic ties

You can catch more than a glimpse of nature at Blackwater National Wildlife Refuge. You can also see what Harriet Tubman likely saw when she grew up in this area of Maryland's Eastern Shore. Parts of the current migratory bird sanctuary once were part of the landscape where Tubman, a hero of the Underground Railroad and activist, spent her early years. Born in 1822, Tubman spent her childhood as a slave working on farms that are thought to be within the boundary of the refuge. As a young adult Tubman worked as a timber laborer on the north side of the Blackwater River. The natural habitats of the refuge, wetlands, waterways, swamps, and upland forests that visitors can experience today are very similar to the landscape that Tubman grew up in and experienced so long ago. Something else to consider as you view the landscape . . .

Green Trail during the fall or winter, call the refuge first and make sure hunting on nearby private land won't interfere with your trip.

Purple Trail. The Purple Trail is 9 miles each way and takes most paddlers about four hours to complete. The put-in is at Shorters Wharf. In order to not interfere with waterfowl migration, the trail is closed from October 1 through March 31 each year. In late summer both the Orange and Purple take paddlers past blooming marsh hibiscus. There is also a shorter Purple Trail Spur, which is about a 3-mile round trip and takes about an hour for most to complete.

Orange Trail. This trail is an almost 8-mile paddle round trip and takes about three or four hours for most to complete. The put-in is at Shorters Wharf.

where to shop

Eagle's Nest Book & Gift Shop. (410) 228-2677; friendsofblackwater.org/store.html. Housed in the visitor center, the store stocks all things eagle including children's books, reference books, clothing, and gift items. You can also purchase a nature cam to place in your very own birdhouse or backyard. There also is a special eagle section of the shop. All proceeds from the shop go back to the Blackwater National Wildlife Refuge. You can also find out about walks and education programs sometimes sponsored by the Friends of Blackwater.

southeast

day trip 11

southeast

waterslides & pullman cars:
chesapeake beach, md

chesapeake beach

Chesapeake Beach's heyday started and ended with a train ride. On June 9, 1900, the first railcar pulled into Chesapeake Beach bringing eager visitors to the new beachfront resort destination for a day of entertainment, complete with a game-filled boardwalk, casinos, bathhouse, racetrack, dance pavilion, and, of course, the beach. The colossal Great Derby roller coaster even zoomed over the boardwalk. For thirty-five years crowds flocked to the area for days filled with fun and sun. From DC they arrived by rail and from Baltimore they came by steamboat, docking at the new pier built solely to give more people access to Chesapeake Beach. Once here, many checked into the luxurious Belvedere Hotel, which also went up in 1900 and offered bayside views.

At the same time that Chesapeake Beach thrived as a resort town, the twin town of North Beach grew up next to it as a vacation community. Summer cottages popped up around North Beach in the early years before it became more of a year-round community.

For several decades both towns thrived as local resort destinations, until the Depression hit and people stopped coming, The Chesapeake Beach Railway went bankrupt and the last train pulled away in April 1935.

Today with the grand roller coaster, resort, and casinos gone, both Chesapeake Beach and North Beach have become bedroom communities. But what hasn't changed is that the towns remain seaside destinations offering beaches and bay breezes to those who visit

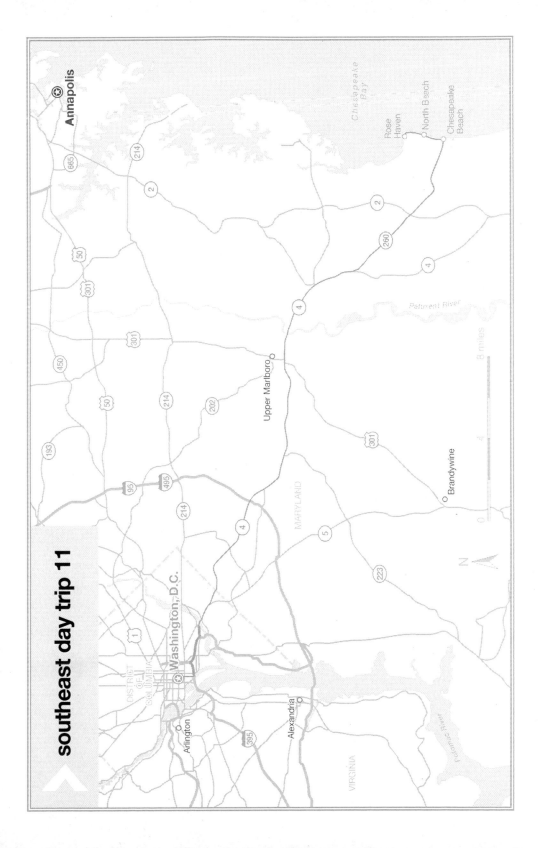

southeast day trip 11

their shores. And sometimes as you stroll along the sandy shoreline, if you close your eyes you can almost imagine the grand Belvedere Hotel rising up in the distance, getting ready for the next trainload of guests arriving for a summer holiday.

getting there

Chesapeake Beach is an easy 30-mile drive from Washington. Take the Beltway to Route 4 South into Calvert County, and just past the county line take Route 260 about 5 miles to Chesapeake Beach. Definitely allow extra time during beach season, as hordes of hot Washingtonians will be taking the same path to the Delaware beaches.

where to go

Breezy Point Beach. 5200 Breezy Point Rd., Chesapeake Beach, MD; (410) 535-0259; co .cal.md.us. Breezy Point is a popular public beach with a netted swimming area, volleyball court, playground, grills, covered picnic area, and fishing and crabbing pier. The park also has camping grounds. Breezy Point is open from May to Oct. Small admission fee.

Chesapeake Beach Railway Museum. 4155 Mears Ave., Chesapeake Beach, MD; (410) 257-3892; cbrm.org. A museum dedicated to the time when the railroad was king and regularly brought Baltimoreans and Washingtonians to the twin beaches. The museum is housed in the restored former Chesapeake Beach Railway Station and displays memorabilia and historical items from the town's glorious railroad era. The museum is free and has limited hours during the non-summer months, but will usually open by appointment if you call ahead.

Chesapeake Beach Waterpark. 4079 Gordon Stinnett Ave., Chesapeake Beach, MD; (410) 257-1404; chesapeakebeachwaterpark.com. All the splash and fun you expect from a water park including tube slides, a lazy river that circles the park, and a water volleyball

geocaching by the sea

Chesapeake Beach has jumped on the geocaching bandwagon. A high-tech scavenger hunt, geocaching requires seekers to use GPS to find hidden treasure. The Town of Chesapeake Beach started participating in the Maryland Municipal League Geocache Trail back in 2009, giving those who embrace the trend one more activity when they are in town. Chesapeake Beach goodies and coupons are among the items hiding in the Chesapeake Beach geocaches. Log on to geo caching.com to get started and for more information.

area. A kids' activity pool has a frog slide and other fun features. Check with the park for current prices and hours. No food is allowed in the park but there is a snack bar inside. Calvert County residents showing ID get discounted admission.

where to shop

A-1 Antiques Collectibles. 3736 Chesapeake Beach Rd., Chesapeake Beach, MD; (301) 855-4500. Several dealers show and sell their wares at A-1. You really never know what you are going to find here, from antique furniture to vintage jewelry to hard-to-find pottery.

Bayhill Market. 7544 Bayside Rd., Chesapeake Beach, MD; (410) 257-2349. Home accents and furnishings with a nautical theme can be bought here. The store also carries some gourmet goodies.

Tyler's Tackle Shop and Crab House. 8210 Bayside Rd., Chesapeake Beach, MD; (410) 257-6610; tylerstackle.com/crabhouse.html. Locals make sure to stop at Tyler's for fresh fish and seafood by the pound. Specialties revolve around the catch of the day and include Maryland blue crabs, clams, and scallops. The small shop also sells seasonings and premade seafood salad. The requisite wooden red crab sign hangs outside identifying the store, and tackle is sold next door. Closed Mon.

where to eat

Abner's Crab House. 3725 Harbor Rd., Chesapeake Beach, MD; (301) 855-6705; abnerscrabhouse.com. A popular family-run business, Abner's Crab House is something of an institution in these parts. The owner started crabbing when he was eleven and hasn't stopped. Abner's has several hundred crabbing pots in the waters around the bay and serves some of what is caught. Crabs at this casual restaurant are served every which way. $$.

Neptune's Seafood Pub. 8800 Chesapeake Ave., North Beach, MD; (410) 257-7899; neptunesseafoodpub.com. A good place to grab a casual meal or nurse a cold beer, Neptune's is a block from the bay and has TVs for watching the game. The pub serves brunch and a regular menu with seafood touches, such as a buffalo shrimp dip, crab omelets, and mussels with a choice of five dipping sauces. $$.

Westlawn Inn. 9200 Chesapeake Ave., North Beach, MD; (410) 257-0001; westlawninn .com. Housed in a historic building that served as an inn for seventy-five years, Westlawn offers dinner and brunch. The chef uses a lot of seafood and fish and creates desserts that include fried cheesecake. $$$.

where to stay

Breezy Point Campground. 5200 Breezy Point Rd., Chesapeake Beach, MD; (410) 535-0259; co.cal.md.us. The public campground at Breezy Point can be reserved for anyone who wants to sleep out under the stars and near the beach for a night, week, or longer. Pets are not allowed and there is a two-night minimum on weekends. Open May 1 to Oct 31. $.

Chesapeake Beach Resort and Spa. 4165 Mears Ave., Chesapeake Beach, MD; (410) 257-5596; chesapeakebeachresortspa.com. The Chesapeake Beach Resort and Spa offers visitors access to its indoor pool, marinas, restaurants, game room, and spa. The Rod 'N' Reel Dock offers boat enthusiasts and sailors 120 slips, boats to charter, two head-boats, a fuel dock, and a tackle shop. The dock even has a fish-cleaning table. The mostly suites hotel often offers packages online. $$.

The Inn at Herrington Harbour. 7161 Lake Shore Dr., Rose Haven, MD; (410) 741-5100; herringtonharbour.com. The Inn at Herrington Harbour in nearby Rose Haven makes it easy to be green. The "ecolifestyle" resort has been providing an environmentally friendly beach lodging option since 1978, back when green was just a color for most people. The marshes here have been planted and restored by digging out rotting boats, engines, cars, and other debris. The marshes filter storm water runoff and recycle wash water. There are even recycling areas for used motor oil, diesel fuel, and antifreeze. $$$.

day trip 12

southeast

sittin' on the dock of the bay:
tilghman island, md

tilghman island

Cross the Knapps Narrows Drawbridge into Tilghman Island and enter the zone of island-brand relaxation. Only 3 miles long, the nineteenth-century waterman town on the Chesapeake Bay and Choptank River offers the chance to truly get away from it all. Walking, biking, and sailing are preferred modes of transportation on the island, and sitting and watching the world go by is a treasured Tilghman Island pastime. From the island's southern tip you can even catch a glimpse of the cast-iron-caisson Sharps Island Lighthouse as you gaze out at the water. Bring a stack of good books and some tension to release and you're set for a day or more on the tiny island known to many as the pearl of the Chesapeake.

getting there

Tilghman Island is about 11 miles west of the town of St. Michaels and is separated from the mainland by Knapps Narrows. Drivers need to cross a drawbridge to get to the island, which can also be reached by boat.

where to go

Chesapeake Bay Skipjack Charters. 21308 Phillips Rd., Tilghman Island, MD; (410) 829-3976; skipjack.org. Captain Wade H. Murphy takes good care of all who come aboard the *Rebecca T. Ruark,* the oldest working skipjack on the Chesapeake Bay. Captain Wade

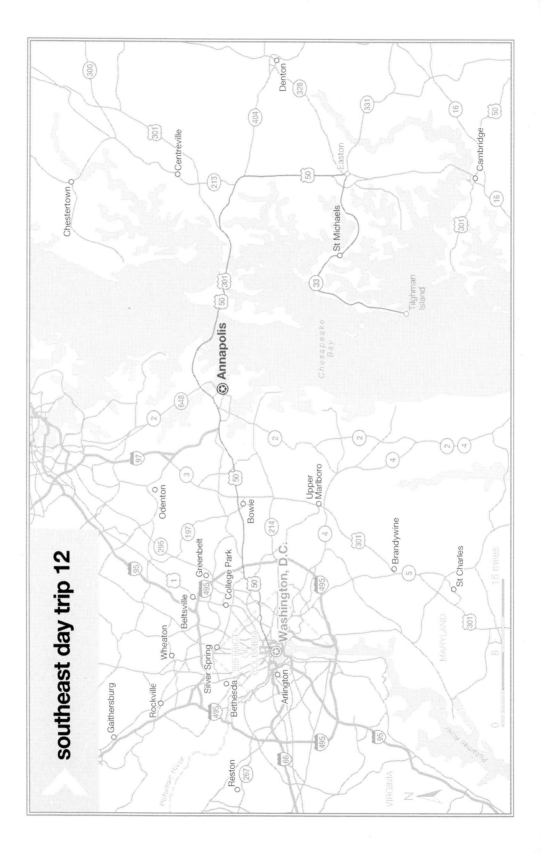

southeast day trip 12

brings guests on two-hour sails along the bay, pointing out sites of historic significance along the way and sometimes he even conducts oyster-dredging demonstrations. The *Rebecca* is also available for fishing charters and sunset sails. Call for the most current schedules and prices.

Phillips Wharf Environmental Center. 21604 Chicken Point Rd., Tilghman Island, MD; (410) 886-9200; pwec.org. Kids get to touch sea critters and learn about the bay at this hands-on experience. The center is housed in the last crab shanty in town and is open Thurs through Mon from 10 a.m. to 4 p.m. Call ahead. Free.

Sail *Lady Patty*. PO Box 248, Tilghman Island, MD; (410) 745-8077; svladypatty.word press.com. Come sail away on the lovely *Lady Patty,* a 1935 canoe stern ketch crafted from spruce, oak, teak, and bronze. The classic boat glides on the bay providing all aboard with wonderful views as its masts soar 56 feet above the water. Visitors can sign up for two-hour daytime trips or two-hour Champagne and sunset sails. Half-day and full-day sailing trips sometimes are also offered. Call for schedule and prices.

where to shop

Crawfords Nautical Books Book Bank. 5782 Tilghman Island Rd., Tilghman Island, MD; (410) 886-2230; crawfordsnautical.com. Water, water everywhere and lots to read about it. If it's a book—old or new—that has anything to do with the sea, chances are Crawfords carries it. Subject categories at the store include bridges, pirates, decoys, yachting, naval history, waves, islands, lighthouses, wrecks, and rivers. The store carries both used and new volumes related to the sea including a small children's section. The Book Bank is open Sat and Sun from Apr through Oct.

Island Treasures. 21445 Chesapeake House Dr., Tilghman Island, MD; (410) 886-2058. A little bit of everything is sold at this island store, including clothing, books, local crafts, and jewelry. Island Treasures also rents bicycles perfect for exploring the island.

where to eat

Bridge Restaurant. 6136 Tilghman Island Rd., Tilghman Island, MD; (410) 886-2330; bridge-restaurant.com. Locally caught seafood has a starring role on the menu at the Bridge Restaurant, which specializes in crab cakes and oysters. Much of the wine served at the casual restaurant with a water view is from nearby wineries. When it's warm out you can eat outside and the restaurant allows those who sail up to dock for free. $$.

So Neat Cafe & Bakery. 5772 Tilghman Island Rd., Tilghman Island, MD; (410) 886-2143. Recharge your batteries with a cup of coffee, a salad, or a fresh-from-the-oven pastry at the pretty So Neat Cafe. The bread baked here is used to make the eatery's sandwiches. Breakfast, which includes eggs and waffles, is also served. A cute card and gift shop is attached to the cafe. $.

where to stay

Black Walnut Point Bed & Breakfast Inn. Black Walnut Road, Tilghman Island, MD; (410) 886-2452; blackwalnutpoint.com. The innkeepers here like to call the property a sanctuary for humans. Set on 57 acres of a wildlife preserve on the island's southernmost tip, the Black Walnut Point is a true getaway. If you crave quiet and water views, the Black Walnut should keep you very happy—not to mention very chill. Spend the day reading or napping in the inn's hammock. For a relaxing change of pace, explore one of the property's trails and engage in a little armchair bird-watching. Guests can also take advantage of the inn's pool, tennis court, and spa. And while all of those activities are fun, sunset watching is probably the most beloved activity at the Black Walnut Inn. $$.

Tilghman Island Inn. 21384 Coopertown Rd., Tilghman Island, MD; (410) 886-2141; tilghmanislandinn.com. The twenty-room inn welcomes guests for a night or two—or ten. Overlooking the water, the guesthouse offers a soothing setting for a getaway and the restaurant serves seafood and other local favorites. $$.

day trip 13

southeast

>>> whimsical art oasis:
annmarie garden sculpture park &
arts center: dowell, md

annmarie garden sculpture park & arts center

If you think magical gardens appear only in storybooks and on movie screens, then you probably haven't spent time at the Annmarie Garden Sculpture Park and Arts Center outside of Solomons Island, Maryland. Here art and nature are married in the outdoor cathedral of whimsy. Contemporary and modern sculpture, much of it on loan from the Smithsonian's Hirshhorn Museum, fills the wooded 30-acre park. The beautiful light-filled Arts Center also sponsors exhibits and houses a gift shop and cafe, but getting lost below the forest's dense canopy and sculpture-adorned paths is the big draw.

getting there

Drive south on Route 4 to exit 11 and follow the signs to Solomons. Make a left on Dowell Road at the Solomons Firehouse. The sculpture garden is on the left.

where to go

Annmarie Garden Sculpture Park & Arts Center. 13480 Dowell Rd., Dowell, MD; (410) 326-4640; annmariegarden.org. Art and nature seamlessly share the stage at the tree-filled

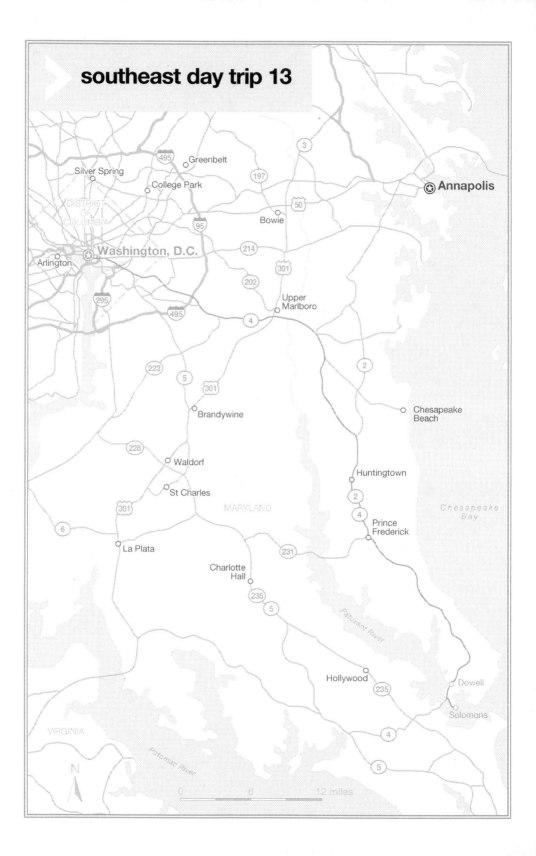

southeast day trip 13

Annmarie Garden Sculpture Park and Arts Center. Walk, wander, and explore the day away at this gem of a spot, perfect for a family day trip, romantic journey, or solo voyage for anyone who wants to spend a few hours getting lost in thought and art. The site also runs a host of programs from family fun days to date nights. On Father's Day, daddies and their darlings can even come out and build their own paint-throwing catapults to create Jackson Pollock–style art. Admission is $3 for adults and $5 for senior citizens and children between the ages of 5 and 12. Children younger than 5 are free.

Here are some of the park's highlights:

John Dennis Murray Arts Building. The winner of several architectural awards, the arts building is a deceptively simple structure. When you see it for the first time, it seems like a straightforward rectangular country building among the trees. But look again and you'll start to see more. In a nod to the region's maritime culture, the architect designed the second floor to look like a boat, complete with a glass-enclosed bow and stern that protrude at the ends. Art exhibits, programs, classes, and parties take place regularly in the arts building, which also houses a cafe and gift shop.

The Butterfly Garden. Just adjacent to the John Dennis Murray Arts Building explore the almost 5,000-square-foot butterfly garden. This once weedy patch now blooms with some three-dozen species of native pollinator plants that make the space come alive with winged creators. Not only is the Butterfly Garden enjoyed by guests but it also serves double duty as teaching garden.

Gateway. The massive ceramic-adorned gates usher visitors into Annmarie's art-filled garden. Handcrafted by two Florida-based potters, the more than 600 ceramic sections that make up the two gates were inspired by the Calvert County landscape and are filled with watery and leafy images. The artists used more than eight tons of clay to finish the gateway.

Permanent collection. In addition to the beautiful gates, Annmarie Garden also plays host to several other significant works of art belonging to its permanent collection. The bronze and granite *A Tribute to the Oyster Tonger, A Chesapeake Waterman* by Francis Koenig was the first piece installed on the grounds and also speaks to the region's strong maritime identity. Further picking up the theme, Baltimore artists Jann Rosen-Queralt and Roma Campanile weave quotes from Calvert County residents into their design for *A Surveyor's Map,* a wood and steel boardwalk that winds through the woods. In a nod to the experience of personal memories, spots along the boardwalk offer different views of the garden.

Work on loan from the Smithsonian Institution's Hirshhorn Museum & Sculpture Garden. Beginning in 2003 the Smithsonian Institution began lending

Annmarie outdoor sculpture from the world-renowned Hirshhorn Museum and Sculpture Garden in Washington, DC. Several of the Hirshhorn collection's striking pieces can be seen throughout the garden, including works by artists from the United States, Mexico, Israel, and Africa. Such sculptors as James Wolf, Michael Todd, and Nelli Bar are represented in the garden.

Women's Walk. A celebration of the female form and experience define the Women's Walk. Evocative bronze figures representing different types of women and different stages of life line the path. Curators have also provided benches for visitors to stop and reflect on the artwork and perhaps even to recall significant women in their own lives.

Tree Pops. While it's almost impossible to miss the park's larger-than-life bronze and steel installations, the hidden-in-plain-sight tree art can be harder to find. Small sections of famous paintings have been painted onto the knots and bark of tree trunks throughout the park. Some are only a few inches wide. If you look very carefully you can find trees sporting pieces of Georges Seurat's *A Sunday Afternoon on the Island of La Grande Jatte* or one of Dalí's famous melting time-pieces from *The Persistence of Memory*. Walking guides and scavenger hunts (a few created especially for toddlers and kids) will direct you to all the painted-tree treasures and other fun spots along the way.

Rooms to Rest & Refresh. At Annmarie Garden, art turns up in the most unlikely of places. Even the bathroom walls are turned into an artist's canvas. Volunteers and staff members used the walls in the restrooms to create an improvisational mosaic. After being instructed only to leave no wall showing, the artists for a day used spare tiles and other found objects to create a surprising piece in a surprising location.

Public installations. The Rooms to Rest and Refresh project is not the only example of the public creating art at Annmarie Garden. Every summer a call goes out to interested parties of all ages to participate in creating a huge outdoor art installation. Recycled and found materials play a big role in the project and in the past have included a series of pillars made from plastic bottles and decorated graffiti-style with the artist's wishes for the world. Another year what is thought to be the world's largest wind chime was fashioned from decorated old jar lids (officials are still verifying whether a true record was set). The community projects remain on display until Halloween.

Annual Fairy & Gnome Home Festival. During this yearly spring event an already magical place become downright enchanted as all things fairy and gnome take up residence in the garden. A crowd favorite is the exhibit of whimsical handmade fairy and gnome homes. The festival also features a Fairy Lolly, a play

amg for free

Throughout the year Annmarie Garden waives its admission fee on special occasions. So grab your mom on Mother's Day, your nana on Grandparents' Day, and your favorite serviceperson on Veterans Day and treat them to a free day of art and nature. Here are AMG's free days:

Mother's Day: Moms are free.

Father's Day: Dad's turn to put away his wallet.

Grandparents' Day: (the first Sunday after Labor Day) Grammy and Papa's much-deserved turn for free admission.

Veterans Day: All who served or are serving our country get in for free.

Martin Luther King Jr. Day: Show proof that you performed community service that day and AMG will say thank you by letting you in for free.

area where young guests can climb, explore, build, and dream. Guests can also build their own fairy houses and gnome homes as well as create their own magical props and crafts. Along the Wooded Path, listen to live music and hold court with Fairy Queen Ambrosia and Princess Cricket who are on hand to greet visitors. A selection of the whimsical homes created for the event can be bid on during a silent auction.

Glenn Dale Hybrid Azalea Collection. Former Director of the National Arboretum B. Y. Morrison started tinkering with the hybridization of azaleas in 1935. His many years of work resulted in a magnificent collection of bold and colorful blooms revered by the horticultural community and known as Glenn Dale Hybrids. Every spring more than 500 of the same types of hybrids developed by Morrison set the garden ablaze with color. The red, pink, white, and purple flowers tend to blossom from April to June.

Annmarie Garden in Lights. All the light sculptures for the annual December lights show are made at Annmarie so expect to see anything from mythical beasts to circus performers at this show. If you have kids, stop by the arts building and ask for a "Holiday I Spy Game" before you start out. The light fun also includes nightly entertainment, sweet treats, and other seasonal activities.

where to shop

Gift Shop at Annmarie Garden. Since you can't haul home one of the bronze or steel sculptures in the garden (and even if you could figure out how, security wouldn't let you get very far with it) you can legally purchase some of the garden's artful inspiration at the Annmarie Garden Gift Shop in the Arts Center. Fun and often handmade jewelry, scarves, and housewares can be purchased here along with a selection of books and art kits. The shop also carries a selection of one-of-a-kind merchandise from Southern Maryland artists. Open weekdays from from 10 a.m. to 5 p.m. and weekends from noon to 5 p.m. with abbreviated hours during the winter.

Grandmother's Store Antiques. 13892 Dowell Rd., Dowell; (410) 326-3366; grandmothers store.com. Housed in part of the town's former post office, Grandmother's Store Antiques is part of the Dowell family's long shopkeeping history. In addition to the many antiques and collectibles sold here, the store also displays a large collection of antique items from the original Dowell General Store that are not for sale but still are fun to admire.

Kool Kangaroo. 14636 Solomons Island Rd., Solomons, MD; (410) 326-2310; kool kangaroo.com. Antiques, eclectic items, and eccentricities make up Kool Kangaroo's anything-but-ordinary inventory.

where to eat

The Back Creek Bistro. Calvert Marina, Solomons, MD; (410) 326.9900; backcreekbistro .com. Housed in a former World War II power plant, the bistro serves a seafood heavy menu, jazz-heavy musical performances, and sunset-heavy waterfront views. The Bistro owners also take great pride in the local artwork around the restaurant. $$.

The Cafe Gallery. The cafe at Annmarie serves coffee and light fare and its walls serve as a gallery space for local artists. A new artist is showcased every month. You can also sit among the trees and enjoy your cup of tea or a cold drink at the cafe's outdoor plaza. $.

Kim's Key Lime Pie and Lotus Kitchen. 14618 Solomons Island Rd., Solomons, MD; (410) 326-8469. Locals flock to this funky little coffee shop for its great breakfast, creative lunch sandwiches, and, of course, its much-loved key lime pie. Grab a seat inside the small but quaint house or on the heated porch outside. $.

where to stay

Dowell does not have much in the way of indie hotels and inns but nearby Solomons does. Here are a couple of choices:

Back Creek Inn Bed & Breakfast. 210 Alexander Ln., Solomons, MD; (410) 326-2022; backcreekinnbnb.com. A full cookie jar in the kitchen and friendly hosts await all those who are lucky enough to check in to the Back Creek Inn Bed & Breakfast. Rooms are named for different kinds of herbs and have cozy beds, private baths, and coffeemakers. Original artwork by one of the innkeepers adorns many of the walls. $$.

Solomons Victorian Inn. 125 Charles St., Solomons, MD; (410) 326-4811; solomons victorianinn.com. Overlooking the harbor, the main house of the 1906 Victorian Inn was built by an early twentieth-century yacht builder. The cozy house offers guests a library, a porch, and water views. There is also a spa room and the innkeepers keep a list of recommended massage therapists for guests in search of some extra relaxation. $$.

day trip 14

southeast

archaeological explorations:
calvert cliffs state park, flag ponds
nature park, jefferson patterson
park, st. mary's city, md

By Washington standards a fossil is anyone who didn't perform well in yesterday's election. But beyond the Beltway along the Calvert Cliff shoreline, the fossils found most recently date back some 15 million years before the last primary. Both young and the not so young now trek to the Calvert Cliff area in search of petrified treasures from the Miocene Era, which took place about 6 to 20 million years ago. During that time, warm shallow water covered southern Maryland. Marine mammals thrived in these conditions, making it a popular feeding spot for sharks. As a result, while more than 600 fossil species have been found and identified from the cliffs, shark teeth are the most common fossilized objects found here. The fossils from the cliffs make it to the shoreline most often by chipping off into the water and then washing up on shore.

Most of the land along the cliffs is privately owned but there are a few spots to search for fossils. (Please remember that digging into the cliffs is both illegal and dangerous.) Calvert Cliffs State Park and Flag Ponds Nature Park are two spots open to the fossil-loving public. The day after a big storm and low tide tend to be the best times to hunt for fossils, so check the weather and a tide map before heading out.

While more modern than the teeth that dot the cliffs, the archaeological discoveries made at Jefferson Patterson Park and Historic St. Mary's City shed light on the life of native populations and early colonial settlers in Maryland. At Jefferson Patterson Park visitors can even get in on the action by helping scientists uncover or catalog artifacts, while at Historic

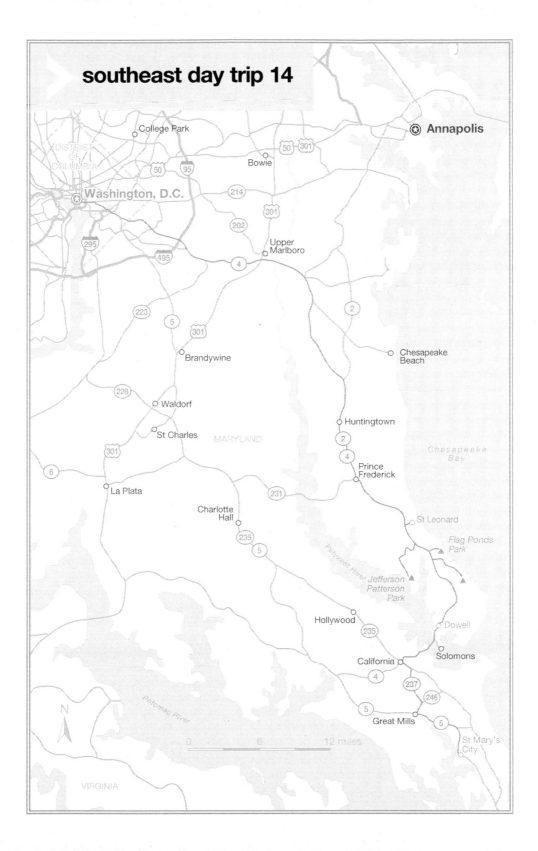

southeast day trip 14

St. Mary's City, staff reenact the past to help convey a sense of life in southern Maryland hundreds of years ago.

calvert cliffs state park

getting there

Calvert Cliffs State Park is 14 miles south of Prince Frederick off Maryland Routes 2/4 South.

where to go

Calvert Cliffs State Park. 9500 H. G. Trueman Rd., Lusby, MD; (301) 743-7613; dnr.state .md.us/publiclands/southern/calvertcliffs.asp. Calvert Cliffs State Park contains 13 miles

kids saving nature

Some of the best advice I found about the local fossils-finding scene came from a now-defunct website started by an eight-year-old and her six-year-old sister. I accidently landed on the blog several years ago and immediately was smitten. Although it hasn't been updated in some time its stories and tips from its young founders' still hold true for nature-focused adventures.

Annika and Cori started Kids Saving Nature in 2003 as a summer project and it grew from there. The girls came up with the domain name, thought up the content, and drew all the cute pictures on the site, including Cori's most excellent fossil map detailing fossil-rich sites around DC. Mom and Dad chime in occasionally with "parents' notes," but it's Annika and Cori who clearly drive the content, as on the Q&A page when they offer advice on what to pack for a fossil trip. For the record, the two recommend "a sieve, a colander, spare time, a collecting jar or something to put the fossils in, a bathing suit, sunscreen, and . . . water shoes."

They also give these easy-to-follow instructions on how to find fossils along the water: "Sieve out the sand that's in the wash (where the waves wash the shore)," they share. "Look for shiny black shapes (triangles with lines on the bottom), about the size of a kid's thumbnail—sometimes they get even smaller or bigger—sometimes they get to the size of a kid's hand—only if you're extra lucky!"

The sisters also have pages about raising tadpoles, butterflies, and sea turtles. I have a feeling that Kids Saving Nature will be bookmarked on my computer for a long time to come.

of hiking trails, picnic areas, and fishing spots, and hundreds of acres of state-designated wildland. But the most popular draw here is the small beach below the fossil-rich cliffs. An almost 2-mile hike from the parking area takes curious fossil finders to the tiny beach. Visitors are allowed to take what they find hidden among the sand (the park's "Leave No Trace" ethical guidelines request taking no more than a handful of fossils) but are strictly prohibited from digging or climbing on the cliffs. The unstable cliffs are constantly eroding from the sea, so large, heavy pieces can and do fall. Shark teeth are the most popular find here and have been identified as coming from a range of sharks, including mako and tiger sharks. Two creatures that still are alive but on the endangered species list can be found on the beach—the puritan tiger beetle and the northeastern beach tiger beetle. Other animals large and small found elsewhere in the park include wild turkeys, deer, rabbits, turtles, butterflies, and snakes.

flag ponds nature park

where to go

Flag Ponds Nature Park. 1525 Flag Ponds Pkwy., Lusby, MD; (410) 586-1477; calvert parks.org/fpp.html Only a couple of miles north of the better-known Calvert Cliffs State Park, Flag Ponds Nature Park also houses a beach rich with fossils and cliff views. The sandy beach here is significantly larger than the one in Calvert Cliffs and is a half-mile from the parking area. It's more than easy to spend a whole day swimming, walking, digging, and relaxing on the beach here. But for those who want non-beach-related activities there are plenty of those, too. Several trail routes run through the more than 450-acre park, and in the spring, summer, and fall, they wind past an array of wildflowers, including the Blue Flag Iris, which gives the park its name. Observation platforms can be found at two different ponds and there is a fishing pier for those who want to try their hand at catching dinner from the bay. Visitors also have good luck crabbing here, so bring along a net. If you do, you will hardly be the first to drop a line in these waters. For about 50 years up until 1955 the area housed a fishery. One of the shanties that popped up during that time to house the fishermen still remains. Inside, a small exhibit provides an overview of the early history of the bay's fishing industry.

where to eat

Vera's White Sands Beach Club. 1200 White Sands Dr., Lusby, MD; (410) 586-1182; verasbeachclub.com. Vera's is a place with a view and a point of view. The view is of the nearby beach and cove and the point of view is fun. The casual seafood restaurant is known for its weekend dance music and lively atmosphere. The menu centers around local delicacies from the sea, including year-round crabs by the dozen and the much beloved house crab cakes. $$.

where to stay

Matoaka Beach Cabins. 4510 Matoaka Ln., St. Leonard, MD; (410) 586-0269; matoaka beachcabins.com. During the late spring, summer, and early fall, several cabins with kitchens can be rented at the privately owned bayfront property. There is also a campground and a fossil-rich beach. $.

jefferson patterson park & museum

As you drive from the Calvert Cliffs to Jefferson Patterson Park, your state of mind moves from shark teeth to pottery shards. The Jefferson Patterson Park and Museum presents the opportunity to explore archaeology of a decidedly different sort than what can be found near the cliffs. The more than 500 acres of farmland here contain some seventy archaeological sites, dating from around 6500 B.C. to the 1940s. And, new discoveries still are being made. The parkland itself has many different identities. It is all at once a museum, working farm, archaeology lab, excavation site, community gathering place, and park. JPPM even has walking trails, including almost 3 miles of shoreline paths along the beach.

getting there

Take Route 4 (exit 11) south toward Upper Marlboro, through Prince Frederick to Route 4. Pick up Route 264 and follow it to Route 265 for 6 miles. The entrance is on the right.

where to go

Jefferson Patterson Park and Museum. 10515 Mackall Rd., St. Leonard, MD; (410) 586-850; jefpat.org. Situated between the Patuxent River and St. Leonard's Creek, Jefferson Patterson Park and Museum offers visitors a look back into Maryland's history. Way back. Some of the artifacts uncovered at the Calvert County park come from prehistoric times and help tell the story of thousands of years of human history on this site. Archaeologists have also found objects from early plantations, Native American villages, and colonial times. Scientists at the park study and preserve the millions of artifacts found both here and throughout Maryland at the state-of-the-art archaeology conservation lab housed here. The site of the 1814 Battle of St. Leonard Creek, fought during the War of 1812, is also part of the multifaceted state park. The exhibit barn and many of the other building are open from

Apr 15 through Oct 15. Admission is free. During the off-season the buildings are closed to the public but visitors can still enjoy some of the grounds.

Maryland Archaeology Conservation Laboratory. The MAC Lab is one of the stars of the Jefferson Patterson Park and Museum. An estimated seven million archaeological artifacts, most found in Maryland, are stored and studied here. Guided tours of MAC may be arranged in advance for a small fee during open season. A behind-the-scenes look can also be had during the free monthly MAC Lab open house. Check the website (jefpat.org/mac_lab.html) for the current open house schedule or call (410) 586-8562 to arrange a tour during another time.

Public Archaeology Program. Archaeology does not have to be a spectator sport. Each spring JPPM sponsors its Public Archaeology Program, giving interested volunteers the chance to assist park archaeologists during an actual

open season on celebrations

Jefferson Patterson Park and Museum's open season is chock-full of yearly festivals. Here are a few of the highlights:

Discovering Archaeology Season. The park kicks off a new season with hands-on activities, tours, and a chance to meet archaeologists from the region.

Annual Children's Day on the Farm. Every June little ones get a taste of life on the farm during this celebration of Maryland agriculture, which includes an antique tractor parade.

Patuxent River Wade In with Bernie Fowler. Every year for more than a quarter century, former state senator Bernie Fowler takes an unusual index of the water quality by seeing how far he can wade into the Patuxent River while still seeing his white high-top sneakers. Join in or watch and participate in the day of fun programming around this event.

The War of 1812 Annual Reenactment. Every year a battle reenactment takes place here. There is also a celebration of life in the early 1800s.

Annual American Heritage Day. The festival, which takes place in the fall, includes Native American crafts, storytelling, music, and dance.

excavation. Volunteers can also help out in the lab. Check the website (jefpat.org/publicarchaeology.html) or call for details or to register.

st. mary's city

If Jefferson Patterson Park and Museum whetted your appetite for colonial architecture, then Historic St. Mary's City might just turn your interest into a mild obsession. The hundreds of archaeological sites here are brought to life through historic re-creations of the city. Staff members in period costumes perform everyday tasks as they would have been done hundreds of years ago. Visitors often get the chance to get in on the act by trying their hand at churning butter, spinning wool, or shooting a bow and arrow. You might even pick up a hint or two about surviving the long winter ahead in the new world.

getting there

Historic St. Mary's City is less than two hours from DC, in southern Maryland. Take Route 4 southeast for about 60 miles to Route 5 and then follow the signs for St. Mary's City.

where to go

Historic St. Mary's City. 8751 Hogaboom Ln., St. Mary's City, MD; (240) 895-4990; stmaryscity.org. In the 1600s colonists arrived in what is now Historic St. Mary's City and settled on the land the Yaocomaco Indians lived on at the time. St. Mary's City served as Maryland's first capital for 61 years until 1695, when it was moved to Annapolis. The colonists all but abandoned the town they built in St. Mary's, leaving it literally to crumble to the ground. For almost 300 years the remains of the former capital were hidden under tobacco, corn, and wheat fields. Unbeknownst to those who planted and tended them, the fields wound up preserving much of the hidden village beneath the surface. Today Historic St. Mary's City serves as a living-history museum based on the vast number of archaeological sites it contains. Many of the buildings have been reconstructed and staff members in period costumes interact with visitors, answering questions and offering tidbits about early American life. Among the new/old sites that can be visited are a square-rigged ship, a tobacco plantation, the 1676 statehouse, and a Native American hamlet.

Researchers have found several hundred archaeological sites at Historic St. Mary's, including ones from prehistoric, colonial, and postcolonial times. Visitors often have the chance to explore the process of unearthing treasures from the past at this National Landmark. Excavations are ongoing and with only 30 percent of the area investigated so far, it's never known what new discovery will be made. The living-history exhibits at St. Mary's City are open to the public from March to November, while the St. John's Site Museum and the visitor center are open year-round. Admission is $10 for adults with discounts for kids, seniors, and students.

native land

While the colonists who arrived on the shores of Maryland were the first Europeans to settle on the land, they were hardly the first people to call it home. The Yao-comaco Indians lived in the area the new settlers named St. Mary's City for many years before the colonists arrived. Members of the Yaocomaco tribe were known as Woodland Indians because their shelter, food, clothing, tools, medicines, and weap-ons came from material found in the nearby forests.

Today at Historic St. Mary's City, visitors can walk through and explore a re-creation of a Woodland Indian hamlet typical of those the Yaocomaco Indians lived in during the seventeenth century. It includes witchotts, or longhouses, that tribe members lived in at the time.

where to shop

Cecil's Country Store. 20853 Indian Bridge Rd., California, MD; (301) 994-1510; cecils countrystore.com. Housed in an old mill dating back to 1812, Cecil's Country Store serves as a place for local artists and craftspeople to display their creations. The mill still has a working water wheel.

where to eat & stay

Brome Howard Inn. 18281 Rosecroft Rd., St Mary's City, MD; (301) 866-0656; stmarys city.org/BromeHoward. The romantic Brome Howard Inn puts you close to Historic St. Mary's City and will lull you into a colonial dream-filled sleep. Rooms have fireplaces, down comforters, feather beds, and pretty views. All guests can relax in the inn's parlor, where there is a high-speed Internet port, cozy seating, and a selection of board games. The innkeepers also keep bicycles on hand so guests can ride along some of the nearby wooded and beach trails. Breakfast includes made-to-order omelets and fresh fruit from the garden. $$.

The Brome Howard Inn offers patrons two pretty dining rooms to choose from when they come for dinner. A porch, perfect for sunset watching, is coveted during warm weather. Inn and restaurant openings schedules depend on the season so call ahead before you go. $$.

south >>>

day trip 15

south

new port of call for fun & food:
national harbor, md

national harbor

Weathered cobblestone paths and historic houses hold a place of honor in the life of a day-tripper, but sometimes even the most devoted roadside historian wants to be somewhere bright, shiny, and new. National Harbor is that place. George Washington never slept, swam, or hitched his horse here. Everything from the hotels to the sidewalks to the street signs is brand spankin' new. When it opened in 2008 the massive 2,000-room Gaylord National Resort and Convention Center was the first hotel on the scene and still anchors the development. Today the area has multiple hotels, a long promenade that runs along the water, and an increasing number of restaurants, galleries, stores, and clubs. Plans for additional sites and attractions are always in the works. (The current development is the first stage of a twenty-five-year plan.) A 175-foot Ferris wheel a la the London Eye is next for National Harbor. But whether you are on the ground or up above it, it's the waterfront with its spectacular city view that is National Harbor's true star. Several kinds of boat rides leave from the marina or you can watch the world go by from one of the cafes overlooking the water.

getting there

Take MD 295 South for about 5.5 miles and get off at exit 1B, National Harbor. There is no street parking but several paid parking options are available. Rush hour traffic will slow you

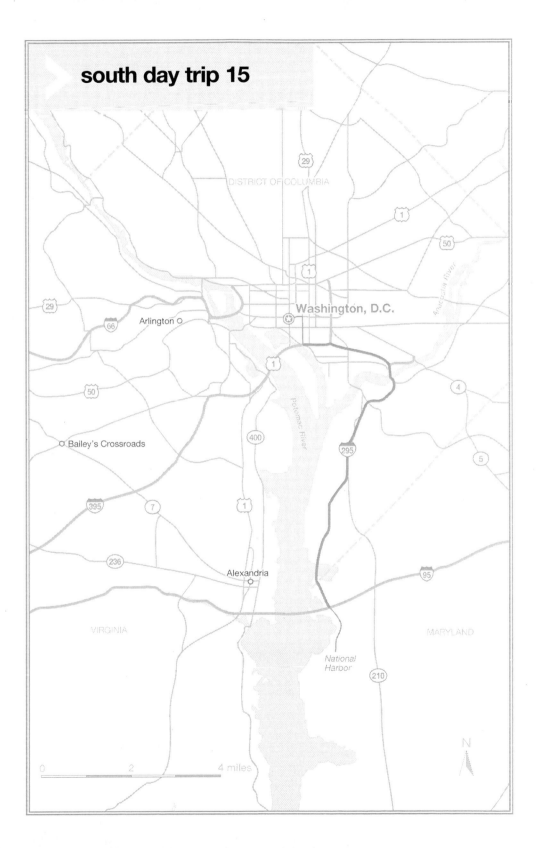

DISTRICT OF COLUMBIA

Washington, D.C.

Arlington

Potomac River

Anacostia River

Bailey's Crossroads

Alexandria

VIRGINIA

MARYLAND

National
Harbor

0   2   4 miles

N

down. You can also take a water taxi to National Harbor from Georgetown, Mt. Vernon, and Old Town Alexandria. The NH-1 National Harbor Metrobus also runs to and from the Southern Avenue Metro stop every half hour.

where to go

Art Whino. 73 Waterfront St., National Harbor, MD; (301) 567-8210; artwhino.com. The bright white walls, high ceilings, and concrete floor set the tone for this über-modern art gallery dedicated to the styles of pop-surrealism, lowbrow, and urban contemporary. Open daily.

The Awakening. National Plaza, National Harbor, MD. This larger-than-life piece of public art depicting a giant rising out of the earth moved from Hains Point to National Harbor in 2008. The cast-aluminum sculpture is actually five separate pieces—head, hand, knee, foot, and arm—that together give the impression of one bearded giant attempting to break free from beneath a plot of sand on the waterfront. Visitors can climb on the statue and the sculpture in general makes for some fun photo ops.

Bobby McKey's. 172 Fleet St., National Harbor, MD; (301) 602-2209; bobbymckeys.com. Satisfy your inner piano man and experience the dueling pianos at Bobby McKey's. Genres can be anything from Bach to the Beach Boys to Beyoncé. You can order signature cocktails and bar-style food at this locally owned and operated club.

The Carousel at National Harbor. 137 National Plaza, National Harbor, MD; (301) 203-4170. Round and round you go on the harbor's Americana-themed carousel.

Guided Bass Fishing Tours. National Harbor, MD; (703) 360-3472; nationalbass.com. Embrace your inner sea captain on this catch-and-release bass fishing charter on the Potomac. Prices vary.

Movies on the Potomac. National Harbor, MD; nationalharbor.com. Free movies are shown most Friday and Sunday nights on the Plaza's big screen (near *The Awakening* statue) during nonwinter months. Bring a lawn chair but leave your cooler at home, as they are not allowed.

National Children's Museum at National Harbor. 112 Waterfront St., National Harbor, MD; (301) 686-0225. A children's museum designed for children eight and younger. Admission is $10 and free for babies younger than twelve months.

Seadog Speedboat & Sightseeing Tour. Commercial Pier, National Harbor, MD; (866) 443-9283; seadogcruises.com/dc. A 45 minute speedboat tour not intended for the land-lubber. The boat cruises past famous sites as a guide with a sense of humor shares facts and trivia about the landmarks before turning up the music and zooming around. Tickets are $20 for adults and $15 for children.

ice, ice baby

Every year more than 2,000 sculptors carve a dazzling walk-through city crafted out of ice for the International Ice and Snow Festival in Harbin, China. People from all over the world come to marvel at the frozen city. For those who can't make it all the way to China, National Harbor presents a taste of the festival every December. The Gaylord National Resort brings over 400 master carvers from the Harbin festival to create a winter wonderland crafted from more than a million pounds of ice. It takes the artists a month to create scenes that often include a life-size horse-drawn sleigh to sit on, a two-story ice slide to glide down, and an ice bridge to walk across. The specially designed exhibit area is kept at a chilly 9 degrees to keep the artwork from turning into puddles but worry not, guests can bundle up in oversize coats loaned out at the entrance. Call the Gaylord for more information, exact dates, and ticket prices.

where to shop

CakeLove. 160 National Plaza, National Harbor, MD; (301) 686-0340; cakelove.com. Whoever doesn't love CakeLove cupcakes must have icing running through their veins. One of Washington's favorite made-from-scratch bakeries has a location at the Harbor that sells the cupcakes, cakes, and other sweet treats that have come to make it famous.

Occasions. 185 Waterfront St., National Harbor, MD; (301) 298-8016; otrgifts.com. A bright, happy store filled with such whimsical gift items as handmade picture frames, crafts, and gourmet candy. The store also makes and ships custom gift baskets.

Peeps & Co. 150 National Plaza, National Harbor, MD; (301) 749-5791; justborn.com. This is the first store dedicated to those delicious squishy yellow sugarcoated marshmallow chicks and their brand cousins Mike and Ike, Hot Tamales, and Peanut Chews. Here at this 3,500-square-foot marshmallow store you can find everything Peeps from china to sweatshirts to toys.

where to eat

Cadillac Ranch. 186 Fleet St., National Harbor, MD; (301) 839-1100; cadillacranchgroup .com. Barbecue, country music, and a mechanical bull. Really, need I say more? $$.

Grace's Mandarin. 188 Waterfront St., National Harbor, MD; (301) 839-3788; graces restaurants.com/mandarin.html. The grand restaurant plays with traditional American and Asian flavors in a creative menu that includes such dishes as coconut ginger braised beef, black bean shrimp, and a crab cake and lamb chop version of surf and turf. In addition to the food and the attentive service, the dining room is marked by a three-story waterfall and 33-foot Buddha. $$$.

Mayorga Coffee Roasters. 150 American Way, National Harbor, MD; (301) 686-0284; mayorgacoffee.com. The leather chairs and dark wood make Mayorga a good place to nurse a cup of fresh coffee. Some pastries, light fare, and teas are also served and an alcoholic bar is adjacent to the coffee counter. The shop sponsors live music on some evenings and hosts happy hours. $.

Old Hickory Steak House. 201 Waterfront St., National Harbor, MD; (301) 965-4000; marriott.com/hotels/hotel-information/restaurant/wasgn-gaylord-national-resort-and-convention-center. An upscale steakhouse in the Gaylord made to look like an elegant Georgian home, where the maître de fromage selects and recommends a selection of artisanal cheeses. Old Hickory also has a cigar terrace. $$$.

Rosa Mexicano. 153 Waterfront St., National Harbor, MD; (301) 567-1005; rosamexicano .com.com/Locations/NationalHarborMD. The upscale modern Mexican restaurant was one of the first eateries to stake its claim here. The menu is pretty much the same as its beloved downtown location and includes its delicious made-at-tableside guacamole. When it's warm out, an outdoor seating area is a nice place to sip one of its famous pomegranate margaritas while watching the boats float by. $$$.

where to stay

Aloft. 156 Waterfront St., National Harbor, MD; (301) 749-9000; alofthotels.com. Aloft, the new, hip urban brand of the W Hotel chain, has set up its chic shop at National Harbor. The new hotel stands alongside the waterfront row of restaurants and shops. A sleek, modern design aesthetic defines all of the common areas and guest rooms, which feature signature beds, high-tech entertainment centers, Bliss Spa toiletries, free Wi-Fi, connectivity stations for your gadgets, and LCD TVs. The hotel also has an indoor pool, fitness center, and cocktail lounge. $$.

Gaylord National. 201 Waterfront St., National Harbor, MD; (301) 965-2000; gaylordhotels .com. The massive Gaylord National looks like the lodging lovechild of the Emerald City and the Mall of America. An eighteen-story glass atrium functions as the hotel's focal point and provides sweeping views of the Potomac and the nation's capital. On the inside of the sky-high glass wall is an area made to look like a village with rivers, street lamps, benches, and colonial-style dwellings that actually house shops. In the evening a regular dancing fountain show a la the Bellagio hotel in Las Vegas takes place in the atrium. The Gaylord also has an indoor pool, spa, fitness center, nightclub, and many dining options. The sports bar here has almost as many television screens as a Best Buy showroom. $$.

Westin National Harbor. 171 Waterfront St., National Harbor, MD; (301) 567-3999; star woodhotels.com/westin. Perched along the waterfront, the Westin National Harbor offers water views along with its signature Heavenly Beds, Heavenly Showers, and Heavenly Baths (and Heavenly Cribs for its youngest guests). The hotel, done in a palette of soothing earth tones, also has an indoor pool and fitness center. $$.

day trip 16

south

embrace your inner farmer:
oxon cove park & oxon hill farm:
oxon hill, md

oxon cove park & oxon hill farm

Oxon Cove Park and Oxon Hill Farm, which is found on its grounds, have a long and storied past. Native Americans planted fields of corn, pumpkins, and tobacco on the fertile land here centuries ago. After the Native American peoples who lived on the land were forced out, the property became a working plantation owned by Samuel Debutts and his wife, Mary Welby Debutts. Samuel named it Mt. Welby in his wife's honor. Although a large slave population was forced to labor on the plantation, Oxon Cove Park is listed as a site on the National Underground Railroad Network to Freedom. It is believed that enslaved African-Americans on the Mt. Welby Plantation along with the slave community on a neighboring plantation helped to shelter Jacob Shaw as he escaped to DC, where slaves could "earn" their freedom by joining the army.

In 1891 the government acquired the property and turned it into a work therapy site for patients at Washington's St. Elizabeth's Hospital, which treated mentally ill individuals. The plot was renamed Godding Croft, and patients under the supervision of instructors worked the ground and grew food for the hospital. The program lasted up to the 1950s.

Today Oxon Hill still is a working farm, an educational one. Visitors can get a feel for early farm life by participating in park-run programs such as cow-milking and chicken-coop

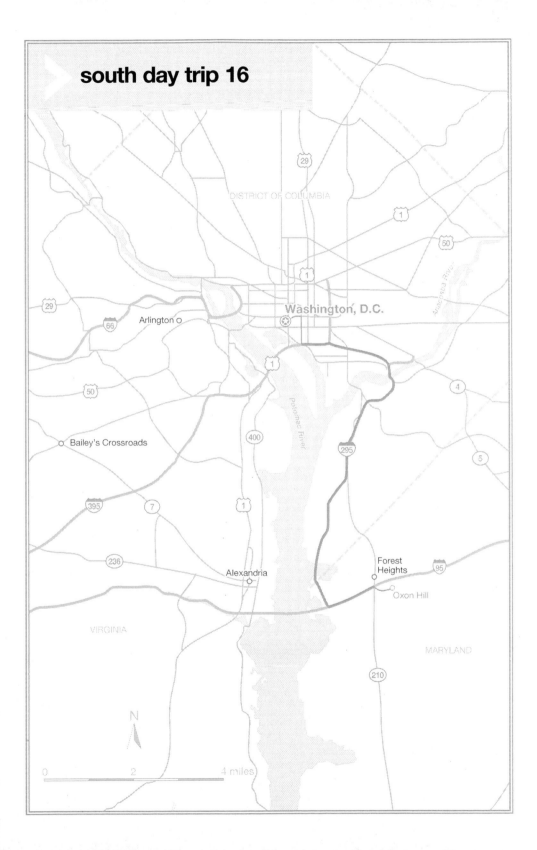

care. Scenic wagon rides and historical programs also are scheduled throughout the year. In addition to the farm, the park has hiking trails and many places throughout it to admire and to picnic (no food is sold at Oxon Hill, so pack your own before you go). If you are coming with kids consider printing out the scavenger hunt from the website before you go, at nps.gov/oxhi/planyourvisit/upload/scavenger.pdf.

getting there

Located in Prince George's County, Oxon Cove is a close 10 miles outside of the DC city limits. Take I-295 South toward Maryland until it ends. Get off at the exit for MD 210, Indian Head Highway, and follow the first ramp toward Indian Head Highway north toward Forest Heights. At the second light make a right onto MD 414, Oxon Hill Road East, and at the next light turn left onto Bald Eagle Road. Follow this road into the Oxon Hill parking lot.

where to go

Oxon Hill Farms & Oxon Cove Park. 6411 Oxon Hill Rd., Oxon Hill, MD; (301) 839-1176; nps.gov/oxhi/index.htm. Both the farm and park are free and open from 8 a.m. to 4:30 p.m. daily, except New Year's Day, Thanksgiving Day, and Christmas Day. Groups of five or more need to make reservations.

   Visitors' Barn. The red barn is a good place to begin exploring the park and farm. Maps, books, and information about the site can be found here, and changing displays tell about farm life past and present. Park rangers staff the barn and can answer questions. You can check out old farm equipment, machinery, and tools in the Farm Museum located to the right of the Visitors' Barn. Wander out back and take a peek at the windmill used to pump well water.

   Self-guided tours can be taken whenever the farm is open. You can show yourself the pigpens, horse stables, root cellar, and feed house. Do keep in mind that Oxon Hill is not a petting zoo and visitors are asked not to touch or feed the animals unless they have the permission of a park ranger.

   Grain exhibit building. Everything you wanted to know but were afraid to ask about grain growing. Learn about the role grains play in the food chain and in farms like this one.

   Programs requiring reservations. Cow milking demonstrations, egg gathering, and wagon rides around the farm take place regularly but require reservations. Check the website for schedules and call ahead to reserve a spot.

   Mt. Welby. The white farmhouse holds the distinction as the oldest structure in the park. The historical exhibits inside the house are open to the public for limited hours on the weekend. Call for details.

power rangers

Visitors between the ages of nine and thirteen can earn the distinction of Junior Ranger next time they visit the park. Stop by the visitor center and ask a ranger for a copy of the special kids' activity book. Once the young visitors finish the exercises, they should bring it to one of the park rangers, who will reward them with a special certificate, badge, and patch.

Woodlot Trail. The 0.3-mile trail guides you along wooded areas near the Potomac River. It's not uncommon to spot foxes, squirrels, beavers, deer, ducks, wild turkey, and other wildlife along the trail.

Hiker-Biker Trail. Just as its name suggests, this 1.6-mile trail is for anyone on two legs or on two wheels who wants to see some of the 512-acre park. Bikers should walk their bikes to the start of the trail to avoid disturbing nearby animals.

Chicken and Egg, Milk the Dairy Cow. Help with farm chores by feeding the chickens and collecting the eggs. Or learn about the cows before helping to milk one as part of these occasional programs. This is for groups of five or more, who must make reservations at least two weeks in advance. Check the website for schedules.

worth more time

Fort Foote Park. 13551 Fort Washington Rd., Fort Washington, MD; (301) 763-4600; nps .gov/fofo. Before you head out to Oxon Hill, check the schedule for nearby Fort Washington. The National Park holds monthly Civil War artillery demonstrations from April to October. Fort Foote is one of sixty-eight forts that were built to protect Washington during the Civil War and has two massive cannons on display that were used during the war. The park also has hiking trails and picnic areas. The park is open daily from 9 a.m. to dusk.

day trip 17

south

>>> **city streets:**
richmond, va

richmond

In recent years Richmond, Virginia, has been embracing its urban appeal with tremendous success. The former capital of the Confederacy seems to have hit its stride as both an American and Southern city and now stands as an ideal destination for those who don't want to decide between historic sites and city streets filled with modern restaurants, theaters, clubs, and shops. The city is even set to host its very own minor league baseball team, adding one more item to the long list of things to do while you are in town.

getting there

It takes just under two hours to drive to Richmond from Washington, with the majority of the trip spent on I-95 South. Take I-395 South to I-95 South and start looking for signs directing you toward the city. Amtrak also runs between Washington and downtown Richmond.

where to go

American Civil War Center at Historic Tredegar. 500 Tredegar St., Richmond, VA; (804) 780-1865; tredegar.org. The museum strives to tell the story of the Civil War from three distinct perspectives—the African-American perspective, the Southern perspective, and the Northern perspective. Located on the James River, the living-history campus contains eight buildings and outdoor areas where educators dressed in period costumes

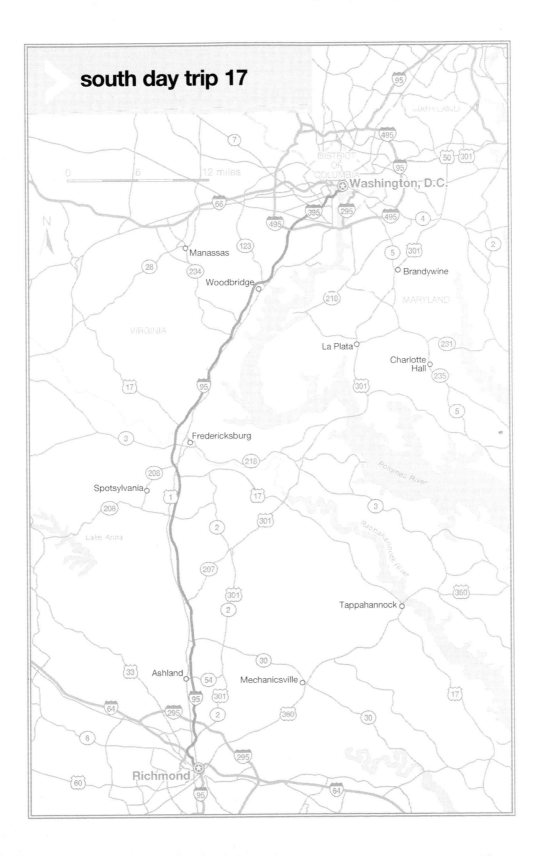

south day trip 17

present information and insights about life during the Civil War era. Tredegar Iron Works once thrived here and served as the heart of the Confederacy. The center's main exhibit is housed in a restored 1861 gun foundry. Admission fee is charged.

Byrd Theatre. 2908 W. Cary St., Richmond, VA; (804) 353-9911; byrdtheatre.com. The Byrd Theatre is a tribute to when a movie theater was truly a theater. The grand movie palace built in 1928 boasts gold-leaf arches, marbled walls, and original paintings. But perhaps the best known feature of the Byrd is its Wurlitzer organ, which has played along to many a screening over the years. The organ is played every Saturday night before the scheduled film and on holidays for the theater's famous sing-alongs. Christmas Eve and Christmas Day organ concerts are paired with showings of *It's a Wonderful Life.*

Camel. 1621 W. Broad St., Richmond, VA; (804) 353-4901; thecamel.org. Up-and-coming Southern rock and bluegrass bands and other musicians take the stage here and offer the audience a chance to say they saw them when. Poetry readings and political forums also share the spotlight here during the week. The Camel offers a menu filled with subs, pizza, and creative appetizer choices like sweet potato cheese fries, fried artichoke hearts, and sausage stars.

Canal Walk. 14th and Dock Streets, Richmond, VA; (804) 788-6466. A more than mile-long path in the city that runs along Haxall Canal, the James River, and the Kanawha Canal.

CenterStage Performing Arts Complex. 600 E. Grace St., Richmond, VA; (804) 225-9000; richmondcenterstage.com. Downtown's brand-new performing arts center boasts three performance venues and a full calendar of shows and concerts. The Richmond Symphony often plays at CenterStage, which also hosts ballets, operas, and Shakespearean productions.

Lewis Ginter Botanical Garden. 1800 Lakeside Ave., Richmond, VA; (804) 262-9887; lewisginter.org. About fifteen minutes from downtown you can find an oasis of floral and plant wonders at the Lewis Ginter Botanical Garden. Among the many themed areas here are rose, healing, Victorian, sunken, Asian Valley, children's, and wetland gardens. There is also a visitor center and beautiful domed conservatory on the property. Admission is charged to enter the gardens.

Maymont. 2201 Shields Lake Dr., Richmond, VA; (804) 358-7166; maymont.org. Maymont is many things at once, all of them stunning. A historic Victorian home, acres of manicured gardens (including magnificent Japanese, Italian, and even cactus gardens), nature center, and park are some of the highlights here. The 100 acre country estate also offers tours by carriage and tram. During the summer Maymont also sponsors hay wagon rides around the property.

The Museum of the Confederacy & White House of the Confederacy. 1201 E Clay St, Richmond, VA 23219; (804) 649-1861; www.moc.org. Civil War buffs won't want to leave

frozen in time: the statues of richmond

When taken together or alone, the diverse collection of statues found in Richmond helps tell the city's story. Keep an eye out for these:

Arthur Ashe Monument. *The monument to the tennis champion and Richmond native stands on Monument Avenue, which is lined with statues of Virginia-born Civil War participants from the Confederate side.*

Robert E. Lee Statue. *A statue of the general of the Confederate Army on horseback stands as the focal point of Monument Avenue.*

Lincoln in Richmond. *When the first statue of President Abraham Lincoln was dedicated in Richmond in 2003, it caused controversy in the former capital of the Confederacy. Today the bronze statue of the sixteenth president and his son Tad is on the grounds of the American Civil War Center and commemorates his visit to the city to "bind up the nation's wounds."*

Bojangles Monument. *The statue of dancer Bill "Bojangles" Robinson stands near the traffic light he donated to his hometown in the 1930s as part of his effort to help keep the children of Jackson Ward safe while they crossed the street. The statue, which shows Robinson tap dancing, can be found at Adams Street and Chamberlayne Parkway.*

Poe Statue. *The statue of the famous writer stands on the grounds of the Virginia State Capitol next to Bell Tower Visitor Center and is not far from two of the homes Poe lived in during his life.*

Thomas Jefferson Statue. *A life-size white marble statue of Thomas Jefferson graces the Palm Court at Richmond's historic Jefferson Hotel.*

Black Iron Dog Statue. *The statue guarding the grave of a little girl at Richmond's Hollywood Cemetery at 412 S. Cherry St. attracts many visitors, some of whom leave gifts by the child's headstone. The sprawling Hollywood Cemetery is the final resting place of two American presidents and many Confederate generals and soldiers, including Confederate States president Jefferson Davis. A 90-foot granite pyramid memorial to Civil War soldiers also can be seen at the cemetery.*

Richmond without spending time here. The museum houses a collection of manuscripts, artifacts, and images associated with the Confederacy period including some personal effects of Robert E. Lee, Jefferson Davis, and others. You can also take a guided tour of the White House of the Confederacy, home to Jefferson Davis, who served as the president of the Confederacy when the southern states seceded, and his family throughout the Civil War. The mansion contains over half the furnishings that were here during the war. A fee is charged and a combination ticket may be purchased.

Poe Museum. 1914-1916 E. Main St., Richmond, VA; (804) 648-5523; poemuseum.org. Located in an old stone house not far from the famous American author's first Richmond home, the Poe Museum celebrates his literary legacy and life. Inside the Poe Museum visitors can see manuscripts, letters, first editions, memorabilia, and personal items belonging to the writer known for his dark tales. The museum is closed Mon and charges a small admission fee. If you can't get enough of *The Raven* author's life and times, head to Richmond's Library of Virginia (lva.virginia.gov), which houses one of the largest collections of Poe artifacts.

Science Museum of Virginia. 2500 W. Broad St., Richmond, VA; (804) 864-1400; smv.org. Housed in the city's grand former train station, the museum offers a hands-on approach to science. It also houses an IMAX style theater, gift shop, and cafe.

Virginia Museum of Fine Arts. 200 N. Boulevard, Richmond, VA; (804) 340-1400; vmfa.museum. The stunning art museum houses a collection representing just about every culture in the world. Especially noteworthy are the museum's collections of Art Nouveau, Art Deco, modern and contemporary American, French Impressionist, and Post-Impressionist art, and Fabergé jeweled objects. The museum's holdings of South Asian, Himalayan, and African art also stand out among the finest in the nation. Docent-led highlight tours are given most days and the museum even has a special program that offers group tours for individuals with dementia and Alzheimer's. On the third Thursday of the month, the museum sponsors a popular program that combines music, cocktails, and a creative twist on an artistic theme. Museum admission is free.

Virginia State Capitol. 910 Capitol St., Richmond, VA; (804) 698-1788; virginiacapitol.gov. A newly restored Virginia State Capitol building shines like never before. A recent extensive restoration process preserved Thomas Jefferson's vision for the beautiful building. The newly opened building now blends its historic elements with modern themes and amenities, like a state-of-the-art visitor center. Free tours are given every hour from 9 a.m. to 4 p.m. Mon through Sat and from 1 to 4 p.m. Sun.

where to shop

Bygones Vintage Clothing. 2916 W. Cary St., Richmond, VA; (804) 353-1919; bygones vintage.com. Because you never know when life will require you to don a retro evening gown and tiara. Bygones has been making a name for itself on the vintage clothing scene since it first opened in 1979. Here you can find men's and women's clothing from the 1900s to the 1970s. Fishnets, fedoras, and formal. Oh my!

Chop Suey Books. 2913 W. Cary St., Richmond, VA; (804) 422-8066; chopsueybooks .com. Bibliophiles will not want to leave Chop Suey, which sells an eclectic assortment of secondhand volumes and takes its name from the restaurant once housed at its original location. Expect to find a little bit of everything on the shelves here including the latest best sellers—and that's the appeal.

Fountain Bookstore. 1312 E. Cary St., Richmond, VA; (804) 788-1594; fountainbook store.com. What's better than a town with one great independent bookstore? A town with multiple great indie bookshops. The small shop houses a selection of well-written prose and sponsors author talks and readings.

Metro Modern. 1919 W. Cary St., Richmond, VA, (804) 353-1921; metromodern.biz. The store carries enough original mid-twentieth-century pieces to build your very own *Mad Men* set. New items are put on display every week and if you are on the hunt for something in particular let the staff know. They might be able to help you track it down. Closed Mon and Tues.

River City Cellars. 2931 W. Cary St., Richmond, VA; (804) 355-1375; rivercitycellars.com. The artisanal cheese counter, exquisite wine selection, and staff of connoisseurs can help you pack a perfect sunset picnic. Staff will happily offer you samples at the cheese counter, with its impressive array of raw milk and artisanal cheeses. Wine tastings and other fun events are held regularly. Check the website or call for more information.

World of Mirth. 3005 W. Cary St., Richmond, VA; (804) 353-8991; worldofmirth.com. Often described as Dr. Seuss meets *Pee-wee's Playhouse,* World of Mirth sells novelty gift items, toys, and games for kids of all ages. If you've been in the market for a Betty Boop wobblehead, a "How to Speak Zombie" phrasebook, or a baby onesie sporting a three-eyed monster, this is the place for you.

for your amusement

*Not far from all the history and urban attitude of Richmond is **Kings Dominion,** a place that historically keeps kids and adults happy. The huge amusement park has everything from crazy roller coasters to a gentle merry-go-round to an enormous splash-filled water park. Kings Dominion, 16000 Theme Park Way, Doswell, VA; (804) 876-5000; kingsdominion.com.*

where to eat

Acacia Mid-Town. 2601 W. Cary St., Richmond, VA; (804) 562-0138; acaciarestaurant .com. Much buzz and praise surrounds Acacia and for good reason. The family-run restaurant shows up again and again on published best-of lists, and, perhaps more significantly, the lists of best Richmond diners. Acacia takes pride in its steadfast commitment to local sourcing of ingredients particularly when it comes to its seafood and fish selection. $$$.

Bev's Homemade Ice Cream. 2911 W. Cary St., Richmond, VA; (804) 204-2387. On a hot summer night you can spot Bev's by the long line. Her homemade ice cream is worth the wait. $.

Buz and Ned's Real Barbecue. 1119 North Blvd., Richmond, VA; (804) 355-6055; buz andneds.com. In a barbecue-loving town, Buz and Ned's stands out from the competition and a meal of barbecued brisket or pork ribs out on the back patio here is something of local point of pride. $$.

Cafe Rustica. 414 E. Main St., Richmond, VA; (804) 225-8811. New on the city's dining scene, Cafe Rustica repeatedly gets high marks for its menu of "European comfort food," its three-course, $15 prix-fixe deal, and its Mediterranean short-stack salad. The cozy neighborhood restaurant is decorated with local artwork. $$.

Kuba Kuba. 1601 Park Ave., Richmond, VA; (804) 355-8817; kubakuba.info. Fantastic Cuban food right in the heart of Richmond. Kuba Kuba serves breakfast, lunch, dinner, and weekend brunch but does not take reservations. $$.

Lemaire Restaurant. 101 W. Franklin St., Richmond, VA; (804) 649-4644; lemairerestaurant .com. The historic restaurant at the city's iconic Jefferson Hotel recently underwent a transformation, taking it from stuffy and formal to trendy and hip. The new menu embraces the farm-to-table philosophy and includes small plates and no entrees costing more than $30, which is a big change from the restaurant's former incarnation. Jackets and ties are no longer required. $$.

Mekong Restaurant. 6004 W. Broad St., Richmond, VA; (804) 288-8929; mekongisfor beerlovers.com. Pho, Asian food, and beer. Lots and lots of beer. $.

Mezzanine. 3433 W. Cary St., Richmond, VA; (804) 353-2186; mezzanine3433.com. The kitchen here prides itself on using only in-season ingredients and flavors and as a result writes its always changing menu on a chalkboard. $$$.

where to stay

Jefferson Hotel. 101 W. Franklin St., Richmond, VA; (804) 788-8000; jeffersonhotel.com. The Jefferson Hotel is considered one of the country's finest hotels. Take one look at its grand lobby and you'll begin to understand why. In addition to its elegant rooms, the hotel offers guests an indoor pool and spa. Its downtown location completes the package. For many years alligators lived in the marble pools in the hotel's Palm Court. But worry not, an alligator hasn't resided at the Jefferson since 1948. $$$.

Linden Row Inn. 100 E. Franklin St., Richmond, VA; (804) 783-7000; lindenrowinn.com. A lovely small historic hotel in downtown filled with Victorian and Empire period antiques and reproductions. The historic building built in the 1840s boasts high ceilings, working fireplaces, and cozy sitting areas. Complimentary continental breakfast is included in the room rate and the inn is within walking distance to many of the city's attractions. $$.

Maury Place on Monument. 3101 W. Franklin St., Richmond, VA; (804) 353-2717; maury place.com. Done in soothing earth tones and marble, this charming bed-and-breakfast puts you near many of the city's museums and attractions. The 1916 home has been beautifully renovated to combine old-world charm and unobtrusive modern amenities and touches. All the rooms have private baths, and two have private balconies. There is an outdoor pool. $$.

William Miller House B&B. 1129 Floyd Ave., Richmond, VA; (804) 254-2928; william millerhouse.com. Everything about the William Miller House B&B exudes hospitality. The two guest rooms—the Regency Room and the Touch of France Room—share the light, bright feeling of the beautifully decorated house. The Touch of France Room has a clawfoot tub, while the Regency Room has a spa tub. Both have plush linens, flat-screen televisions, and free Wi-Fi. One of the innkeepers is a trained chef and prepares a gourmet breakfast every morning. Inviting rocking chairs line the porch and a fireplace crackles in the beautiful parlor. The inn offers a 10 percent discount to military personnel. $$$.

southwest

day trip 18

southwest

civil war battlefield:
manassas national battlefield:
manassas, va

manassas national battlefield

As you drive into Virginia, it's hard not to notice how steeped the area is in Civil War history. Many of the old homes and buildings in the region sheltered soldiers or served as makeshift hospitals during the war and historic site markers dot the landscape. Virginia's strategic location meant that the cities and towns along the way to Washington suffered huge losses of life and property as Union and Confederate forces clashed.

For anyone who wants to learn more about the role the region played in the War Between the States, a trip to Manassas Battlefield Park is a must. The first major land battle of the Civil War took place at Manassas in 1861. Both sides went into the encounter thinking it would be a quick, casualty-free war, only to be proven very wrong by the bloody fighting that ensued. It is for this reason that soldiers labeled the event "baptism by fire." A little more than a year after the first deadly conflict, a second one started here. It too resulted in a great loss of life. Some visitors claim they have seen the ghosts of soldiers while touring Manassas.

Confederate forces named battles after the closest town or railroad junction and there-fore refer to the first encounter as the Battle of First Manassas. Union soldiers named their battles after the closest river, stream, or creek, which is why this conflict is sometimes also called Battle of Bull Run. The park uses the Manassas names when referring to the two battles.

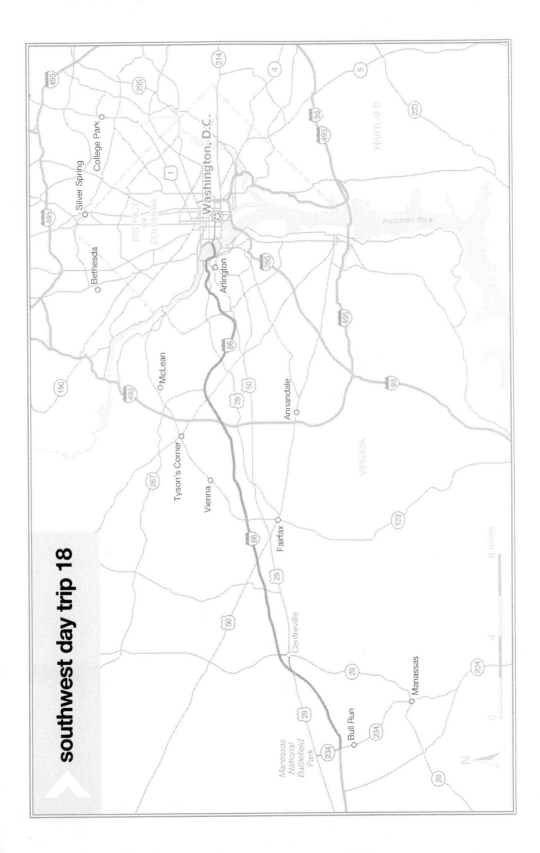

southwest day trip 18

The museum, rangers, and guides at Manassas have created something of a living monument to the events that occurred on the site. Twice a year reenactments are held at Manassas to help tell the story of the two major battles that took place on what is now 5,000 acres of national parkland. Reenactments take place in the summer and coincide with the anniversary of each battle.

getting there

It takes a little less than an hour to get to the battlefields at Manassas. Go west on I-66 to exit 47B, Route 234 North. The entrance to the Henry Hill Visitor Center is on the right.

where to go

Manassas National Battlefield. 12521 Lee Hwy., Manassas, VA; (703) 361-1339; nps .gov/mana/index.htm. The battlefield park covers a massive amount of land. True Civil War buffs will want to spend many hours or days touring the various historic points while others can get a good sense of the events that took place here with a single visit. No matter which category you fall into, you'll probably want to start your trip at the Henry Hill Visitor Center. The museum here displays uniforms and weapons used during the war along with other artifacts from both sides. Every hour on the hour, the film *Manassas: End of Innocence* is shown, providing a good background of the Civil War and the battles that took place here. An electronic map, which shows field strategies and tactics, is one of the center's more popular attractions. Ranger-led tours are held most days and begin at the visitor center. (Check the website for current schedules and fees. Admission is $3 and it is free for those sixteen and younger.)

The Stuart's Hill Center on the west side of the park focuses more on the second battle and is open only during the summer. A car audio tour of the Second Battle of Manassas may be purchased at the park year-round. You can also download a cell phone tour by dialing (703) 253-9002.

Other historic sites at Manassas include:

Groveton Confederate Cemetery. This cemetery sits on the land that is now Manassas National Battlefield and was the final resting place for many Southern soldiers who died here.

Henry Hill Loop Trail. The 1-mile pathway lets visitors take a self-guided tour of some of the sites significant to the First Battle of Manassas. Among the places of interest on the trail is the house of Judith Henry, an elderly woman who refused to leave her home when the fighting began and was killed by a stray bullet. She is buried in the Groveton Cemetery. You will also see the remains of the house belonging to James Robinson, a free African American whose farmhouse got caught up in the long war. Field artillery placements, monuments, and troop markers can also be seen along the way. If you are there on a summer weekend, you likely will coo a cannon demonstration. Give yourself about an hour to complete the loop and read the detailed signage along the way. The tour starts and ends at the Henry Hill Visitor Center.

Locust Shade Park. 4701 Locust Shade Dr.; Triangle, VA; (703) 221-8579; pwcparks.org. Next door to the Marine Corps Heritage Center sits the family-friendly Locust Shade Park, which (no surprise given its name) is a mostly wooded park. Some 290 acres of wooded parkland to be exact, complete with a lake for boating and fishing, large picnic pavilions, mini golf, a driving range, batting cage, fitness and hiking trails, horseshoe pits, and a 400-seat amphitheater. If you want to change your auto-responder to "gone fishin" before heading to Locust, you do need to purchase the appropriate fishing licenses. If you are 15 or older, a Freshwater Virginia State Fishing License is required year-round and a Virginia State Trout License is required during the winter season, which is from Nov 1 to Apr 30. The pond is stocked with trout by from Nov to Apr and channel catfish during the spring season. Additionally, there is a native population of blue gill, largemouth bass and crappie.

Manassas Industrial School & Jennie Dean Memorial. 9601 Wellington Rd., Manassas, VA; (703) 368-1873; manassascity.org. A memorial to Jennie Dean, a former slave who chartered a secondary school for African Americans in 1893. The 5-acre archaeological park covers the land where the school once sat and includes historical markers, a model of the school, a re-creation of its gates, and an exhibit kiosk.

Manassas Museum. 9101 Prince William St., Manassas, VA; (703) 368-1873; manassas museum.org. The city's museum focuses on the area's agricultural and social history. Open Tues through Sun from 10 a.m. to 5 p.m. Admission is charged.

National Museum of the Marine Corps. 18900 Jefferson Davis Hwy., Triangle, VA; usmcmuseum.com. The museum strives to bring to life more than 200 years of US Marine

nature's healing

It's sometimes hard to reconcile the great carnage that took place at Manassas with the park's great natural beauty. Meadowlands, woodlands, and grasslands fill many of the 5,000 acres. Runners, hikers, and bikers flock to the trails at Manassas and two picnic areas make for scenic alfresco dining—one is located at the Stuart's Hill Center and the other is in the Brownsville area off Groveton Road. The park even holds the distinction of being named an Audubon Important Bird Area because of the numerous bird species, including several rare ones, that live in the park.

Corps history as well as honor the commitment, accomplishments, and sacrifices of all Marines. Regular family days along with special events take place throughout the year.

Old Rose Garden. Ben Lomond House, 10311 Sudley Manor Dr., Manassas, VA; (703) 367-7872. Even the flowers are historic in this part of the country. The majority of the delicate roses that bloom on this antebellum farm date back to varieties created hundreds of years ago. Only a few of the garden's blooms are from the twentieth century—most are flowers that grew in the 1800s. Tours of the antique blooms are given from May through Oct for a small fee. Call to make sure the roses are in bloom and the grounds are open. The Federal-style Ben Lomond house played a role in the Civil War and is also open to visitors.

Quantico National Cemetery. 18424 Joplin Rd., Triangle, VA; (703) 221-2183; cem.va .gov/cems/nchp/quantico.asp. Quantico is the final resting place for many of the men and women who gave their lives serving their country. Seemingly endless rows of small American flags mark the military gravestones. Among the individuals buried here is World War II combat photographer Louis R. Lowery, who won the Pulitzer Prize for capturing on film the iconic photo *Raising the Flag on Iwo Jima*.

Stone bridge. The stone bridge that spanned the deep creek of Bull Run was a strategic target during the war for both sides. The bridge was destroyed and damaged several times during the Civil War and rebuilt in 1884.

Stone House. This is one of only a few pre–Civil War buildings that remain at Manassas today. A tavern before the war, the Stone House served as a hospital during both battles of Manassas.

where to shop

Echoes. 9101 Prince William St., Manassas, VA; (703) 368-1873; manassasmuseum.org. The shop at the Manassas Museum, Echoes specializes in local and Virginia-made crafts and products, such as handmade soaps and lotions. The shop also carries a wide variety of Manassas Battlefield souvenir items, including pins, spoons, and Christmas ornaments.

Manassas Clay. 9122 Center St., Manassas, VA; (703) 330-1040; manassasclay.com. The exquisite and often whimsical creations of dozens of potters fill the downtown gallery. Clay regularly sponsors classes and programs at its studio and also sells clay, brushes, glazes, and other pottery-making supplies.

Opera House Gourmet. 9126 Center St., Manassas, VA; (703) 330-9636; operahouse gourmet.com. Opera House Gourmet is one part specialty foods, one part fine wines, one part handmade house gifts, and all parts adorable. The pretty downtown shop also runs an international wine-of-the-month club.

in every life some water park must splash . . .

Throw a bathing suit in your bag before you head for Manassas because after a few hours of hot and humid, SplashDown Waterpark may seem as appealing as the Riviera. The giant water park is the area's largest and loaded with wet fun. A lazy river ride, two cannonball slides, and four-story waterslides are just a few of the highlights. The park is open during the summer and charges admission. Call or check the website for the most current details. SplashDown Waterpark; 7500 Ben Lomond Park Dr., Manassas, VA; (703) 361-4451; splashdownwaterpark.com.

where to eat

Carmello's & Little Portugal. 9108 Center St., Manassas, VA; (703) 368-5522; carmellos .com. The kitchen at this restaurant in historic downtown Manassas cooks both Italian and Portuguese dishes. Local musicians perform on weekends and Carmello's often holds special events like Portuguese wine sampling. $$$.

City Square Cafe. 9428 Battle St., Manassas, VA; (703) 369-6022; citysquarecafe.com. City Square Cafe bills itself as an international bistro serving dishes with influences from around the globe. During the week from 3 to 7 p.m. the special tapas menu is available along with beer, wine, and sangria. In warm weather, dine outside on the patio. $$$.

Malones of Manassas. 9329 Main St., Manassas, VA; (571) 208-1246; malonesofmanassas .com. Malones' profile has been rising thanks to its chef and a stream of praise and great reviews. The menu is steak-heavy but includes some interesting salads and fish dishes. Don't forget to take in the historic building, dating back to 1874, which once served as the Manassas Presbyterian Church and was built from locally quarried red sandstone. $$.

Okra's Louisiana Bistro. 9110 Center St., Manassas, VA; (703) 330-2729. Downtown Okra's serves up Cajun- and Creole-style cooking with dishes like seafood gumbo, jambalaya, and pan-blackened filet mignon on its extensive menu. Every Fri and Sat night the sounds of live jazz, blues, and zydeco music fill the downtown restaurant. $$$.

where to stay

Bennett House Bed & Breakfast. 9252 Bennett Dr., Manassas, VA; (800) 354-7060; virginiabennetthouse.com. This light-filled bed-and-breakfast is in the heart of Old Town, putting it within walking distance of shopping and restaurants. The refrigerator upstairs is stocked with soda, juices, and bottled water, and fresh flowers and cookies are placed in your room before you arrive. A full home-cooked country breakfast is served every morning in the downstairs dining room. $$.

Manassas Junction Bed and Breakfast. 9311 Prescott Ave., Manassas, VA; (703) 216 7803; manassasjunction.com. The owners of the Manassas Junction B&B usher guests back in time when they visit the two-room Victorian located in Old Town Manassas. Period antiques fill the quaint 1902 home with the wraparound porch. The inn is known for its hospitality and its homemade breakfast, which often includes house-made jellies and other goodies. $$.

day trip 19

southwest

>> **brunch & browsing near the blue ridge:**
culpeper, va

culpeper

Something happens when you enter Culpeper. The iced tea gets sweeter, the y'alls start flowing more freely, and the Blue Ridge rises up to greet you in the distance. Before long you might even get a hankerin' for fried okra or maybe even some grits. Don't worry, it's perfectly normal in these here parts. Because when you're in Culpeper you start to feel like you're in the South.

The town has a long history that dates back to colonial times. During the American Revolution a group of men from the region banded together to form the Culpeper Minute Men Battalion and carried a version of the now iconic pre-American flag with the motto "Liberty or Death—Don't Tread on Me." Because of its location, Culpeper was enmeshed in the Civil War. More than a hundred battles and skirmishes took place in the town and just about every house and building was used at some point as either a makeshift hospital or to house soldiers. In the mid-twentieth century the town fell into disrepair and in the 1980s a movement began to bring new life to the historic downtown. Today as you walk the charming streets of Culpeper you can see for yourself that the movement was indeed a success. Culpeper has become increasingly well known for its restaurant scene, with many tasty choices along its main street. Movie buffs also are drawn to this quaint town for its rich film offerings from the Library of Congress at the new State Theatre and also at Mount

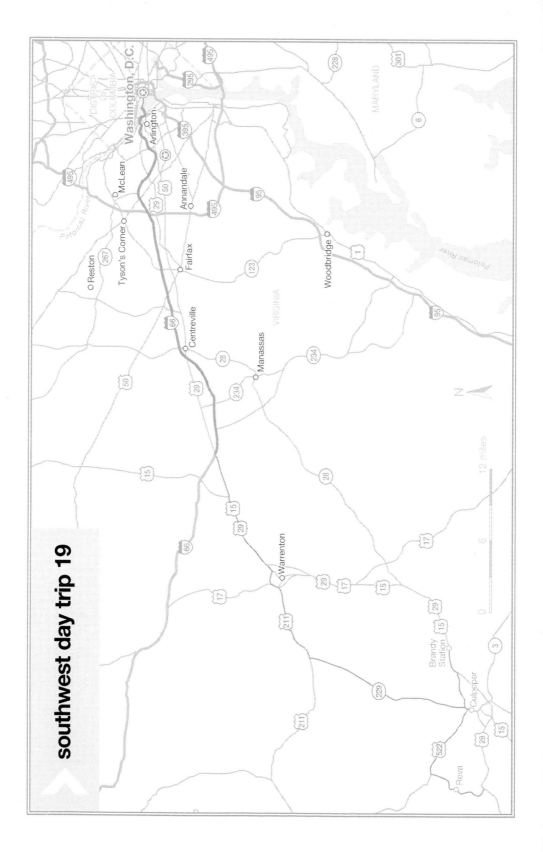

southwest day trip 19

Pony (a 200-seat Art Deco–style movie theater that holds weekly free screenings from its amazing collection).

getting there

Culpeper is about an hour and a half from DC, depending on traffic. Take I-66 West to exit 43A, Route 29 South toward Warrenton, and continue on Route 29 South for approximately 40 miles to the first Culpeper exit. Follow the signs to the historic district. Culpeper also is an easy hour-and-a-half-long train ride from DC on Amtrak, and the majority of the town's highlights are in walking distance from the station.

where to go

Belmont Farm Distillery. 13490 Cedar Run Rd., Culpeper, VA; (540) 825-3207; virginia moonshine.com. You don't need a secret password or a special knock to see how local moonshine is made. You don't even need to come under the cover of darkness. All you need to do is take a tour of the Belmont Farm distillery and see how the facility has been turning out fresh corn whiskey for generations. The moonshine is prepared in a solid copper pot still, which owners claim as the secret ingredient in their twice-distilled Virginia Lightning. Tours are given from Apr to Dec. Sip what all the fuss is about with a tasting, which costs $5 per person. Call ahead for schedules and holiday closures.

Culpeper County Court House. 35 W. Cameron St., Culpeper, VA. The current working courthouse is the third to stand in Culpeper (the first was built in 1749 shortly after the county was formed). On the courthouse lawn two monuments pay tribute to local fallen soldiers—one to those who died in Vietnam and one to Culpeper's Confederate soldiers who were killed during the Civil War.

Culpeper County Library. 271 Southgate Shopping Center, Culpeper, VA; (540) 825-8691; tlc.library.net/culpeper. Civil War buffs might want to detour over to the Culpeper County Library, which has a large collection of Civil War books, including some rare titles. Open daily but hours vary, so check the website before you go.

Culpeper Train Depot & Culpeper Visitor Center. 111 S. Commerce St., Culpeper, VA; (540) 727-0611; visitculpeperva.com. The Culpeper Train Depot harkens back to a time when the rail was king. In 1998 ownership of the depot was officially transferred from Norfolk Southern to the town of Culpeper and the depot began its new life as the town's visitor center. (It's also a functioning Amtrak station.) The walls of the visitor center are lined with pamphlets, brochures, and maps for attractions in and around Culpeper and Virginia. In one back corner a display case houses china from the golden days of the railroad, when meals were served in formal dining cars. Outside visitors can climb on the back of a restored old red caboose.

top-secret cinema

A precious film collection filled with rare treasures gets moved into a former government high-security currency warehouse once owned by the Federal Reserve Board and fortified with lead-lined shutters, walls that are a foot thick, and a steel-reinforced bunker. Sounds like the plot of an obscure old flick. It's not. But if it was ever filmed or recorded it likely would be housed at the Library of Congress Packard Campus of the National Audio-Visual Conservation Center in Culpeper.

A few years back the audio-visual department of the Library of Congress moved its extensive film and recording collection to Culpeper to a 45 acre campus that once served as an emergency headquarters for the government. Today the building no longer houses top-secret stuff but instead protects the library's collection of more than 1.1 million film, television, and video items and about 3.5 million audio recordings. It takes more than 90 miles of shelving to store the massive collection, which includes a motion picture from the 1890s.

In 2008 the library opened Mount Pony, a 200-seat Art Deco–style movie theater that regularly holds free screenings of its extensive collection of classic films. Showings tend to be on Thursday, Friday, and Saturday evenings with a matinee and evening showing on Saturday afternoon. While there is no cost to see the flicks, reservations are required. You can call up to a week before a screening to reserve a seat. The line is open Mon through Fri from 9 a.m. to 4 p.m. Mount Pony is one of only a handful of theaters in this country capable of projecting nitrate film stock, so you never know what might be on the marquee. Mount Pony Theater, 19053 Mount Pony Rd., Culpeper; (540) 827-1079 ext. 79994 or (202) 707-9994; loc.gov/avconservation/theater.

Museum of Culpeper History. 111 S. Commerce St., Culpeper, VA; (540) 829-1749; culpepermuseum.com. The Culpeper museum displays artifacts and items as a way of tracing the Virginia town's history from prehistoric times, with a locally excavated pair of 215-million-year-old dinosaur tracks, up to the present. The museum owns a large collection of maps, photos, artifacts, and items from the Civil War era. A working Native American village and a fully restored eighteenth-century log cabin are also on museum grounds and open to the public. A small admission fee is charged for adults but the museum is free for children under 18 and all Culpeper residents regardless of age. Open daily in its new space in the in the Culpeper Train Depot.

Old House Vineyard. 18351 Corkys Ln., Culpeper, VA; (540) 423-1032; oldhousevineyards.com. When you look at the Old House Vineyard today, it's hard to imagine that what is now a charming Victorian home and lush vineyards was once an abandoned old farmhouse and overgrown alfalfa fields. Regular tours are given of the winemaking process at Old House. Visitors also get to ride through the vineyards and fields hayride-style. Tastings and tours are held daily for a fee.

The State Theatre. 305 S. Main St., Culpeper, VA; (540) 829-0292; culpepertheatre.org. The State Theatre's carefully restored Art Deco marquee once again lights up Main Street after an extensive $9 million restoration and expansion effort. First opened in 1938, the state-of-the-art entertainment and educational venue hosts a range of live performances. You can also catch a range of film here including a popular classic film series put on with the Library of Congress and has featured such flicks as *Raiders of the Lost Ark, The Wizard of Oz* and *An Affair to Remember*. The State Theatre also is listed on the State and National Registers of Historic Places.

where to shop

The Cameleer. 125 E. Davis St., Culpeper, VA; (540) 825-8073; thecameleer.com. International giftware, aboriginal art, and crafts. This large, light and bright store with the great big camel in the window started out just selling Australian aboriginal art and now sells items from across the globe. The store is stocked with a nice mix of international clothing, crafts, children's items, and housewares.

Clarke Hardware. 201 E. Davis St., Culpeper, VA; (540) 825-9178. Clarke Hardware is the anti-box-store store. The family-owned old-fashioned hardware store features an array of goods, from hammers to wooden sleds, and specializes in Aladdin Mantle Lamps, Radio Flyer wagons, and large cast-iron cookware. The establishment also offers professional knife and scissor sharpening.

Culpeper Downtown Farmers' Market. East Davis Street and Commerce Street parking lot, Culpeper, VA; (540) 825-4416; culpeperdowntown.com. Every Saturday from May to October from 7:30 a.m. to noon, this otherwise unassuming parking lot turns into an outdoor market filled with local produce, farm-fresh eggs, and home-baked goods. Local musicians play as shoppers fill their baskets.

Found. 162 E. Davis St., Culpeper, VA; (540) 825-4694; foundantiquesandvintage.com. Found sells fun and functional antiques and vintage pieces. You truly never know what you might find here and that is exactly the point.

The Culpeper Cheese Company. 141 E. Davis St., Culpeper, VA; (540) 825-8025; www .culpepercheese.com. A carefully curated selection of cheeses begs customers to try them at this local gourmet shop. Some fifty different types of local, domestic, and international cheese can be sliced or ordered. The store also has an extensive wine and beer selection.

Green Roost. 141 E. Davis St., Culpeper, VA; (540) 829-6378; shopgreenroost.com. A pretty, light-filled gift shop that only sells products that are kind to the earth while at the same time being stylish and trendy.

Sara Schneidman Gallery. 122 E. Davis St., Culpeper, VA; (540) 825-0034; saraschneidman .com. The bright, vibrant colors of Sara Schneidman's work practically pull you off the street and into this lovely store showcasing her pottery, paintings, and hand-knotted rugs. Works by other potters and artists also are for sale here.

where to eat

Davis St. Pier. 302 E. Davis St., Culpeper, VA; (540) 317-5072. Seafood is the name of the game here at this casual eatery near the train depot. $.

Foti's. 219 E. Davis St., Culpeper, VA; (540) 829-8400. Chef Foteos "Frank" Maragos perfected his culinary skills at the acclaimed Inn at Little Washington. And his wife and Foti's co-owner, Sue Maragos, cultivated her restaurant management skills at the famed inn where the two met. Many of the dishes on the menu at the well-reviewed Foti's have a Mediterranean influence. Lunch and dinner Thurs through Sun and on Tues. $$$.

Frost Cafe. 101 E. Davis St., Culpeper, VA; (540) 829-034. Old-school diner complete with a long counter, red booths, and tabletop jukeboxes. In addition to the regular menu, breakfast is served all day and includes a few distinctly Southern options, such as scrapple omelets, scrapple sandwiches, and fresh grits. $.

It's About Thyme and Thyme Market. 28 E. Davis St., Culpeper, VA; (540) 825-1011; thymeinfo.com. This pretty, European-style eatery sells salads, pizzas, and a host of dishes that start out on Thyme Market's wood-fed rotisserie. You can eat in at the restaurant, which also has a sweet little outdoor seating area next to the downtown storefront it occupies. Gourmet goodies and prepared meals can be purchased at the market. $$.

Lucio. 702 S. Main St., Culpeper, VA; (540) 829-9788; luciorestaurant.net. Homemade pastas, antipasto, and seafood are staples at this downtown Italian restaurant housed in a turn-of-the-twentieth-century home. Amorous couples will love the romantic atmosphere while families with young children might not be loved by said couples. If you're dining with little ones this isn't a great choice. $$.

The Restaurant in Culpeper. 110 E. Davis St., Culpeper, VA; (540) 825-6500; therestaurant inculpeper.com. A simply named restaurant with a simply delicious concept: Southern-style home-cooked meals with flair. Everything from the ketchup to the corned beef is made in house and is locally sourced. Menus change based on the season and what is available. The Restaurant serves lunch, dinner, and Sunday brunch and also carries a variety of local beers and wines. $.

where to stay

Cheesecake Farms Bed, Barn & Breakfast. 4085 Sumerduck Rd., Sumerduck, VA; (540) 439-2188; cheesecakefarms.com. If you are not ready to leave city life behind but want to spend a night or two in a cozy barn suite, this is the place for you. The suite is adjacent to an actual hayloft and has air conditioning, a private bath, microwave, refrigerator, and a Sleep Number bed. You are welcome to explore the grounds and come meet some of the animals that call Cheesecake home. Breakfast is served to all guests, as is a substantial afternoon snack that often includes homemade soups, chili, macaroni and cheese, and, of course, cheesecake. Whenever possible, local ingredients, many grown on the farm, are used. $$.

Fountain Hall Bed & Breakfast. 609 S. East St., Culpeper, VA; (540) 825-8300. This grand old Colonial Revival home in the historic district boasts the title of Culpeper's first B&B. Inside you will find 10-foot-high ceilings, a sweeping walnut staircase, three parlors, and six guest rooms. Each room has a private bath and air-conditioning and some have private porches and spa tubs. Breakfast is served from 7 to 10 a.m. and features fresh croissants. $.

Funny Farm Inn. 2437 Funny Farm Rd., Reva, VA; (540) 547-3481; thefunnyfarminn.com. The European-style cottage on this 75-acre horse farm has two levels that can be rented either separately or together. Each level sleeps six people and comes with a kitchen stocked with dishes, flatware, glassware, and cookware, along with pantry and refrigerator staples. Pets and children are welcome, as are horses, which can bunk in the farm's deluxe barn. Just think of the fun you can have telling your friends the Funny Farm is only 10 crazy miles south of Culpeper. $$.

Hazel River Inn Bed & Breakfast. 11227 Eggbornsville Rd., Culpeper, VA; (540) 937-5854; hazelriverinn.com. The Hazel River Inn Bed and Breakfast sits on 5 acres of land on the morning side of the Blue Ridge Mountains. The innkeeper also wears a horticulturalist hat and her gardens share the property. Guests staying in any of the three rooms at the nineteenth-century inn can enjoy the heated swimming pool behind the house. The owners also run the Hazel River Inn Restaurant (195 E. Davis St., Culpeper, VA; 540-825-7148) in downtown Culpeper in a historic corner building thought to be the oldest standing commercial structure in town. $.

Suites at 249. 249 E. Davis St., Culpeper, VA; (540) 827-1100; suitesat249.com. The Suites at 249 combines an urban vibe with small-town charm. Each of the six suites here is individually decorated and the decor incorporates the restored redbrick building's lines and angles. Private balconies, gas fireplaces, flat-screen TVs, and king-size feather beds with down comforters and Italian linens are among the many amenities found in every room. The boutique hotel stands near the base of the main street in Culpeper's historic district, putting it steps away from restaurants and shops. Suite 249 does not allow pets, smoking, or children. $$.

Thyme Inn. 128 E. Davis St., Culpeper, VA; (540) 825-4264; thymeinfo.com. Three pretty rooms above the downtown Thyme Market can be yours for the night or more. The three rooms—named what else but Rosemary, Sage, and Thyme—have fireplaces, balconies, and private baths. A nice, quiet place to spend an evening or to set up a home base while you explore the area. $.

worth more time

Graffiti House. 19484 Brandy Rd., Brandy Station, VA; brandystationfoundation.com. The old red house functioned as a field hospital during the Civil War and many of its walls were filled with the doodling, signatures, and musings of the soldiers who passed through. Local lore says the hospital was used by both Union and Confederate troops. Many of the scribbles have been preserved and historians have identified some of the authors. You can check out some of the graffiti on the second floor of the two-story house.

day trip 20

southwest

caving in:
luray caverns, va

luray caverns

When I pulled up to Luray Caverns for the first time, I must admit I thought it looked a bit like a tourist trap. But past the huge parking lot, gift shop, and row of soda machines I found a natural wonder worth every drop of gas it took to get here. The seemingly endless formations in the vast caverns are breathtaking. In places they are massive while in others they are delicate and artistic.

The more than 400-million-year-old caverns were discovered in 1878. When news of the underground find got out, journalists and scientists came to see for themselves. And as they began to spread the word to the public about Luray, people came by horse, stage-coach, and carriages to see for themselves. Cavern-bound folk dressed up to see the site and even in the 1950s and 1960s visitors donned their Sunday best to come here. Today you don't need to press your pants or starch your shirt to come to Luray—jeans, sneakers, and a zip-up sweatshirt will do just fine. But whatever you decide to wear you'll likely be very pleased that you made the trip.

getting there

Luray Caverns is about 90 miles from the Beltway. Luray is in the Shenandoah Valley, which makes for a beautiful drive in any season. From Washington take I-66 West to Gainesville

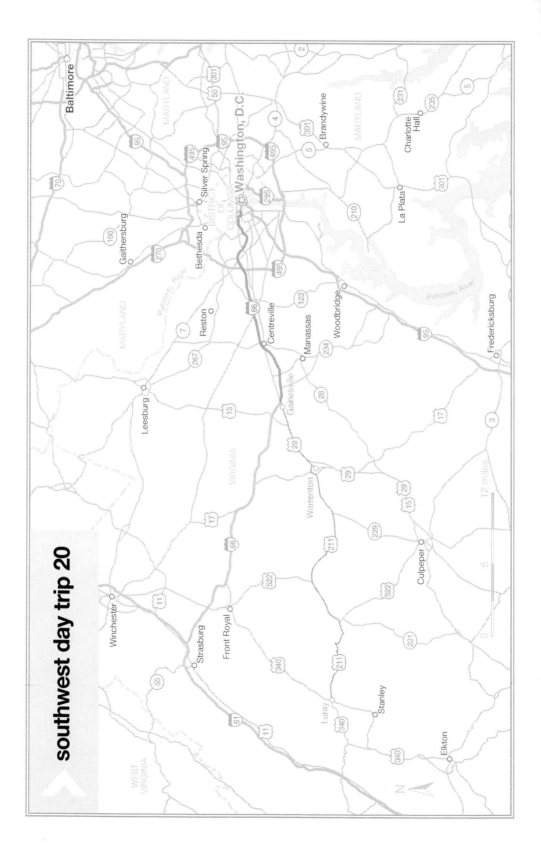

southwest day trip 20

and get on US 29 South to Warrenton. Follow US 211 West to Luray Caverns. The caverns are about ten minutes past the entrance to Skyline Drive.

where to go

Luray Caverns. 101 Cave Hill Rd., Luray, VA; (540) 743-6551; luraycaverns.com. When you pay the entrance fee to get into Luray you are entitled to an audio headset tour, which explains the various formations and gives background and interesting facts about the caverns. There is also a kids' version of the tour, which my seven-year-old gave a review of forty thumbs up, his highest rating. Nature has divided the limestone caverns into large room-like spaces, each tending to have one major focal point. Remember to not touch the formations, stay on the pathways, and use the hand railings when necessary. Here are a few highlights:

> **Dream Lake.** At first glance Dream Lake appears to be an intricate city of stalagmites rising up from the ground toward an equally stunning group of stalactites hanging from the ceiling. But look again and see that Mother Nature is playing a trick on you. The stalactites on the ceiling are reflected into the mirror-like pool of water below it to create this striking illusion.

> **Fried Eggs.** Some formations throughout Luray Caverns serve as a kind of Rorschach test, looking like different objects to different people. But the vast consensus is that two small, round formations near the end of the tour look just like two sunny-side-up eggs. Rubbing the eggs used to be considered good luck but turned out to be bad luck for the National Landmark caverns, as oil and such from hands can erode the surface. So please, don't touch.

> **Stalacpipe Organ.** The caverns house the world's largest instrument, the Stalacpipe Organ. The one-of-a-kind instrument relies on a series of rubber mallets tapping various stalactites spread across the caverns to create the notes. The unusual organ was the brainchild of a Pentagon scientist who worked for thirty-six years to perfect his design. More than 5 miles of wiring connect the organ to various stalactites. Visitors can listen to the eerie music in the room called the Cathedral, which has been the site of many a wedding.

> **Titania's Veil.** This gleaming white, pure calcite formation shares its name with the fairy queen from *A Midsummer Night's Dream* and can be seen from many angles in the caverns. This type of deposit if often referred to as flowstone and occurs when crystalline deposits spread.

Car & Carriage Caravan Museum. 101 Cave Hill Rd., Luray, VA; (540) 743-6551; luray caverns.com/Attractions/CarandCarriageCaravanMuseum/tabid/535/Default.aspx. Included with admission to the caverns is a visit to the Car and Carriage Caravan Museum. Filled with vintage cars, coaches, and carriages, this small museum includes an impressive number of vehicles, including a very rare operating 1892 Benz. Other highlights include an 1840 Cones-toga wagon, a 1913 Stanley Steamer, and a 1925 Rolls-Royce once owned by Rudolph Valentino. The museum is open daily from 9 a.m. to an hour and half after the last cavern tour.

Garden Maze. 101 Cave Hill Rd., Luray, VA; (540) 743-6551; luraycaverns.com/Attractions/GardenMaze/tabid/536/Default.aspx. Get lost among the twists and turns created by 8-foot-high and 4-foot-wide shrubbery. The maze is a half-mile long and admission costs $6 for adults and $5 for children six through twelve.

Luray Singing Tower. Belle Brown Northcott Memorial; 970 US 211 West, Luray, VA; (540) 743-6551; luraycaverns.com. Against the backdrop of the magnificent Blue Ridge Mountains, a carillon of forty-seven bells sings out from a 117-foot-high tower across the road from the caverns. Free outdoor recitals are given regularly throughout the year except during the winter. Check the website for the current concert schedule.

Luray Zoo. 1087 US 211 West, Luray, VA; (540) 743-4113; lurayzoo.com. This is a little zoo with a big heart. The zoo provides a safe haven for animals that were either abandoned or abused. It also takes in so-called exotic pets that have been confiscated. You can feed and interact with some of the animals at the petting zoo. Admission is $10 for adults and $5 for children and the money goes to help with the care of the animals.

The Rope Adventure Park. 970 US 211 West, Luray, VA; (540) 843-0319; ropeadventurepark.com. A somewhat new addition to the area, Rope Adventure Park features a two-level course—a low ropes course and a more challenging high ropes course. The park is family-friendly and you don't need any specific rope experience or skills set to give it a try.

Valley Star Farm. 1140 Springfield Rd., Luray, VA; (540) 860-8040; valleystarfarm.com. During the fall and early winter this family-owned farm lets the public come and peruse its pumpkin patch and Christmas tree farm. Visitors can pick their own pumpkins and choose their very own Christmas tree. Valley Star Farm also has a play area and corn maze for kids. Check the web site for dates and times.

The Warehouse Art Gallery. 15 Campbell St., Luray, VA; (540) 843-0200; warehouseartcenter.net. This 7,000-square-foot space is part visual art gallery, part performance space, and all parts dedicated to nurturing and celebrating the creative process. The Warehouse encourages visitors to bring a lunch and enjoy it in the Brown Bag Cafe. Hours vary depending on the season so please check before you go.

where to shop

Apple Cottage Gourmet Health Foods. 51 W. Main St., Luray, VA; (540) 743-7299; applecottagefoods.com. The Apple Cottage stocks its shelves with an array of organic and gourmet foods and items. It's also a good place to pick up locally grown cider and honey or some custom-made herbal tea.

> ## candlelit anniversary

When the lucky explorers stumbled upon Luray Caverns in 1878, the only way to illuminate the magnificent formations was by lantern and candlelight. One day every year to celebrate the discovery, the staff lights portions of the caverns with candles and lets visitors tour the caverns by the flickering light. The celebration is held the Saturday closest to the August 13 discovery day. In addition to the candlelight tours, fireworks, entertainment, and other festivities help to mark the day.

Bank Street Books. 201 W. Main St., Luray, VA; (540) 843-0690. You never know what literary treasures you may discover at this secondhand bookstore.

where to eat

Artisans Grill. 2 E. Main St., Luray, VA; (540) 743-7030; artisansgrill.com. Housed in a historic downtown building, the two-level Artisans Grill specializes in subs, sandwiches, burgers, and salads. The restaurant uses local produce and naturally raised beef in its kitchen. $.

Circa '31. 401 W. Main St., Luray, VA; (540) 743-5105; mimslyninn.com. This elegant restaurant housed in the Mimslyn Inn serves both Southern classic and modern dishes. The chef changes the menu frequently to reflect seasonally available ingredients and flavors. $$$.

Gathering Grounds Patisserie & Cafe. 55 E. Main St., Luray, VA; (540) 743-1121; ggrounds.com. A cute spot to pop in for a homemade coffee cake, a loaded wrap, or something hot from the espresso bar. Gathering Grounds makes all its baked goods fresh each day and offers a big pie selection. The cozy cafe also has Wi-Fi and serves beer and wine. $.

Triple Crown BBQ. 1079 US 211 West; Luray, VA; (540) 743-5311. Roadside barbecue done right. No frills but lots and lots of flavor and a super-loyal following that the owners attribute to their wood-fired Southern Pride smoker and old family recipes. Food can be eaten at the picnic tables outside or taken to go. Closed in the off-season and open Wed through Sun most weeks during the on season. $.

Uncle Buck's Restaurant. 42 E. Main St., Luray, VA; (540) 743-2323. Affordable, big portions and friendly service are the order of the day at this family restaurant. $.

West Main Market. 123 W. Main St., Luray, VA; (540) 743-1125; westmainmarket.com. This deli and sandwich shop is a good place to pick up provisions for a picnic or to have a casual sandwich or bowl of the soup of the day. Salads and hot and cold sandwiches can be ordered or you can just purchase meats and cheeses by the pound to go. $.

antiquing in luray

Luray's small but charming downtown is home to several antiques stores. Some only sell things from days gone by and others have a mix of new and old collectibles. If antiquing gets your heart rate up, here are a few shops you might want to visit while you are in town:

- *Bren's Antiques, 24 E. Main St., Luray, VA; (540) 743-9001.*

- *Court House Antiques, 12 W. Main St., Luray, VA; (540) 743-2333.*

- *Luray Antique & Design Center, 26 N. Broad St., Luray, VA; (540) 743-7900.*

- *Luray Antique Mall, 56 E. Main St., Luray, VA; (540) 743-1298; antique malls.com/stores/10168.aspx.*

- *Mama's Treasures, 22 E. Main St., Luray, VA; (540) 743-1352; tias.com.*

where to stay

Mayne View Bed & Breakfast. 439 Mechanic St., Luray, VA; (540) 743-7921; mayne view.com. The Mayne View Bed and Breakfast is steeped in history. Two of the men who discovered Luray Caverns originally built it in 1865 as a hunting lodge, and during the Civil War the property functioned as part of the Underground Railroad. Today visitors can choose from five rooms, all with private baths, soak in the outdoor hot tub, and stroll Mayne View's 3 acres with mountain views. $$.

Mimslyn Inn. 401 W. Main St., Luray, VA; (540) 743-7921; mimslyninn.com. A grand old 1930s Southern hotel, Mimslyn Inn recently underwent a multimillion-dollar renovation. The forty-five-room inn counts among its amenities an outdoor pool, fitness center, winding staircase, extensive gardens, restaurant, and spa. Mimslyn Inn is listed on the Historic Hotels of America registry. $$.

Victorian Inn of Luray. 138 E. Main St., Luray, VA; (540) 743-1494; woodruffinns.com. The pretty yellow and white Victorian home houses three elegant guest suites with antique furnishings, Jacuzzi tubs for two, and other romantic touches. The front porch and wraparound porch on the second floor make for great spots to relax and take in the scenery. Southern cuisine is the house specialty at the inn's restaurant. Right behind the inn, the French Country Cottage offers four additional room choices. $$$.

west

>>>

day trip 21

west

middleburg

Nestled in the heart of Virginia's horse and hunt country stands the charming town of Middleburg. The affluent colonial town is home to about 600 residents but since the early 1900s has been welcoming large crowds during foxhunting and steeplechase season. Middleburg counts one street as its downtown and it's perfectly acceptable to trot down the street on horseback.

getting there

Middleburg is about an hour from Washington and is a pretty easy drive. Take I-495 to I-66 West and exit at Route 50 West. Continue about 25 miles west to Middleburg.

where to go

Great Meadow. 5089 Old Tavern Rd., The Plains, VA; (540) 253-5000; greatmeadow.org. On 250 picture-perfect acres are the field and steeplechase of Great Meadow. A nonprofit organization owns and maintains the property, which hosts races and events like its annual Fourth of July celebration and the Virginia Scottish Games and Festival. Great Meadow also serves as the permanent home of the Virginia International Cup and the Virginia Gold Cup, the country's oldest steeplechase races.

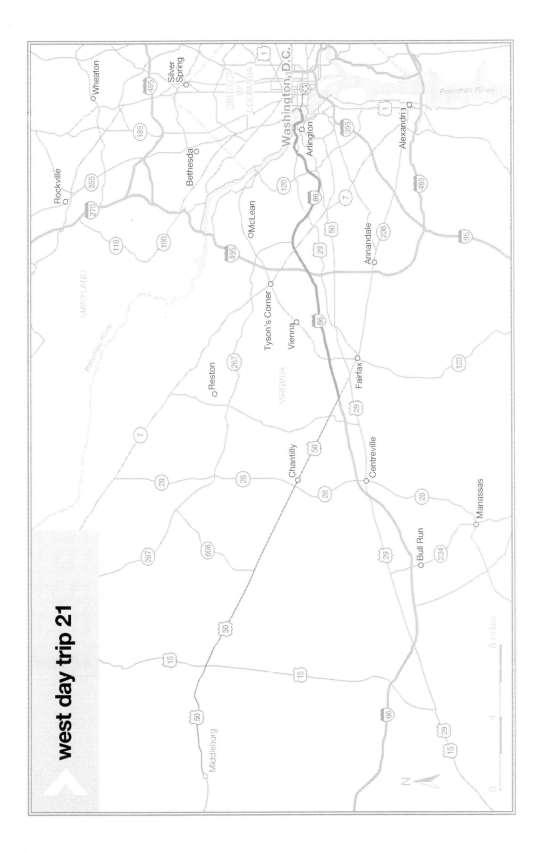

west day trip 21

National Sporting Library. 102 The Plains Rd., Middleburg, VA; (540) 687-6542; nsl.org. Riding devotees come to the National Sporting Library to get lost in its extensive collection, which deals with everything from foxhunting to polo to thoroughbred racing to dressage. Books about fishing and shooting are also catalogued at the research library. A rare-book room includes thousands of old and unusual works, some from as far back as the sixteenth century. The nonlending library is free and open to the public. The National Sporting Library also sponsors exhibits and readings.

Serene Acres. 19312 Walsh Farm Ln., Bluemont, VA; (540) 554-8618; SereneAcres.com. The activities in horse country do not need to be only spectator sports. Hourlong trail rides are offered at Serene Acres, a farm that also gives pony rides and horse boarding and training services. You can even buy the pony your parents would never get you when you were a kid—the farm generally has several for sale. Rides must be reserved in advance and start at around $65.

where to shop

Clothes Minded. 8 E. Washington St., Middleburg, VA; (540) 687-4774. Trendy, hip fashions and accessories fill this cute downtown boutique. Labels like BCBG, Michael Stars, Alice & Trixie, and other fashionista favorites fill the light-filled shop.

Duchess. 100 E. Washington St., Middleburg, VA; (540) 687-8898; duchessaofmiddleburg .com. Look your finest at the races with an outfit from this downtown women's clothing boutique. Clean lines, fine fabrics, and classic designs define the styles here that help you step out in an impeccably proper ensemble that would make Ralph Lauren smile.

off to the races

Every year Middleburg hosts two steeplechase races. Held the third weekend in April, the Middleburg Spring Races started in 1911 and have attracted such dignitaries as President John F. Kennedy. Spectators come with picnic baskets and binoculars to watch the horses and help raise money for the local hospital. The Virginia Fall Races also have a long and distinguished past. President Dwight D. Eisenhower watched the first running of the annual races in 1955. Both races require tickets and are held at Glenwood Park, 36800 Glenwood Park Ln., Middleburg. Online you can find more information at middleburgspringraces.com for the spring races and vafallraces.com for the fall races.

Betsey. 102 W. Washington St. in Middleburg, VA; (540) 687-5748; betseyshop.com. Betsey holds true to its mission of selling clothes and home accessories that "styles with moxie."

The Fun Shop. 117 W. Washington St., Middleburg, VA; (540) 687-3861; thefunshop .com. With its rocking-horse sign outside greeting shoppers, the Fun Shop is a lovely little department store with home goods and items to fill the elegant homes found in horse and hunt country. A family-owned business, the store that sells everything from copper kettles to Egyptian-cotton towels first set up shop in 1956 and was a favorite of First Lady Jackie Kennedy.

Hastening Antiques. 7 E. Washington St., Middleburg, VA; (540) 687-5664; hastening antiques.com. Exquisite eighteenth- and nineteenth-century Italian, French, and English furniture and accessories fill Hastening's showroom. The owner began Hastening in the Cotswolds and moved it to Virginia about ten years ago. Delicate antique restoration work is also performed here.

Middleburg Tack Exchange. 103 W. Federal St., Middleburg, VA; (540) 687-6608; middleburgtack.com. This is a consignment store like no other. Middleburg Tack Exchange sells previously owned English hunting tack apparel. The large store has an entire floor dedicated to used saddles, boots, and blankets, and it's not uncommon to find such items as glass hunting flasks, handmade leather sandwich boxes, and frock coats in the rest of the ever-changing inventory. Closed Sun.

Second Chapter Books. 10 S. Liberty St., Middleburg, VA; (540) 687-7016. Second Chapter Books is a sweet little bookshop that sells new and used volumes for adults and children.

where to eat

Common Grounds. 114 W. Washington St., Middleburg, VA; (540) 687-7065; middleburg commongrounds.com. A great family-run indie coffee shop where you can sip your coffee while grabbing a bite to eat.

Cuppa Giddy Up. 8 E. Washington St., Middleburg, VA; (540) 687-8122. Pop into the tiny Cuppa Giddy Up coffee shop for a caffeine fix before the hunt. And, really, what's a latte without one of those delicious-looking pastries? $.

The French Hound. 101 Madison St., Middleburg, VA;, (540) 687-3018; thefrenchhound .com. Relaxed French-style bistro with outdoor patio seating. Many of the selections from the restaurant's extensive wine list are sold at the Wine Cellar, the eatery's nearby sister store at 15 S. Madison St. $$.

The Restaurant at the Goodstone Inn. 36205 Snake Hill Rd., Middleburg, VA; (540) 687-3333; goodstone.com. The Restaurant at Goodstone's is considered one of the best restaurants in the area, so if you plan on dining here reserve a table at the intimate French restaurant in advance. The estate's own organic herb and vegetable gardens provide many of the ingredients used in the kitchen. The Sunday Champagne brunch is a popular way to celebrate a special moment. No jeans or sneakers. $$$.

where to stay

Briar Patch Bed & Breakfast. 23130 Briar Patch Ln., Middleburg, VA; (703) 327-5911; briarpatchbandb.com. Guests can choose from eight light-filled guest rooms (some with private baths and some with shared ones) at the Briar Patch B&B. A one-bedroom cottage with its own kitchen offers even more privacy. Children and pets are welcome and monthly cooking classes are offered. $$.

Goodstone Inn & Estate. 36205 Snake Hill Rd., Middleburg, VA; (540) 687-4645; good stone.com. The Goodstone is the closest many of us will get to having a fabulous wealthy uncle with a country estate. Five elegant guesthouses sit on the more than 200 acres of rolling hills, romantic pathways, and babbling brooks. Each building has its own personality, with all the rooms sharing the overall theme of sophistication. In the Manor House guests will find the inn's formal dining room and a nineteenth-century mural, while the French Farm House boasts two log-burning floor-to-ceiling fireplaces and stone patios. Every afternoon an elegant tea is served at the Carriage House, which once upon a time housed fourteen horse stables. A beautiful outdoor pool sits on the property and the inn's world-class restaurant serves dinner in an intimate and romantic setting. $$$.

Middleburg Country Inn. 209 E. Washington St., Middleburg, VA; (540) 687-6082; middle burgcountryinn.com. From the fireplace in the sitting parlor to the four-poster beds to the complimentary ice cream out back, everything at the Middleburg Country Inn makes guests feel at home. The charming downtown inn has seven antiques-filled guest rooms, including at least one suite that can accommodate a family. Apple spice waffles, eggs Benedict, and grits are among the inn's breakfast choices. In good weather the pergola in the back makes for a pretty spot to eat breakfast or enjoy a glass of wine. $$$.

Red Fox Inn. 2 E. Washington St., Middleburg, VA; (540) 687-6301; redfox.com. The Red Fox Inn and Tavern has been part of the hunt country landscape since Middleburg's beginning. The original fieldstone section of the inn dates back to 1728 and is listed on the National Register of Historic Places. Inside, the inviting guest rooms reflect the inn's prestigious pedigree with carefully chosen eighteenth century–style furnishings and art. $$$.

worth more time

Cows-n-Corn. 5225 Catlett Rd., Midland, VA; (540) 439-4806; cows-n-corn.com. From one farming experience to another decidedly different one. Not far from Seven Oaks, you can visit a 1,800-acre working dairy farm. The family-owned Cows-n-Corn lets the public get an up-close look at milk production. While you are on the farm you can see cows being milked, take a hayride tour, and learn how to make butter. The farm store sells butter and cheese made from milk produced by the cows on the farm. Homemade dipped ice cream is also for sale. It too uses Cows-n-Corn fresh milk. Yum. The farm is open spring, summer, and fall. Small admission fee. Call for hours and prices.

Seven Oaks Lavender Farm. 8769 Old Dumfries Rd., Catlett, VA; (540) 788-4257; seven oakslavenderfarm.com. Get lost in a gentle sea of purple at the Seven Oaks Lavender Farm, where acres upon acres of fragrant lavender soothe the soul. Every spring when the pastel crop is in season, the mother-and-daughter farmers who make pastel magic bloom from the ground let visitors come to pick their own lavender. Edith and Deborah Williamson also host a few open houses and parties during the off-season and sell products such as sachets, lotions, and culinary lavender made from their harvest. Most years, lavender season runs from the end of May through the beginning of July.

day trip 22

west

scenic small towns:
warrenton, paris, the plains, va

As you get deeper into Virginia's horse and hunt country, there seem to be more charming small towns than you can shake a historic marker at. Grand old homes carefully restored to perfection, quaint main streets bordered by brick sidewalks, and friendly residents happy to point you in the right direction define the landscape out here. Each town offers Southern small-town charm with its own spin. A few like Paris, Virginia, with a population of only fifty-one, make "small" sound like something of an overstatement. But what Warrenton, Paris, and The Plains all do equally well and with bravado is provide a glimpse back in time while at the same time offering a peek into the current state of small-town life.

warrenton

Rolling hills and picturesque farmland lead the way to Warrenton, and the big, old historic homes let you know that the center of the historic district is near. Incorporated in 1810, Warrenton is steeped in history, having played a role in the Civil War like most of the neighboring communities here. Today the quaint town that sits within eyeshot of the Blue Ridge Mountains claims about 9,000 residents as well as many more visitors.

getting there

It takes just about an hour to drive to Warrenton. Take the Beltway to I-66 West to US 29 South. Follow VA 643/Meetze Road toward Lee Street/Warrenton.

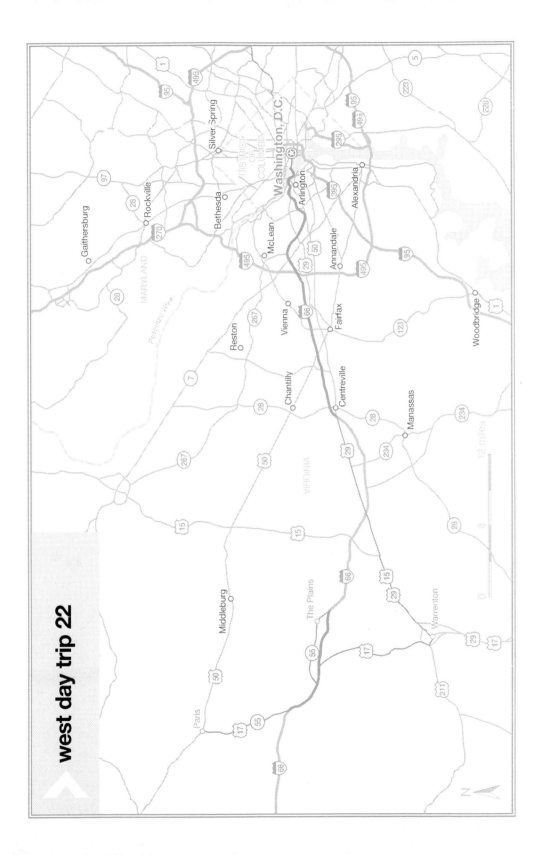

west day trip 22

where to go

Mediterranean Cellars. 8295 Falcon Glen Rd., Warrenton, VA; (540) 428-1984; mediter raneancellars.com. The founder and owner of Mediterranean Cellars first learned his craft and developed a passion for winemaking in his homeland of Greece. He brought his skills and secrets to northern Virginia to start the beautiful Warrenton winery, which produces thirteen varieties that can be sampled on the winery's patio or in the tasting room.

Old Courthouse. Courthouse Square, Warrenton, VA. Built in 1890, the old court-house stands on the highest point in town and replaces three earlier structures that were destroyed. Just to the left of the courthouse you will find a statue of Chief Justice John Mar-shall, a Warrenton native who began his law practice in town. Also outside the courthouse sits the remnants of a slave auction block, used to sell African-American men, women, and children into bondage. It is one of the few remaining examples of a slave block in Virginia.

Old Jail Museum. 10 Ashby St., Warrenton, VA; (540) 347-5525. Built in 1808, the building that now houses the Fauquier Historical Society served as a county jail up until 1966. Out back you can see the exercise yard, which was also the site of prisoner hangings. Located in Courthouse Square, the building also contains a small museum with exhibits about nineteenth-century toys, Fauquier County's Native American community, and the town's role in the Civil War. You can also pick up a brochure for a self-guided walking tour at the Old Jail Museum, which is closed Mon.

Rady Park. 725 Fauquier Rd., Warrenton, VA; (540) 347-6896. A fun place to picnic with some of the gourmet goodies that can be picked up in town. Rady Park has a large picnic shelter, playground, sports fields, and paved trails for biking, walking, and Rollerblading.

Warrenton Caboose. South 4th Street just off Main Street, Warrenton, VA; (540) 347-6896; warrentoncaboose.org. A restored 1969 Norfolk & Western steel cupola red caboose makes its permanent home at the head of a walking and biking trail that once served as the old Warrenton Branch spur line. More than 3,000 volunteer hours have been invested in the restoration of this caboose. The caboose is open mornings on the first Saturday of the month from Apr through Oct.

Warrenton-Fauquier Visitor Center. 33 N. Calhoun St., Warrenton, VA; (540) 341-0988. The obvious place to start an exploration of historic Warrenton and the surrounding area. Pick up information, maps, and brochures here to get started. You can also pick up the route for the self-guided driving/walking tour of eleven local Civil War sites.

Weston Farmstead. 4447 Weston Rd., Casanova, VA; (540) 788-9220; historicweston .org. The nineteenth-century farmstead at Weston gives a glimpse into what agricultural life in the area was once like in this region. Ten buildings remain on the property including the smokehouse, overseer's cabin, blacksmith shop, stable, and two barns. A collection of letters, documents, photographs, and diaries from the family who lived here helps piece together their story. Weston Farmstead is about 5 miles from the historic district. Tours are given by appointment and there is a nominal fee.

where to shop

Carter & Spence. 41 Main St., Warrenton, VA; (540) 347-9189; carterandspence.com. Selling things that sparkle and shine, the downtown jewelry shop sells gold, silver, and precious and semiprecious stones in designer settings. The family-owned business focuses on regionally handmade collections and prides itself on its friendly service.

Christine Fox. 47 S. 3rd St., Warrenton, VA; (540) 347-3868; christinefox.com. This women's clothing boutique in Warrenton's historic district sells ready-to-wear and affordable yet stylish clothing and accessories.

The Galloping Grape. 143 E. Shirley Ave., Warrenton, VA; (540) 428-1002; gallopinggrape .com. The store with the fabulously fun name combines the local passions for wine and riding. One part of the shop sells new and used Western and English saddles along with other riding-related accessories, while the other side sells more than 800 varieties of wine.

Red Truck Rural Bakery. 22 Waterloo St., Warrenton, VA; (540) 347-2224; redtruck bakery.com. A break-your-diet-worthy bakery housed in a former 1920s Esso filling station. The smell of freshly baked bread will lure you in and the taste of the homemade sour cherry jam will keep you coming back for seconds and thirds. Brian Noyes, the bakery's owner and a former art director for several national magazines, purchased a farm after moving to Washington. He planted some fruit trees, tried his hand at making jams, and started selling his culinary creations. The jams caught on and so Noyes turned his attention to baking. The rest, as they say, is history. Noyes named his bakery (and his jam business) after the 1954 Ford farm truck he purchased from fashion designer Tommy Hilfiger.

The Scoti. 35 Main St., Warrenton, VA; (540) 351-0309; thescoti.com. Need a new kilt pin? Then look no further, the Scoti sells everything Irish and Scottish including kilts, knit sweaters, and Nicholas Mosse Pottery. You can even purchase your very own set of bagpipes here. No matter what items catch your fancy you can be sure that everything sold here was chosen because it evokes the rolling green hills and landscape of the home country.

The Town Duck. 100 Main St., Warrenton, VA; (540) 347-7237; townduck.com. Pâtés, chocolates, wines, cheeses, teas, and other gourmet goodies fill this little shop, which also makes custom gift baskets. The staff here prides itself on offering personal service that makes every shopper feel like a welcomed guest. The Town Duck sells many culinary gifts at a variety of price points so you don't have to spend a lot to get something interesting or fun at The Town Duck.

where to eat

Claire's at the Depot. 65 S. 3rd St., Warrenton, VA; (540) 351-1616; clairesrestaurant .com. A popular local restaurant housed in a turn-of-the-twentieth-century train depot that once served Warrenton. Claire's ever-changing menu features eclectic Southern and local flavors with a twist, resulting in dishes like Coca-Cola-braised pork loin and cornmeal-crusted fried oysters. $$.

Hidden Julles Cafe. 70 Main St., Warrenton, VA; (540) 216-3121. A favorite place among locals to pop by for a slice of banana bread, burrito, or some eggs Benedict. The breakfast, lunch, and coffee shop has a small, covered outdoor seating area and is committed to using local and organic ingredients. $.

Iron Bridge Wine Company. 29 Main St., Warrenton, VA; (540) 349-9339; ironbridge wines.com. The atmosphere at this downtown wine bar is casual and friendly. Customers can pair wines with a light meal of tapas, salads, soups, and desserts. You can order from the large cheese selection throughout the day. Special tasting events, coupled with special menus, are held on Mon and Tues night. $$.

where to stay

Black Horse Inn. 8393 Meetze Rd., Warrenton, VA; (540) 349-4020; blackhorseinn.com. The nine regal guest rooms at the recently restored Black Horse Inn are done in a style evocative of the horse and hunt country around it. All the rooms have private baths and many also feature fireplaces, Jacuzzi tubs, and four-poster beds. Boxwood gardens and beautiful landscaping fill the grounds, which include a stable where guests' horses can board overnight. $$$.

paris

If you've been dreaming of strolling along the River Seine but just can't cross the Atlantic anytime soon, you can still always have Paris. Paris, Virginia, that is. Although the Louvre and the Eiffel Tower are nowhere to be found in this tiny village nestled among Virginia's horse and hunt country, it is still a charming destination. Paris has one main street but its scenery has endless appeal.

getting there

Paris is found at the eastern base of Ashby Gap at the intersection of Route 17 and Route 50 and is about an hour from DC.

where to go

Sky Meadows State Park. 11012 Edmonds Ln., Delaplane, VA; (540) 592-3556; dcr .virginia.gov/state_parks/sky.shtml. Not even 2 miles from Paris stands Sky Meadows, a stunning park complete with rolling pastures, woodlands, and access to the Appalachian Trail. From the park you can embark on a three-day hike to Harper's Ferry or a two-day hike to Shenandoah National Park. In addition to hiking, the park also offers places to fish, picnic, ride horses, and camp.

where to shop

American in Paris. 694 Federal St., Paris, VA; (540) 592-9008; american-in-paris-antiques .com. The lone shop in Paris, American in Paris specializes in American country and high-country pieces as well as original folk art. The shop is open weekends, and during the week "by chance."

where to stay & eat

The Ashby Inn and Restaurant. 692 Federal St., Paris, VA; (540) 592-3900; ashbyinn .com. So many city slickers make the hour-plus drive to Paris for a meal at the acclaimed Ashby Inn Restaurant that the inn is often referred to as a restaurant with rooms. And Ashby's jumbo lump crab cakes have a reputation all their own. Menus revolve around seasonal flavors and many of the herbs and summer vegetables come from the garden at Ashby. The inn dates back to the early 1800s and many of its furnishings come from that time period. Many of the guest rooms in the main house have four-poster beds and antique quilts. There are also four rooms in the schoolhouse behind the inn. $$.

the plains

With a population of almost 300, The Plains is six times bigger than Paris but not larger than much else. The picturesque town is centered on Route 55 (John Marshall Highway) and Route 245 (Old Tavern Road) and has an out-of-a-movie-set main street to stroll.

where to go

Afro-American Historical Association of Fauquier County. 4243 Loudoun Ave., The Plains, VA; (540) 253-7488; aahafauquier.org. The Afro-American Historical Association of Fauquier County is dedicated to preserving the history of the African-American community in the region. The organization also serves as a research resource for individuals and groups and has a small museum on site that has limited hours, so call first.

Great Meadow Foundation. 5089 Old Tavern Rd., The Plains, VA; (540) 253-5000; great meadow.org. Great Meadow Foundation, a nonprofit organization, was formed in the early

1980s to prevent this massive space from being developed. And as a result, the public can still enjoy the 250-acre field events center and steeplechase course operated by the foundation. It also acts as the permanent home of the Virginia Gold Cup steeplechase classic.

where to shop

Crest Hill Antiques & Tea Room. 6488 Main St., The Plains, VA; (540) 253-5790; cresthillantiques.com. Traditional tea and just about anything make a delightful combination, and this tea-slash-antiques shop is just shy of brilliant. Shop for hidden treasures and indulge in tea with a fresh scone or muffin at Crest Hill.

Hunt Country Yarns. 6482 Main St., The Plains, VA; (540) 253-9990; skeins.com. A needle and fiber arts supply store housed in a friendly old home with a table up front for knitting and a porch outside for knitting and relaxing. The store also holds workshops and classes, and its employees are a knowledgeable team.

Live an Artful Life. 6474 Main St., The Plains, VA; (540) 253-9797; liveanartfullife.com. Fine arts and American crafts fill the light, bright store. Wearable art, whimsical garden decorations, and artful jewelry are some of the handcrafted items sold here.

Zigzag Crafts Gallery & Shop. 6477 Main St., The Plains, VA; (540) 253-5364; zigzagtheplains.com. Zigzag displays and sells crafts, art, and wearable art from a host of interesting local and national artists. The gallery also hosts art shows and a range of classes, including many for children.

where to eat

Forlano's Market. 6483 Main St., The Plains, VA; (540) 253-5456; forlanos.com. Two accomplished epicureans who also happen to be a husband-and-wife team run Forlano's, a part deli, part butcher, and part bakery shop in The Plains. Meats are locally raised and corn-finished and the poultry is free-range. Hearth-baked breads are used to create the made-to-order sandwiches sold here. The store also holds cooking classes. $$.

Girasole. 4244 Loudoun Ave., The Plains, VA; (540) 253-5501; girasoleva.com. A quaint Italian restaurant that has been getting a lot of good attention in recent years. Short menu that fortunately is not short on flavor. And there always seems to be a long list of specials. $$$.

The Rail Stop. 6478 Main St., The Plains, VA; (540) 253-5644; railstoprestaurant.com. The Rail Stop serves up hearty country meals in a family atmosphere. Try the outdoor seating area on a nice day. $$.

day trip 23

west

Quaint. Picturesque. Charming. It's near impossible to steer away from these words when describing Washington, Virginia. Often referred to as Little Washington, the tiny village in the foothills of the Blue Ridge Mountains counts only about 150 people as residents yet it attracts a steady stream of visitors from places large and small, including many from the District of Columbia. The pull to come to this pretty little dot on the map has much to do with its quaint, picturesque, and charming qualities (yes, those words again). The entire town, which serves as the seat of government for Rappahannock County, is listed on the Virginia Landmarks Register and the National Register of Historic Places. Many of its buildings date back to the late 1700s.

Perhaps the biggest draw in town is the famed 5-star Inn at Little Washington. Considered one of the best and prettiest restaurants in the country, people travel far and wide to experience a meal at Chef Patrick O'Connell's world-renowned restaurant and inn, which happily marries luxury and whimsy. Little Washington also boasts art galleries, B&Bs, shops, a theatre, and wineries, and sits only a few minutes away from Shenandoah National Park.

washington

The historic Town of Washington was founded in 1769 and surveyed by George Washington for whom it is named. From Washington to Washington is a must for any true DC day tripper.

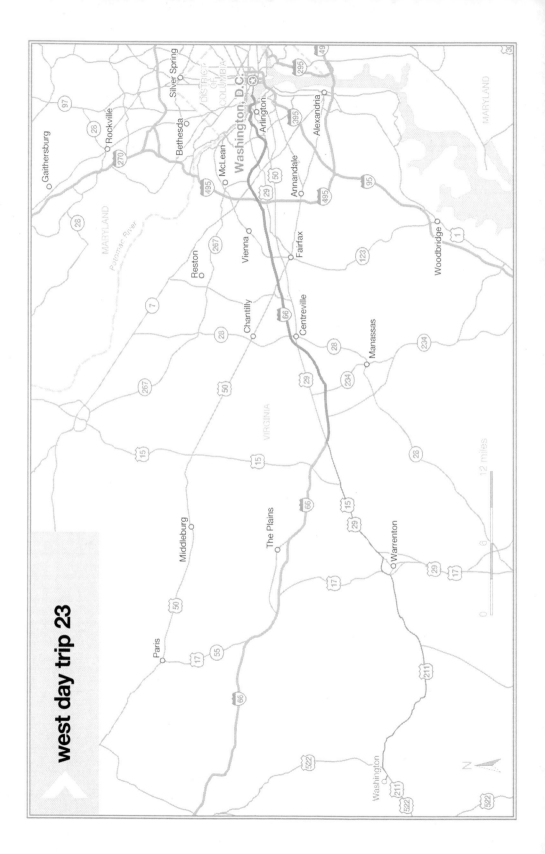

west day trip 23

getting there

Little Washington is only about seventy minutes From "Big" Washington. Take 66 West to exit 43A Gainesville/Warrenton. Then get on 29 South for about 12 miles to Warrenton. At the third stoplight take the ramp to Warrenton/29 Business. Drive for 2 miles and at the fifth stoplight turn right onto 211 West. Then follow 211 West for about 25 miles until you reach Washington, Virginia.

where to go, stay, eat & stop

The Inn at Little Washington wins best in show of these categories but the other suggestions below also should not be missed.

The Inn at Little Washington. Middle and Main Streets, Washington, VA; (540) 675-3800; theinnatlittlewashington.com. Happy people make happy food, Chef Patrick O'Connell likes to say. And O'Connell, the world-renowned chef and founder of The Inn at Little Washington, makes certain that this mantra of sorts touches every ingredient, utensil, and decision made in his Windsor castle–inspired kitchen. Gregorian chants fill the air as chefs dressed in Dalmatian-print pants, an homage to O'Connell's beloved pups, expertly prepare dishes. Within these lovely walls no detail is too small to garner attention and, as a result, an atmosphere of calm perfection permeates the award-winning restaurant and inn. The Inn also has a legendary wine cellar, lovely shops, and even employs a farmer in residence.

The Inn's eighteen bedrooms and suites are a similarly sumptuous hideaway. Joyce Evans, a London stage and set designer, is responsible for the look and feel of the inn and has made doing so her life's work. Breathtaking views, impeccable service, and just the right amount of fancy define the entire property. The Inn at Little Washington is one of those places worth saving and planning for so you can experience it at least once. And, once you have you will see why The Inn at Little Washington finds itself on many a culinary bucket list.

where to go

Little Washington Winery. 72 Christmas Tree Ln., Washington, VA; (540) 987-8330; littlewashingtonwinery.com. At the Little Washington Winery you can settle into an Adirondack chair as you sip a glass of artisan wine and stare out at the Blue Ridge Mountains. As if that weren't enough, the Little Washington Winery also offers fun tasting experiences during its daily Dirt Road Wine Tour or in its Wine Loves Chocolate Tasting Room. Wine Immersion Bootcamp happens year round and is a fan favorite.

Rappahannock County Visitor Center. 3 Library Rd., Washington, VA; (540) 675-3153. The Visitor Center is a spot to start your Washington visit. Visitors have access to the brochure-filled kiosk located right outside the center throughout the year. Fri through Sun (although more limited during the winter) a staff person can be found inside the center to

sky and wine

File the Skyline Wine, Dine & Recline Trail map under good ideas. The map combines the location of hikes, waterfalls, scenic overlooks, picnic areas, restaurants, and lodging within Shenandoah National Park with the location of the vineyards, restaurants, and inns that dot the foothills below. Download a copy of the must-have map at skylinewinetrail.com.

help answer questions provide information on the Town of Washington and Rappahannock County.

The Theatre at Washington, Virginia. 291 Gay St., Washington, VA; (540) 675-1253; theatre-washington-va.com. The Theatre hosts a variety of professional musical and dramatic performances as well as some films and community events. Shows tend to be only on weekends.

where to shop

Eastwoods Nurseries. 634 Long Mountain Road, Washington, VA; (540) 675-1234; japanesemaples.com. Eastwoods is a small tree nursery specializing in Japanese maples (more than 300 different varieties), Ginkgos (about thirty different cultivars) and selected conifers (about eighty different selections). Call ahead to check on hours and or to schedule a time to stop in and talk to the knowledgeable staff.

Ginger Hill Antiques. 12625 Lee Hwy., Washington, VA 22747; (540) 987-8440; ginger hillantiques.com. You never know what treasure you might find waiting for you at Ginger Hill Antiques. And that is the fun it. Explore the collections of the multiple antiques dealers who sell here.

where to eat

Country Cafe. 389 Main St., Washington; (540) 675-1066. Simple country cooking is the order of the day here. Country Cafe cooks up lunch and dinner, is within walking distance of town, and doesn't mess with reservations. $.

Griffin Tavern & Restaurant. 659 Zachary Taylor Hwy., Flint Hill, VA; (540) 675-3227; griffintavern.com. Home-style cooked meals and pub favorites make up the menu here—think fish-and-chips, wings, burgers, and shepherd's pie. A kids' menu also is available. For those not ordering from the children's menu, The Tavern also offers a full bar. $$.

where to stay

Gay Street Inn. 160 Gay St., Washington, VA; (540) 316-9220; gaystreetinn.com. Gay Street Inn makes its home in a 1850s farmhouse in historic Washington complete with a quiet garden, library, and home-cooked breakfasts. The cozy inn is within walking distance of the The Inn at Little Washington, and is also close to the other area highlights. There is one pet-friendly room here for those traveling with Rover in tow. $$.

Middleton Inn Bed & Breakfast. 176 Main St., Washington, VA; (540) 675-2020; middletoninn.com. A stay at the Middleton Inn Bed & Breakfast may be the closest you can get to a stay on English countryside without actually crossing the pond. Dating back to 1840, the country estate sits on a knoll facing the Blue Ridge Mountains. A favorite pastime for those who stay here is sipping wine while gazing out at the mountain splendor. Each of the 7 rooms here has a working fireplace and marble bath. Guests wake up to an elegant gourmet breakfast served each morning in the dining room. $$$.

Parma in Little Washington. 105 Christmas Tree Ln.; Washington, VA; (540) 987-8588; parmainlittlewashington.com. Parma is many things at once: An elegant inn with beautiful views, a relaxation-steeped ayurveda spa, and a holistic health center. And guests may come for one, some, or all of the above. $$.

northwest

day trip 24

northwest

pick your own pie filling:
germantown, poolesville, md

Some of my favorite childhood memories revolve around my family's yearly apple-picking trip in upstate New York. Something magical seemed to happen when we hopped on the tractor that drove us out to the tall trees. Climbing to a high branch to find apples to toss into the bushels below felt like pure bliss. When I moved to Washington I was thrilled to learn that I could still go apple picking in the fall, even if the more southern locale means leaving coats at home and that most of the leaves on the ride up will still be green. The Maryland trees look smaller than the ones I remember through the lens of childhood but I suppose that is always the case. What hasn't changed is the fun of twisting ripe apples off the branches and biting into the first Red Delicious of the season while standing among the rows of fruit trees. And I still think it's pretty funny to bite an apple while it's still on the tree, but now I know better than to leave it hanging there for someone else to discover.

Today with the popularity of pick-your-own produce farms, apples are just one fruit on a long list of crops that can be picked locally. Within an hour of the city you can collect everything from berries to snap peas to pumpkins. Many farms even let you select and cut down your own Christmas tree.

germantown

The first time I headed up to Butler's Orchard more than twenty years ago, I drove past farmland and empty fields pretty much the entire way between the highway exit and the

176

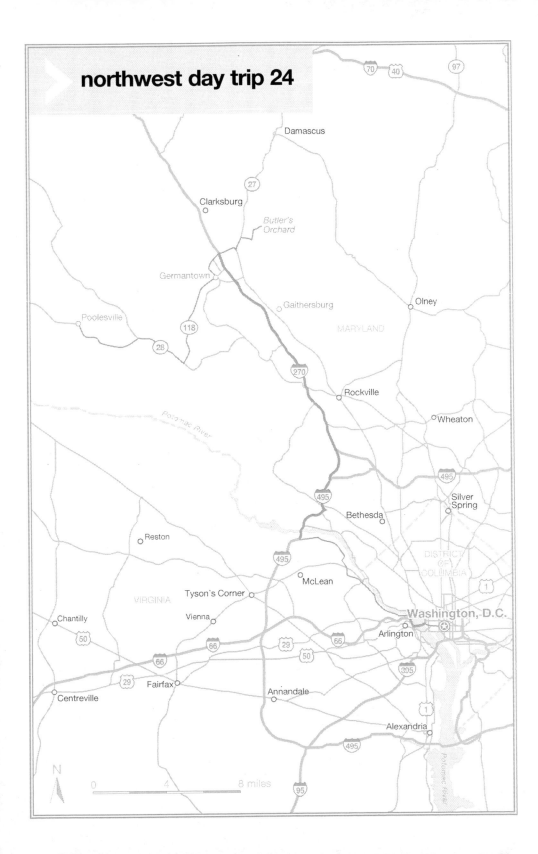

northwest day trip 24

orchard. I remember one gas station and maybe a church along the way but other than that it pretty much seemed like the middle of nowhere to a city kid like me. I made a point of coming back to the pick-your-own farm every year or two to collect apples or berries out in the country. With each trip I spied more and more box stores, garden apartments, and strip malls creeping up along the landscape. On my last trip almost the entire route between the highway and the Germantown orchard had been developed. But even with a Target and a Best Buy along the way, Butler's still feels like a little farmland oasis. Once you turn onto the narrow road leading to the farm, the tree canopy and fields make all the city-slicker stuff disappear. Even though the farm can be crowded at the peak of season, it still beats a crowded Metro platform during Monday morning rush hour.

getting there

Germantown is an easy ride from DC that takes about 40 minutes unless you hit rush hour traffic, which will slow you down significantly. Go north on the Beltway to I-270 North toward Frederick. Get off at exit 16, Father Hurley Boulevard, and bear right onto Route 27. Take Route 27 to Brink Road, make a left onto Wildcat Road and follow until you reach Davis Mill Road. Butler's Orchard is on the left.

where to go

Butler's Orchard. 22200 Davis Mill Rd., Germantown, MD; (301) 972-3299; butlers orchard.com. When George and Shirley Butler purchased a 37-acre peach farm in 1950, a log house was the only structure on the property. The couple literally grew the farm and today Butler's Orchard spans 300 acres and harvests more than twenty-five different crops, including the popular pick-your-own fruit and vegetable fields.

The Butlers first opened their farm to the public some fifty years ago with a crop of pick-your-own strawberries. At the time, the concept was brand new but the Butlers watched it catch on quickly and expanded their PYO offerings. Today the farm plans an almost year-round PYO calendar that starts in May with strawberries and ends in December with cut-your-own Christmas trees. In between everything from snap peas to tart cherries to pumpkins can be picked at the massive Germantown farm.

I think over the years I have picked just about everything Butler's will let me. While everything they grow is fresh and delicious, the enormous thornless blackberries are my favorite. (The Butlers first planted the crop in the 1970s, for which I am seasonally grateful.) I must admit I'm not sure how many blackberries my family has smuggled out in their stomachs over the years but I have a feeling the number is significant. Really, you have never seen such a big berry or tasted such a sweet one. The farm also runs evening hayrides from May to December and holds a popular pumpkin festival in the fall.

Red Wiggler Community Farm. 23400 Ridge Rd., Germantown, MD; (301) 916-2216; redwiggler.org. The Red Wiggler farm is a shining star of the community-supported

agriculture movement. Developmentally disabled adults tend to the farm, growing vegetables, herbs, and flowers for the community and for local food banks. Red Wiggler is
also home to a solar farmhouse built by University of Maryland students in 2005 for the US
Department of Energy Solar Decathlon, held on the National Mall every year. The twenty-
first-century structure uses green energy to generate power for the house for everything
from heating and cooling to lighting and cooking. The house was donated to the farm by the
university and serves as a staff residence. Tours of the farm and the solar farmhouse can be
arranged in advance—please don't just show up. The farm also has programs throughout
the year like yoga and a farm-to-table dinner and ongoing volunteer opportunities that are
listed on its website. Also on the website is information on how and when to apply for a
Red Wiggler CSA share.

where to shop

Butler's Orchard Farm Market. 22200 Davis Mill Rd., Germantown, MD; (301) 972-3299;
butlersorchard.com. Stop at the market on your way out of the farm to weigh and measure
your haul but also take some time to browse and shop. An array of farm-fresh produce can
be purchased here, including corn, melon, squash, kale, and tomatoes. Jams, jellies, local
honey, relishes, dressings, and sauces are also sold. Tempting homemade fudge, pies, and
caramels are displayed dangerously close to the check-out stands. The market also sells
some country gift items and carries ingenious cherry pitters made from jelly jars.

Phillips Farm Produce. 13710 Schaeffer Rd., Germantown, MD; (301) 540-2364; phillips
farmproduce.com. A family with a Maryland farming history that stretches back more than
350 years runs the Phillips Farm. The most recent Phillips Farm has been at its current
Germantown location since 1977 and not long ago the family opened the Red Barn, a new
sales facility where visitors can purchase fresh produce, flowers, and such down-home
goodies as preserves. A few rocking chairs sit on the front porch, calling to shoppers to sit
and enjoy a crisp Gala apple or the view of Sugarloaf Mountain in the distance. The family has also put together a display of vintage farm machines inside the barn that provide a
glimpse into the history of local agriculture. During the fall you can take a hayride out to the
pumpkin patch and pick your own jack-o'-lantern. In the fields you will also find haystacks
for jumping and animals for petting.

Rock Hill Orchard. 28600 Ridge Rd., Mt. Airy, MD; (301) 831-7427; rockhillorchard.com.
The farm stand at Rock Hill Orchard sells seasonal fruits and vegetables grown on its farm
along with jams, jellies, fresh breads, wildflowers, pickles, local honey, and popcorn. The
same family has been tending to Rock Hill since 1969. Rock Hill also keeps some pick-your-
own fields where visitors can harvest strawberries, tart cherries, kale, snap peas, blackberries, okra, eggplant, red raspberries, apples, and pumpkins. The Woodbourne Creamery at
Rock Hill Orchard became the first Grade A dairy processing facility in Montgomery County.
Bottles of the farm's Creamline Golden Guernsey milk are for sale in the market.

where to eat

Lancaster County Dutch Market. 12613 Wisteria Dr., Germantown, MD; (301) 515-1019; lcdutchmarket.com. The Lancaster County Dutch Market brings a little bit of Amish Country to Germantown three days a week. About a dozen vendors share the indoor market space and sell everything from fresh meat to cheese to Amish soft pretzels. People line up for the fried chicken and ribs. The ice cream also tends to be a big hit. The market holds limited hours and is only open Thurs, Fri, and Sat, so check the website (yes, really, the Amish market has a website) before you head over. The vendors have a reputation for polite, friendly service and some only accept cash, so stop at the ATM before you arrive. $$.

poolesville

Consider yourself warned. Pick-your-own farms have a tendency to become addictive. It must be something they put in those organic tomatoes. If you find yourself craving more PYO experiences, try some comparison farming over in Poolesville at Homestead Farms, another local PYO favorite. It's practically a rite of passage for kids in the region to take a fall field trip to Homestead to pick apples and pull up grass from the ground to feed to Elmo the calf. The trip between DC and Homestead is beautiful, particularly when the leaves are changing colors.

getting there

It takes about a half hour to drive between Germantown and Poolesville, and when you map out the two towns they make a triangle with DC. From Germantown take MD 118 South to MD 28 to MD 107. If you are coming from DC, you pretty much are heading up River Road most of the time.

where to go

FarmAtHome Produce. 15350 Partnership Rd., Poolesville, MD; (240) 372-0674; farmathome.com. It's a very exciting day in my house when blueberries come back in season. And if you have as much trouble keeping the supermarket pints of the blues around for more than ten minutes, then you might find yourself wanting to spend a significant amount of time at FarmAtHome. The pick-your-own Poolesville farm only grows blueberries and during June and July visitors can come and pick to their hearts' content. Blueberries are not native to DC, so they are not always found at PYO farms in the region, which is precisely the reason FarmAtHome was started. There is a 1-pound minimum per adult, which will probably last you at least half the drive home.

peachy keen

More than fifty varieties of peaches grow at Kingsbury's Orchard and they can be yours for the picking. Owned by the same family for more than a hundred years, the orchard grows several kinds of fruits but specializes in white peaches. Among the juicy varieties that can be picked here are Peach Tree Road, White Lady, Saturn, Summer Pearl, Lady Nancy, and Scarlet Snow. Kingsbury's Orchard, 19415 Peach Tree Rd., Dickerson, MD; (301) 972-8755; kingsburysorchard.com.

Homestead Farm. 15604 Sugarland Rd., Poolesville, MD; (301) 977-3761; homestead-farm.net. Homestead is a pretty pick-your-own farm that glows under a blue sky on nice days. The farm offers several PYO crops, including strawberries, peaches, and nectarines, but it's the apples that seem to be the biggest draw here. Homestead grows row upon row upon row of apple trees. At last count varieties at the farm included Jonathan, Empire, Golden Delicious, Red Delicious, Jonagold, Stayman Winesap, Braeburn, Rome Beauty, Cameo, Pink Lady, and Sun Fuji. Tractor-pulled wagons take visitors out to the orchard and the farm even provides a wheelbarrow for your haul—or for hauling your kids when they are too tired or too full to walk. Although Homestead is certainly not just for families, it does offer a lot in the way of kid-friendly activities, such as said wheelbarrows. Hay-bale jumping takes place all around the farm and a grouping of friendly animals lives in and near the barn. Many of the chicks found here came from school hatching projects. Goats, ducks, sheep, and pigs can also be visited at Homestead.

Kunzang Palyul Choling (KPC) Maryland Temple. 18400 River Rd., Poolesville, MD; (301) 710-6259; tara.org. Poolesville is also home to a Buddhist temple that welcomes visitors. People of all faiths can take advantage of the 65-acre Peace Park across from the temple. A 35-foot-tall golden Migyur Dorje Stupa statue graces the park, which also has hiking trails and a meditation garden. The facility also houses the Garuda Aviary, which shelters and rehabilitates abused and neglected parrots. Visitors can watch the brightly colored birds fly around the aviary and interact with their handlers. Inside the temple there are many meditation areas and prayer rooms, including one that since 1985 has housed an ongoing 24-hour prayer vigil for world peace.

McKee-Beshers Wildlife Management Area. On River Road about 2 miles west from the Seneca Road intersection, Poolesville, MD; (410) 356-9272; dnr.state.md.us/wildlife/publiclands/central/mckeebeshers.asp. During the summer a field of happiness blooms at the McKee-Beshers Wildlife Management Area. Every year the state plants hundreds of sunflowers. Photographers, painters, birdwatchers, and anyone who needs a dose of yellow

thanksgiving with the turkeys

Every November the Poplar Spring Animal Sanctuary hosts a vegan Thanksgiving feast. The "Thanksgiving WITH the Turkeys" communal dinner is an opportunity for a meat-free celebration during a meat-heavy time of the year. It also gives participants a chance to hang out with the many turkeys, chickens, pigs, sheep, goats, cows, pigs, rabbits, and mules that live on the 400-acre sanctuary. All of the animals here were either abused, abandoned, or neglected before being rescued by the sanctuary's owners. Each participant is asked to bring a vegan (meat-free, dairy-free, and egg-free) dish that can serve eight people. The farm also suggests a small optional donation. Poplar Spring Animal Sanctuary, 15200 Mt. Nebo Rd., Poolesville, MD; (301) 428-8128; animalsanctuary.org.

love the spot but the reason the flowers are planted can be a buzzkill for some. Maryland plants the tall yellow blooms to attract doves for the fall hunting season.

where to shop

Homestead Farm Stand. 15604 Sugarland Rd., Poolesville, MD; (301) 977-3761; homestead-farm.net. Located near the entrance to Homestead, the farm's store sells everything you need to cook, bake, pickle, and stew your way to happiness once you get home. Fresh fruits and vegetables along with the requisite locally made jams, jellies, and preserves also are for sale. The store often carries fresh herbs.

Lewis Orchard Fresh Farm Produce. 18901 Peach Tree Rd., Dickerson, MD; (301) 349-4101; lewisorchardfarmmarket.com. The Lewis family has been farming in the county for more than a hundred years. Located at the intersection of Darnestown and Peach Tree Roads, the family's shop sells a rainbow of seasonal fruits and vegetables along with milk, cheeses, jellies, jams, flowers, dressings, and other country products. The farm also has PYO apples and cut-your-own zinnias. The store is open from mid-June to Thanksgiving.

The Mani Jewel. 18400 River Rd., Poolesville, MD; (301) 710-6259; tara.org. The Mani Jewel is part of the Kunzang Palyul Choling Buddhist temple and sells Buddhism and Buddhist-related books and prayer items. Proceeds from the shop go to support the temple. An ongoing twenty-four-hour prayer vigil for world peace has been taking place at the temple since 1985. The 65-acre Peace Park across from the temple is open for people of all faiths to use during daylight hours. A 35-foot-tall golden Migyur Dorje Stupa statue graces the park, which also has hiking trails and a meditation garden.

Seneca Store. 16315 Old River Rd., Poolesville, MD; (301) 948-5372. Seneca Store is a step back in time. The small white shop with the green shutters and awning sells a little bit of everything, including homemade pulled pork sandwiches, birdseed, and horse treats. Once known as Poole's General Store, the shop is still run by the Poole family and is Montgomery County's oldest general store in continuous operation. Right across the street is a public entrance to the C&O Canal and Towpath, a 187-mile towpath that starts in Georgetown.

where to eat

Bassett's Fine Food & Spirits. 19950 Fisher Ave., Poolesville, MD; (301) 972-7443; bassettsrestaurant.net. Bassett's serves lunch, dinner, and a popular Sunday brunch. The menu includes a lot of seafood and country style dishes. A heated outdoor seating area stays open three seasons out of the year. $$.

day trip 25

northwest

eat, stroll, shop:
leesburg, va

leesburg

A great treasure sits beyond the Dulles Toll Road and its name is Leesburg. Rich with elegantly preserved buildings, boutiques, and an assortment of restaurants, the Leesburg Historic District feels like a true getaway. Founded in 1758, the town itself is steeped in history. The Declaration of Independence was read on the steps of the first courthouse here and the city is part of the Civil War Trail. Stroll along the old redbrick sidewalks and admire the historic storefronts now housing antiques, craft, and clothing shops. Along the way there are plenty of inviting cafes, restaurants, and bakeries, and even a spa or two.

After giving your credit cards a work out enjoy some nature free of charge at the magnificent Morven Park, which is only about a five-minute drive from downtown. The rolling hills and manicured gardens will tickle your senses and add another dimension to a delightful day downtown.

getting there

Getting to and from Leesburg takes less than an hour (unless you're out during rush hour). Take the Dulles Toll Road until it becomes the Dulles Greenway. Take exit 1A to merge onto Leesburg Bypass/US 15 South/VA 7 toward Leesburg/Warrenton. Follow the signs for the historic district—it's well marked. Park in one of the public parking structures rather than

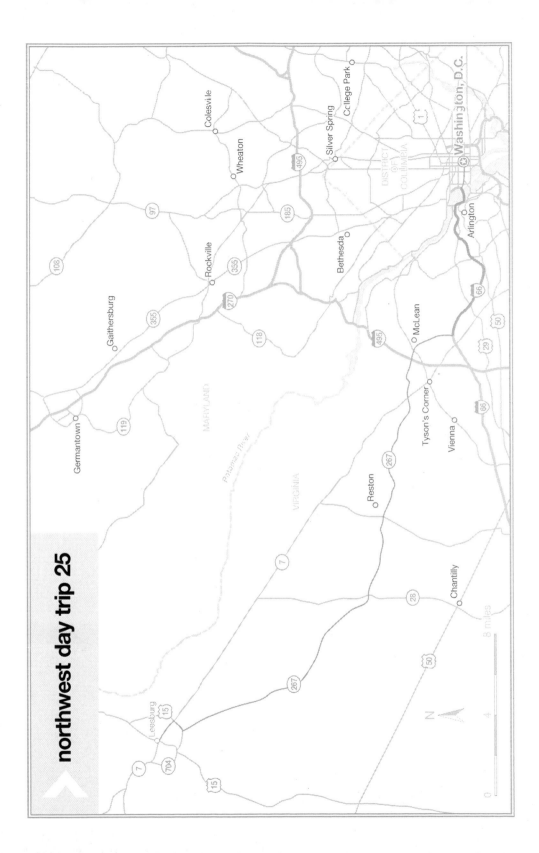

northwest day trip 25

take a chance with the meters on the street (trust me—I have the tickets to show for it). Bikers can pedal to town on the W&OD Trail.

where to go

George C. Marshall International Center at Dodona Manor. 217 Edwards Ferry Rd., Leesburg, VA; (703) 777-1880; georgecmarshall.org. General George and Katherine Marshall lived in the yellow manor from 1941 to 1959. The manor's interior and exterior have been preserved to reflect the way it looked when they were here, including its *Mad Men*–style kitchen. The general served in many executive branch posts including secretary of state and is best known as the architect of the Marshall Plan. Tours are given on the hour from 10 a.m. to 5 p.m. Sat and 1 to 5 p.m. Sun. There are also some afternoon tours during the summer. Admission fee.

Loudoun County Museum. 16 Loudoun St., Leesburg, VA; (703) 777-7427; loudoun museum.org. Housed in two nineteenth-century buildings, one of which is a log cabin, the museum traces the rich 250-year history of the county and the town. Hourlong walking tours are given Mon through Fri by advance reservation. The museum is open Wed through Sat and Mon from 10 a.m. to 5 p.m. and Sun from 1 to 5 p.m.

Morven Park. 17263 Planter Ln., Leesburg, VA; (703) 777-2414; morvenpark.org. Morven Park is many things at once—historic estate, equestrian center, garden collection, Civil War encampment site, museum, and expansive park. Set on more than 1,000 acres, it feels like a true oasis of quiet and beauty. The Marguerite G. Davis Boxwood Garden is particularly lovely. Visitors are welcome on foot anytime the gate is open but only in the areas that are open to the public—several sections are clearly marked as private. Here are some highlights:

> **Mansion.** The white-columned mansion reopened in 2009 after an extensive preservation effort. Group tours are given. Call (703) 777-2414 to schedule. Many famous individuals have been lucky enough to call the mansion home over the years, including B&O Railroad president Thomas Swann Jr. and famed Virginia governor Westmoreland Davis.

> **Winmill Carriage Collection.** More than one hundred horse-drawn vehicles from the nineteenth and early twentieth centuries stand on display here and can be seen from May through Nov during regular tour hours. Counted among the collection is the carriage owned by Tom Thumb of the Barnum & Bailey Circus.

> **International Equestrian Center.** Site of local, national, and world-class equestrian events with both indoor and outdoor arenas. Check the website for a current calendar of events.

Rouge Spa & Store. 17 S. King St., Leesburg, VA; (703) 779-3700; rougespa.com. Melt away the stress with a reflexology massage, moisture-drench facial, or a hot salt wrap at Rouge in the historic downtown area. Lotions and potions are for sale in the shop.

Thomas Balch Library. 208 W. Market St., Leesburg, VA; (703) 737-7195; leesburgva .gov. The Thomas Balch Library archives and preserves printed, written, and photographic documents about the history of Leesburg, Loudoun County, and Virginia. Owned by the Town of Leesburg, the Thomas Balch collections specialize in genealogy, the Civil War, and military history. The once-segregated library now also serves as a designated Underground Railroad research site.

where to shop

The first Friday of every month except January, many of the shops and galleries stay open later and entice shoppers with special sales, refreshments, and live music.

The Cottage: Well Loved Furnishings. 105 S. King St., Leesburg, VA; (703) 443-0058; cottageatleesburg.com. From the minute I walked through the robin's-egg-blue doors of this shop housed in an old Victorian, I wanted to move in. The store is filled with vintage furniture and whimsical decorative objects the owners have found and spruced up with style. Items are artfully displayed in the home's twelve rooms. Old wooden ladders painted in pretty colors (that are for sale) often dot the front porch.

Creme de la Creme. 101 S. King St., Leesburg, VA; (703) 737-7702; shopcremedela creme.com. Crème de la Crème sells a collection of exquisite and pricey French country table linens and handmade pottery and glassware.

Leesburg Antique Emporium. 32 S. King St., Leesburg, VA; (703) 777-3553; leesburg antiqueemporium.net. The corner store houses two floors of antiques from more than fifty independent dealers, with items that range from an old wooden bank teller window to a "Viva Kennedy" campaign button to an Elvis Presley commemorative pocket knife.

Leesburg Vintner. 29 S. King St., Leesburg, VA; (703) 777-3322; leesburg-vintner.com. Wines from around the world and gourmet cheeses are for sale at this shop, which has won many small-business and wine-retailer awards. The owner also stocks a selection of local wines.

Madisonbelle. 5 Loudoun St. SE, Leesburg, VA; (703) 443-1790; madisonbelle.com. Adorable outfits abound at Madisonbelle, which carries designer jeans, tops, and jewelry.

The Old Lucketts Store. 2350 Lucketts Rd., Leesburg, VA; luckettstore.com. The best-friend team that owns Lucketts likes to fill their store with things for the home that mix old and new and match their own vintage style. The shop itself is testimony to that. The store is housed in a restored century-old farmhouse and general store.

where to eat

Eiffel Tower Cafe. 107 Loudoun St. SW, Leesburg, VA; (703) 777-5142; eiffeltowercafe
.com. The menu changes every season at this romantic French restaurant. On warm days, opt to dine on the outside patio or on the deck upstairs. Eiffel Tower Cafe is open for lunch and dinner Tues through Sat and is closed Mon. Reservations are also taken for an a la carte Sunday brunch. $$$.

Lightfoot Restaurant. 11 N. King St., Leesburg, VA; (703) 771-2233; lightfootrestaurant
.com. You might have to remind yourself to look down at the menu your first time here because it's so very tempting to keep gazing upward at the magnificent space, which began life in 1888 as the grand People's National Bank. Details from the Romanesque Revival style have been preserved and the old bank vault has been given new life as a wine cellar. Lightfoot cooks up American fare and is not as formal as its surroundings. $$$.

Shoe's Cup & Cork Club. 17 N. King St., Leesburg, VA; (571) 291-9535; shoescupand
corkclub.com. From the moment you spy the chandelier made of vintage lace-up shoes and the floor-to-ceiling chalkboard (with a ladder so you can scribble on the tippy top) you know you are not in Starbucks anymore. And isn't that nice sometimes? Shoe's Cup & Cork brews fair-trade coffee and espresso beans and serves bagels, salads, and sandwiches. The shop has free Wi-Fi and the requisite cool coffee shop mix-and-match furniture, games, and secret garden out back. $.

Tuscarora Mill. 203 Harrison St., Leesburg, VA; (703) 771-9300; tuskies.com. A restaurant, cafe, bar, and bakery, Tuscarora Mill is a major supporter of the buy local movement. The menu includes the products of several dozen local growers, cheese makers, wineries, farmers. and livestock producers. $$.

where to stay

Idyll Time Farm, Cottage & Stabling. 43470 Evans Pond Rd., Leesburg, VA; (703) 443-2992; bbonline.com/va/idylltime. The log cottage that sits on 50 acres of farmland at Idyll Time sleeps five and can be reserved for a night, a week, or a longer extended stay. Handmade quilts adorn the beds and the pattern the stacked log walls create adds to the cabin's warmth and charm. The modern kitchen comes stocked with breakfast staples. $$$.

Lansdowne Resort. 44050 Woodridge Pkwy., Lansdowne, VA; (703) 729-8400; lansdowneresort.com. The Lansdowne hotel and spa recently underwent a $50 million renovation that touched all the guest rooms, common areas, and outdoor spaces. A new aquatic complex includes waterfalls, a waterslide, and several different pools. The resort also has a golf course and several restaurants. $$$.

day trip 26

northwest

walk this way:
waterford, va

waterford

On my first visit to Waterford, two men chatting in front of a historic building noticed my lost look and asked if they could help. Unsure of exactly where to start my exploration of the garden-filled historic town, I asked for the museum.

They smiled. "The whole town is a museum."

The entire picturesque Village of Waterford is a designated National Historic Landmark District and just about every house sports a historic marker. The two did point me toward the Corner Store, which now houses the Waterford Foundation, the town's preservation society. I picked up a few booklets and some walking-tour brochures and began falling in love with this charming little village that is something of a cross between the English countryside and Martha's Vineyard. Many of the homes here are bank houses, which means they are built into the side of the hills, making for some very pretty structures and gardens.

Waterford began as a Quaker settlement in 1733. During the Civil War the town experienced backlash from both North and South. As pacifists who did not believe in slavery, the Quaker residents were harassed by Confederate troops, often having their farms burned. Union soldiers viewed the spot as Confederate territory. The town never bounced back after the war and most of the structures were left in disrepair. An unintentional by-product of the neglect meant the homes did not suffer the modern fate of teardowns and contemporary

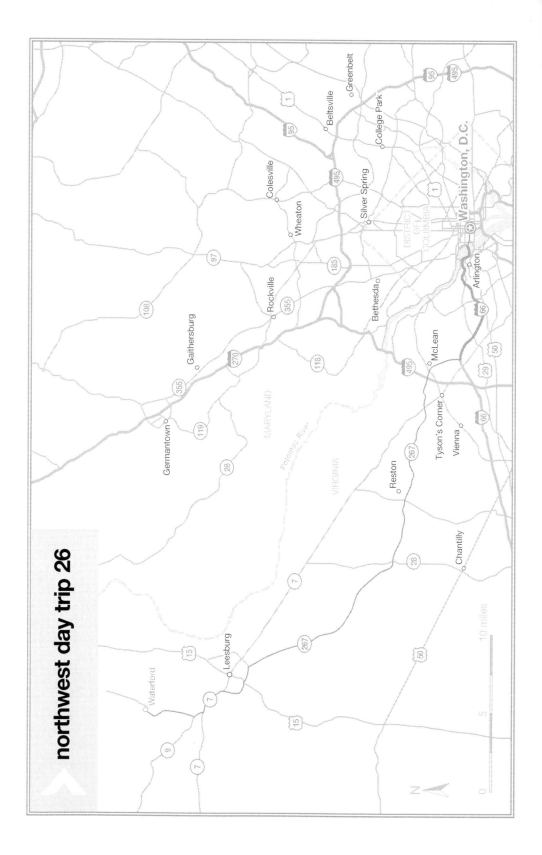

northwest day trip 26

additions. The preservation movement of recent years has helped Waterford regain the look and feel of days past.

While it's ever so tempting to explore the pathways and gardens beyond the main streets, please remember the homes and gardens are private.

Each fall the entire village acts as the backdrop for the impressive Waterford Fair, three days of living history exhibits, food, handicrafts, and house tours. It's worth marking your calendars far in advance to make sure you don't double book that weekend.

getting there

Waterford is about a ten-minute drive from Leesburg and about an hour from DC. Take the Dulles Toll Road to where it becomes the Dulles Greenway. Follow the Greenway to its end to exit 1A and get on 7 West for about 6 miles, exiting at Route 9. Make a right onto Clarkes Gap Road (Route 662). The Village of Waterford starts right after the yellow turn markers.

where to go

Country Store. 40187 Main St., Waterford, VA; (540) 882-3018; waterfordfoundation.org. Once the place for villagers to stock up on supplies, the store now serves as the offices for the Waterford Foundation and is the best spot to start a self-guided walking tour of the town. Volunteers staff the office, happily answer questions about Waterford, and keep help-ful and free information on hand for visitors. The information-filled "Walk With Us Through Waterford, Virginia" booklet will guide you up and down the historic streets. If you are walk-ing with the under-twelve set, ask for the foundation's nicely done children's activity work-book. You can also purchase books, posters, and other items about Waterford as well as tickets to the fair and other events. (The only public bathroom in town is here, too.) The store also sells a variety of gifts that celebrate Waterford, like local honey, books, note cards, wrapping paper, ornaments, and the like. One-of-a-kind and few-of-a-kind works from the juried artisans who exhibit at the Waterford Fair may also be purchased here. Even if you are not buying, the staff at the store encourages visitors to pop by for the "complimentary coffee, tea, cookies and village banter." There are chairs to sit in. The store's winter hours are Sat from 10 a.m. to 2 p.m., and early afternoons on Sun.

The foundation also publishes information about the African-American experience in Waterford. Because of its many Quaker residents who were abolitionists, some theorize that the village was an active spot on the Underground Railroad. Still, life for African Americans in Waterford was far from easy. Slave auctions were held on its main street and segregation existed well into the twentieth century. Other sites of particular African-American signifi-cance include:

John Wesley Methodist Church. 40125 Bond St., Waterford, VA. The black community literally built this church by hand, doing much of the construction at night by lantern light after the workday was done. The congregation moved to this Gothic Revival structure in 1891 and worshiped there until the 1960s, when most of the community moved away.

Phillips Farm Interpretive Trail. The trailhead is at the Old Mill and heads south along the east bank of the Catoctin River. Several years ago the Waterford Foundation bought the town's 144-acre Phillips Farm with the intention of preserving it and preventing development on the land. Since the purchase, the foundation, along with Loudoun Wildlife Conservancy and many volunteers, has helped restore the land by clearing away invasive plants and by putting new trees and plant life in the ground. In 2009 a trail across the southern part of the farm opened. The public walk lets visitors experience the beauty of the farm while at the same time getting a sense of its cultural, national, and historical significance. A brochure for a self-guided trail walk can be picked up behind the Old Mill where the path begins. In keeping with Waterford's strong sense of village pride, all the markers and signs on the trail were designed, constructed, and installed by a Waterford architect and his son.

Second Street School. 15611 2nd St., Waterford, VA; (540) 882-3018. A one-room schoolhouse that served the village's black community from the late 1800s until the 1950s. Black children were not allowed to go to school with white children at the town's larger, better equipped school. Today the Waterford Foundation runs living-history programs for elementary school groups, giving students a sense of what it was like to go to the Second Street School in the 1880s.

Waterford Concert Series. Various locations; waterfordfoundation.org. The Waterford Foundation sponsors a monthly classical music series featuring area musicians. Individual tickets are $25 and a five-concert subscription costs $100.

Waterford Market. 15487 2nd St., Waterford, VA; (540) 882-3631; waterfordconnection .com/waterford-market. Linda Landret can often be found sitting behind her spinning wheel at the Waterford Market. The wool comes from the sheep she raises right outside the market. Inside, Landret sells her handspun wool, some local crafts, organic eggs, local honey, and naturally raised lamb from her sustainable Loudoun County farm. You can also buy soft drinks, candy, and snacks. The market is open from 10 a.m. to 7 p.m. weekdays and from 10 a.m. to 5 p.m. on Sat. If Landret is not in the store during those hours she likely is tending to her sheep and will be right back.

The Waterford Old School. Fairfax Street, VA; waterfordfoundation.org. The Waterford Old School served as the town's white school up until 1957, which was the same year the Second Street School for black children closed its doors. In 2007 a three-alarm fire destroyed the Old School's auditorium, but firefighters were able to save the classroom portion of the historic property. The town celebrated the opening of a rebuilt auditorium in April 2012. A glass atrium now links the new auditorium to the impeccably restored classroom. Waterford's popular concert series takes place in the lovely new side of the building as does a host of programming and events throughout the year.

a glimpse inside

It's hard to resist the urge to peek into the windows of Waterford's historic homes, but once a year visitors not only get to look inside, they get invited inside. Every fall the town hosts a three-day festival and each year a different group of residents opens their doors to the public during the Waterford Homes Tour & Crafts Exhibit, known around these parts simply as the Waterford Fair. The docent-led tours let non-Waterford folks see what lies beyond those pretty façades. A juried craft show featuring traditional such handcrafts as broom making, quilting, and glass blowing also takes place during the fair. Artists, often dressed in period costumes, demonstrate how to do everything from cutting stained glass to molding beeswax to felting a hat. Special children's activities let kids (and sometimes kids of all ages) try their hand at things like tooling a piece of leather, piercing tinware, or stirring apple butter. Like the wares it showcases, the fair itself is steeped in history, with the first one dating back to 1943.

Since all that pewter casting and woodcarving can make a person hungry, there is plenty of food for sale around the town. Pulled barbecue pork sandwiches, homemade doughnuts, and kettle corn are just a few of the many food choices. Sip sweet tea or nibble on a funnel cake while watching a Civil War demonstration, listening to musicians play handmade dulcimers, or humming along with a gospel choir. The Waterford remains one of my favorite fairs and craft shows and is an event I look forward to each year.

Weaver's Cottage. 40188 Water St., Waterford, VA; (540) 882-3018. A two-story log home from the 1700s that was purchased in the 1850s by William Robinson, a free black man. The house remained in Robinson's family for nearly a century. The house is not open to the public.

worth more time

Leave some time to sip, visit, and explore these two wineries with Waterford addresses.

8 Chains North Winery. 38593 Daymont Ln., Waterford, VA (571) 439-2255; 8chainsnorth .com. Finish your day, or spend a good part of it, at this small family-owned and -operated farm winery in its pretty Waterford setting. A renovated barn houses the tasting room, which also displays art by the winery's artist-in-residence. Closed Tues and Wed.

Village Winery. 40405 Browns Ln., Waterford, VA; (540) 882-3780; villagewineryandvine yards.com. The Village Winery proves that good wine does not only come in glass bottles.

In order to create a reduced carbon footprint, the pretty winery just outside the heart of Waterford village sells 3-liter boxes of all its wines. The wines are still produced in oak barrels and the special high-grade liners inside the boxes preserve the integrity of the taste. The winery also produces a range of popular elderberry products—think syrups, teas, and nonalcoholic drinks. The tasting and barrel rooms are housed in a restored farm structure and tours of the pretty winery are given on Sat and Sun.

day trip 27

northwest

"almost heaven" west virginia:

berkeley springs, cacapon resort
state park, wv

berkeley springs

George Washington bathed here and so can you. Right over the Maryland border, this small West Virginia town's claims to historic fame are its naturally occurring mineral springs that were a favorite of the first president. All these years later, you can still soak in the warm waters at the recently renovated bathhouses at Berkeley Springs State Park. Other private spas inspired by the healing waters offer an array of treatments. Once you have de-stressed, you will be in the perfect frame of mind to soak in the rest of the town with its quaint main street, dotted with independent restaurants, wine bars, and shops.

getting there

Take I-270 North to I-70 North to US 522 South via exit 1B.

where to go

Berkeley Springs State Park. 2 S. Washington St., Berkeley Springs, WV; (304) 258-2711; berkeleyspringssp.com. The warm waters of the naturally occurring springs here brought George Washington here many times during his life, and the healing waters continue to lure visitors to this small town. Soak in the park's large Roman baths, which at the time of publication were in the process of being renovated. Massage treatments are also

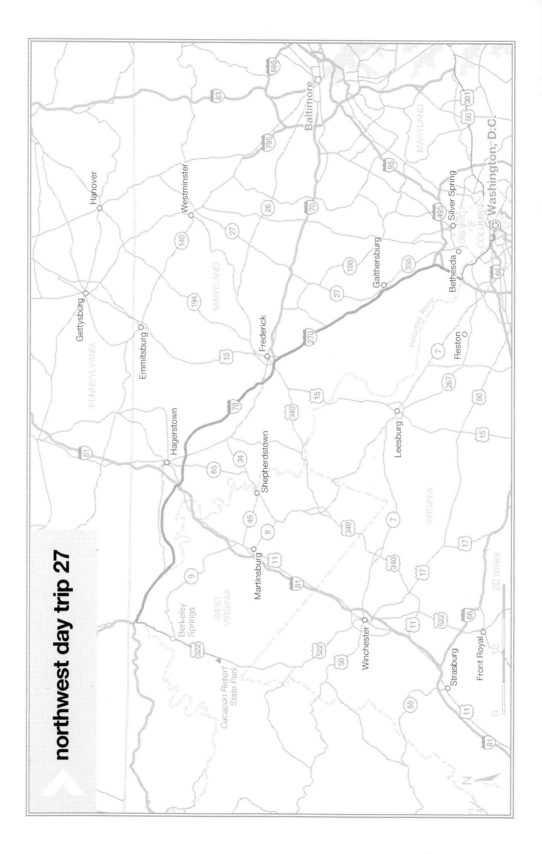

northwest day trip 27

offered at the park. Reservations are strongly encouraged and may be booked up to a month in advance.

Ice House. 138 Independence St., Berkeley Springs, WV; (304) 258-2300; macicehouse .org. Home to the Morgan Arts Council, the Ice House is a place for people to make and enjoy art of every kind, be it painting, dance, or theater.

Morgan County Observatory. 8989 Winchester Grade Rd. (Route 13), Berkeley Springs, WV; (304) 258-1013 or (540) 869-1117; nitesky.org. Gaze at the night sky through the observatory's powerful telescopes during regularly scheduled public star parties. Check the schedule for times, dates, and details.

Star Theater. 137 N. Washington St., Berkeley Springs, WV; (304) 258-1404; starwv.com/ wordpress/star-theatre. The Star movie theater is the anti-multiplex, and that is exactly its appeal. The brick 1928 movie house sports vintage red vinyl seats, striped silk wall coverings, and a fully functioning Manley hot-oil popcorn machine. The Star is known for its fresh homemade popcorn, made in the Manley before each show and topped with real melted butter. The Star shows movies at 8 p.m. on Fri, Sat, and Sun and is a stop on the Historic Theaters of West Virginia Trail.

Troubadour Lounge. 25 Troubadour Ln., Berkeley Springs, WV; (304) 258-9381; troubadourlounge.com. The Troubadour Lounge provides the opportunity to listen to country music in an authentic venue. Started by Jim McCoy, who has spent a lifetime in the business and helped Patsy Cline get on the airwaves, the Troubador hosts live music every Saturday night. There is a stage in the club inside and another one outside, along with a tiki bar and a grill in the shape of a six-shooter. Friday night features steak, and the lounge also sponsors karaoke nights while Sundays are all about NASCAR and football. The Troubadour is open Tues through Sun.

where to shop

Berkeley Springs Books. 21 N. Washington St., Berkeley Springs, WV; (304) 258-6007; berkeleyspringsbooks.com. Bibliophiles will feel right at home in this little treasure of a store, which stocks an interesting array of new and gently used books. The owners look through hundreds of thousands of volumes each year to find the perfect selection for the store.

Berkeley Springs Farmers' Market. Downtown Berkeley Springs at Route 522 and Fairfax Street, Berkeley Springs, WV; berkeleyspringsfarmersmarket.org. It's hard to imagine that this overflowing farmers' market began with just three vendors in 2002. Today local growers sell their produce, flowers, plants, and other goods to the public from 2 p.m. to 5 p.m. every Thurs in July and Aug and from 10 a.m. to 2 p.m. on Sunday from Apr through Dec. Programs like a corn on the cob–eating contest in August and pumpkin decorating in October dot the market's calendar. An added feel-good bonus: Every year participating farmers donate produce to local food pantries.

Heath Studio Gallery. 327 N. Washington St., Berkeley Springs, WV; (304) 258-9840; jheath.com. Heath Studio Gallery displays the works of painter Jonathan Heath and print-maker Jan Heath, husband-and-wife Berkeley Springs artists. The artistic couple are also the parents of Damian Heath, chef and founder of popular local restaurant Lot 21. The gallery is open Sat and Sun from 11 a.m. to 5 p.m. and by appointment.

Homeopathy Works. 33 Fairfax St., Berkeley Springs, WV; (304) 258-2541; homeopathy works.com. An authentic homeopathic pharmacy where most of the natural remedies are made by the staff. The larger company, which has an online component, goes by the name Washington Homeopathic Products.

Mountain Laurel Gallery. 1 N. Washington St., Berkeley Springs, WV; (304) 258-1919; mountainlaurelgallery.com. The works of hundreds of diverse regional artists are sold at this large two-story gallery, which spans 2,500 square feet. The owner works to create relationships with the artisans whose work he chooses to sell here. This results in a diverse selection of handcrafted jewelry, clothing, pottery, and decorative items.

where to eat

Ambrae House at Berkeley Springs. 98 N. Washington St., Berkeley Springs, WV; (304) 258-2333; ambraehouse.com. Ambrae House is a wine bar, restaurant, and bed-and-breakfast all rolled into one and housed in a renovated 1907 house. $$.

Earthdog Cafe. 398 S. Washington St., Berkeley Springs, WV; (304) 258-0500. The Earth-dog Cafe is known for its all-day breakfast menu, barbecue (diners rave about the pulled pork sandwich), and its relaxed vibe. Live-band nights, open-mike nights, and jam nights help keep the late-night crowds happy. $.

Fairfax Coffee Shop. 23 Fairfax St., Berkeley Springs, WV; (304) 258-8019; fairfaxcoffee house.com. The smell of the fresh-brewed coffee and cappuccinos lures unsuspecting passersby into this little coffee shop. Across from the town square, Fairfax uses the famous Berkeley Springs water to brew all of its beloved coffee blends.

Lot 12 Public House. 117 Warren St., Berkeley Springs, WV; (304) 258-6264; lot12.com. Lot 12 is the "it" place to dine in Berkeley Springs and is even earning the coveted culinary tourism label of "destination restaurant." Chef Damian Heath's kitchen creates what he likes to call "seasonal upscale comfort cuisine." Heath, a hometown guy, and his wife, who helps him run the restaurant, also embrace the farm-to-table concept, using many local ingredients and flavors. Lot 21 is housed in a lovely old Victorian home. Porch tables are sought-after real estate during the summer months. $$$.

Panorama at the Peak. 3299 Cacapon Rd., Berkeley Springs, WV; (304) 258-0050; panoramaatthepeak.com. Panorama at the Peak sits on an overlook that National Geographic once praised as one of the east coast's great beauties. Inside you can feast on the view and the dishes created from regional in-season ingredients. Most of the farms that supply the kitchen here are located within a 65-mile radius of the Panorama Peak Panorama Overlook. $$.

Tari's Premier Cafe and Inn. 33 N. Washington St., Berkeley Springs, WV; (304) 258-1196; tariscafe.com. Tari's three dining areas almost function as three restaurants with one shared menu. The cafe is a cozy spot decorated with West Virginia pottery and crafts while the gallery space is brighter, with its long wall of windows and museum-style lighting casting a glow on the local artwork decorating the space. Just as the name suggests, the tavern offers a pub-like setting with a nice beer list and Thursday night jam sessions with area musicians. No matter where you sit, the food is home-cooked and sometimes homegrown, featuring burgers, salads, paninis, and stews.

where to stay

The Country Inn at Berkeley Springs. 110 S. Washington St., Berkeley Springs, WV; (304) 258-1200; thecountryinnwv.com. The Country Inn sits adjacent to the town's famous spring, serves its water, and uses it at its Five Senses Spa. The rooms and common areas have a sweet hometown feel and guests celebrating special occasions or looking for something a bit more private can rent the inn's Treehouse guesthouse. There are four on-site dining options and the inn puts guests within walking distance of the downtown eateries and galleries. $$.

Gobblers Knob Guest House. 2442 Creek Rd., Berkeley Springs, WV; (304) 258-3605; virtualcities.com/vacation/wv/p/wvpa8v1.htm. And now for something entirely different . . . bedding down in Berkeley Springs in an 1820s log cabin. The two-story cabin is nestled atop a mountain at the northern end of the Shenandoah Valley and sleeps up to six people. Although the cabin has current-day amenities, such as a modern kitchen and whirlpool tub for two, its look and charm are authentically 1800s. A large wood-burning stone fireplace serves as the centerpiece to the living room, and many of the furnishings are antiques from between 1820 and 1840. Activities here include napping in the hammock, picnicking among the pine trees, stargazing, and watching the deer, turkeys, foxes, rabbits, and other critters that make regular appearances. $$$.

Highlawn Inn. 171 Market St., Berkeley Springs, WV; (304) 258-5700 or (888) 290-4163; highlawninn.com. Perched on a hilltop overlooking the town's famed springs, the Highlawn Inn offers a quintessential B&B experience down to the floral bedspreads, wraparound veranda, and home-cooked breakfast. Highlawn Inn is a quiet and homey old Victorian and a good spot to get away from it all. $$.

The Manor Inn Bed and Breakfast. 234 Fairfax St., Berkeley Springs, WV; (304) 258-1552 or (800) 974-5770; bathmanorinn.com. The last remaining example of a Second Empire Victorian mansard-roof home in Berkeley Springs, the Manor Inn is listed on the

water, water everywhere but much to sip

I will never sip water the same way again after spending two days as a judge at the Berkeley Springs International Water Tasting. On a cold February weekend I traveled to the historic town to serve as a judge for the final round of the annual competition that showcases water from around the globe. After a few training sessions, the water started pouring. Along with a panel of others, I rated almost a hundred different samples based on clarity, taste, and appearance. And here was the biggest surprise of the weekend: The waters really do taste drastically different from each another. I expected subtle, hard-to-detect distinctions between the glasses and instead tasted bold differences from glass to glass. Both municipal and bottled waters and still and sparkling varieties participate in the competition. The event ends with a much-anticipated "Water Rush" where spectators storm the stage to grab bottles of the entries that have been elaborately set up in front of the judging tables. For more information on this quirky but charming event, click on berkeleysprings.com/water/about.htm.

National Register of Historic Places. Each of the four cozy rooms has 10-foot ceilings and is individually decorated with such items as a vintage marble-top sink and an antique wardrobe. Neither smoking nor drinking alcohol are allowed at the inn. $.

cacapon resort state park

Drive 9 miles south of downtown Berkeley Springs on US 522 and you'll come to the turnoff for Cacapon Resort State Park. And I have two words of advice: Turn off! It's worth it. If you're a city slicker like me (or anyone else, really) who wants a fun, easy, and relatively inexpensive way to hang out in nature without falling off the grid or spending a ton of money on camping equipment, this is the spot for you. The park sits on about 6,000 acres of wooded land in the shadow of the wide expanse of Cacapon Mountain and offers visitors the chance to hike, golf, fish, boat, swim, and ride horses all while being in the great outdoors.

where to go

Cacapon Resort State Park. 818 Cacapon Lodge Dr., Berkeley Springs, WV; (304) 258-1022; cacaponresort.com. Cacapon reminds me of a summer camp for all ages. The park offers many different activities, and here is an overview:

Fishing. Fishing is permitted on the lake and reservoir. Park staff stock the lake with trout in the spring. The reservoir is not stocked but you do have a shot at reeling in a bass, catfish, or bluegill there. Short-term fishing licenses are sold at the lodge and are required for anyone over the age of fifteen who wants to fish in the park.

Golf. Bring your sticks or rent some at the pro shop. The course is open year-round except when the weather gets in the way. Private and group lessons can be arranged in advance with either the PGA pro or LPGA teaching professional, and golf carts and lockers can be rented for an additional fee. Log on to cacaponresort.com/golf.htm for prices, special packages, and course details.

Hiking. Mix up some extra gorp before you come to Cacapon, because with the over 20 miles of hiking trails you are likely to go through a lot of it. The trails range from easy walks to extreme. Park maps and trail guides can be picked up at the lodge. Log on to cacaponresort.com/recreation.htm for more information.

Horseback riding. (304) 258-1022, ext. 170, or (304) 258-4230 after hours. From April through November the park can be experienced on horseback. Riders must be at least ten years old and have an advance reservation with the stable. Guided trail rides, pony rides, midnight rides, lunch rides, and even overnight rides are held during riding season—it's best to call for the schedule and offerings before your visit to the park.

Nature center. Take a walk down to the nature center and introduce yourself to the park's naturalist, who can be a treasure trove of information on the flora, fauna, geology, and other natural elements at the park. The naturalist also organizes and leads a bunch of different programs, such as bird walks, night hikes, and campfires. Nature center programs take place daily from Memorial Day through Labor Day and Tues through Sat during the rest of the year. You can e-mail the naturalist through the park's website for more information.

Swimming/boating. The lake and sandy lakefront referred to as the beach are open from Memorial Day to Labor Day and are an especially big hit with kids who will likely not only love splashing around but also collecting tadpoles at water's edge. Swimming is allowed on the beach side of the lake and lifeguards are on duty every day during the summer. Paddleboats and rowboats can be rented for a nominal fee when the lake is open. Beach hours vary during the summer, so check before you put your suit on. There is also a small snack bar near the gate side of the beach.

Wobble clay (trap) shooting. Reservations: (304) 258-1022. In recent years Cacapon added trap shooting to its list of in-park activities. There is a fee for shooting (check the park's website or call ahead for details), which is done under the authority of a range supervisor. You do not need a hunting license to shoot at the range, but you do need to make a reservation.

where to stay

The park has several lodging options for those who want to hang up their hiking boots for the night.

Cacapon Lodge on the east side of the mountain has forty-eight simple but clean rooms, each with air-conditioning, private bathrooms, and televisions. The lodge itself has plenty of cozy places to curl up with a good book or admire the mountains, including a living room with a big fireplace and a large porch with rockers. Downstairs is an old-school game room complete with an air hockey table. Children younger than twelve stay free, and there is a special senior citizen discount. Rooms facing the golf course cost slightly more than those facing the mountains. The restaurant in the lodge serves standard American fare for breakfast, lunch, and dinner.

There are also three types of cabins available for rent at the park: modern, standard, and bungalows. All three are rustic but vary in degree and size. The modern cabins are built for year-round use and have kitchens, fireplaces, bathrooms with showers, heat, and air conditioning. Standard log cabins are in a more secluded part of the park and can be rented from Mar to Nov, as they have only wall-mounted heat and a/c units. From Apr to Nov small bungalows also are available. Unlike the other cabins, they do not have fireplaces but do have built-in double bunks and a small screened-in porch.

festivals & celebrations

january

Afro-American Historical Association of Fauquier County Dr. Martin Luther King Jr. Day. Celebration held at the museum in The Plains. (540) 253-7488; aahafauquier.org.

Annual Seed Exchange at Brookside Gardens. At this annual event gardeners swap seeds, tools, books, and tips. (301) 962-1400; montgomeryparks.org/brookside.

Babe Ruth's Birthday Celebration. The Babe Ruth Birthplace and Museum in Baltimore celebrates the Bambino's birthday every Jan. (410) 727-1539; baberuthmuseum.com.

february

Berkeley Springs International Water Tasting and Competition. Judges taste bottled, tap, and sparkling water entries from around the globe to name a winner of this watery contest. berkeleysprings.com/water.

Virginia Wine Expo. A huge three-day festival showcasing Virginia wine at the Greater Richmond Convention Center. virginiawineexpo.com.

march

Cunningham Falls State Park Annual Maple Syrup Demonstration. Held during two weekends in Mar, a look into how the sweet stuff gets from tree to pancake. (301) 271-7574; dnr.state.md.us/publiclands/western/cunningham.aspus/publiclands/western/cunningham falls.html.

Richmond Annual French Film Festival. A joint project of Virginia Commonwealth University and the University of Richmond. frenchfilmfestival.us.

april

Baltimore Jewish Film Festival. Movies that speak to the Jewish story and experience are shown during this annual film festival sponsored by the Jewish Community Center of Greater Baltimore. (410) 500-5909; jcc.org/gordon-center/baltimore-jewish-film-festival.

Leesburg Flower & Garden Festival. A celebration and sale of everything garden. leesburgva.gov.

Southern Maryland Celtic Festival & Highland Gathering. Held on the grounds of the Jefferson Patterson Park and Museum, the festival is the state's oldest Celtic celebration. (443) 404-7319; cssm.org.

may

Annual Richmond Greek Festival. A celebration of Greek culture with food, music, dance, crafts, and cathedral tours. (804) 358-5996; greekfestival.com.

Chestertown Tea Party. Commemorate the local merchants' revolt against the British tea tax. A reenactment, parade, concessions, and crafts highlight the day. chestertown teaparty.org.

Delaplane Strawberry Festival. A celebration of all things strawberry. delaplanestrawberry festival.com.

Old Town Warrenton Spring Festival. One-day craft festival held the third Sat of May. fauquierchamber.org/VisitorsGuide/OldTownWarrentonSpringFestival.aspx.

Wings of Fancy at the Brookside Gardens South Conservatory. Butterflies, butterflies, and more butterflies from early May to mid-Sept. (301) 962-1453; montgomeryparks.org/ brookside.

june

Annual Montgomery County Farm Tour and Harvest Sale. A chance to tour some the county's farms including many not usually open to the public. Held the fourth weekend in July. (301) 590-2823; montgomerycountymd.gov/AgServices/agfarmtour.html.

Calvert County Annual African American Family Community Day. calvertcountymd .us.

Chesapeake Beach Railway Museum's Founders Day. The museum kicks off its season every June on the date the historic Chesapeake Beach Railroad used to begin its summer service to the resort town. (410) 257-3892; cbrm.org.

Food & Wine Festival at National Harbor. An annual celebration of fine food and wine. foodandwinenh.com.

Frederick Festival of the Arts. A juried crafts and fine arts festival held the first weekend in June. (301) 662-4190; frederickartscouncil.org.

Honfest. Break out the beehive for Baltimore's annual celebration of all things "hon." honfest.net.

Lavender Farm Festival. A celebration bathed in soft, fragrant purple. (540) 272-7839; sevenoakslavenderfarm.com.

Manassas Heritage Railway Festival. A family-friendly celebration of Manassas's railway history. visitmanassas.org.

Manassas Wine & Jazz Festival. A popular annual event held on Father's Day at the Harris Pavilion in Old Town Manassas. visitmanassas.org.

Old Dominion Gas Engine & Tractor Show. Held on the grounds of the Flying Circus Airshow, this family-friendly event features antique engines, a garden tractor pull, and a petting zoo. (540) 439-8661; flyingcircusairshow.com.

Tilghman Island Seafood Festival. On the fourth Sat in June, island dwellers and visitors gather in Kronsberg Park to celebrate the food from the sea with music, crab races, a parade, and lots of seafood.

War of 1812 Reenactment at the Jefferson Patterson Park & Museum. This important battle is reenacted with precise historical accuracy. The park also holds living history demonstrations and children's activities. jefpat.org/2014-1812fairandreenactment.html.

july

Annapolis Fourth of July Celebration. An old-fashioned parade and US Naval Band concert leading up to a waterfront fireworks display. (410) 263-1183; visitannapolis.org.

Annual Fauquier County Fair. A more than fifty-year-old fair with all the traditional favorites, from livestock shows to carnival rides to lots of deep-fried food on sticks. (540) 351-6086; fauquierfair.org

Chesapeake Beach Annual July 3rd Fireworks Display. Watch the nighttime sky light up the night before Independence Day. chesapeake-beach.md.us.

Culpeper Fourth of July Classic Car & Bike Show. Come see everything from custom cars to hot rods to street rods during this annual celebration of vintage vehicles. culpeper-4thofjuly.com.

First Manassas Anniversary. Civil War encampment, battle reenactment, and other living-history programs. manassasbullrun.com.

Plein Air-Easton. The largest and most prestigious juried plein-air painting competition in the United States. pleinaireaston.com. august

Hot Air Balloon Festival. You can ride in one or just watch them float above the landscape. (540) 439-8661; flyingcircusairshow.com.

Luray Caverns Anniversary Celebration. A celebration of the discovery of the caverns, complete with fireworks and a candlelit tour of some portions of the natural landmark. luraycaverns.com.

Second Manassas Anniversary Living History & Civil War Reenactment at Manassas National Battlefield. The second major battle of the Civil War is brought to life every summer with historically accurate costumes and props. (703) 361-1339; nps.gov/mana/index.htm.

USS *Constellation* Museum Anniversary Celebration. Special tours and artillery demonstrations are held every year to mark the anniversary of the ship's first launch in 1863. historicships.org.

september

Annual Warrenton Horse Show. One of the country's oldest hunter/jumper shows, ending with a hunt. (540) 347-9442; warrentonhorseshow.com.

Baltimore Book Festival. Mt. Vernon. Author readings, children's activities, literary walking tours, live music, and much more at this urban celebration of the written word. (410) 752-8632; baltimorebookfestival.com.

Gay Pride Virginia Annual Pride Festival in Richmond. The GLBT community comes together to celebrate pride day with a colorful parade and festival. (804) 592-1093; vapride .org.

Leesburg Airshow. The skies above Leesburg come alive during the annual general aviation airshow held at the Leesburg Executive Airport. leesburgairshow.com.

Maryland Seafood Festival. A crab soup cook-off and a children's mermaid parade are among the many highlights at this annual Annapolis event. mdseafoodfestival.com.

Middleburg Classic Horse Show. An A-3 competition and one of the region's many horse shows. (540) 253-500; middleburgclassic.com.

Poolesville Day Celebration. A parade, music, livestock competition, 5K race, kids' activities, and performances are just a few of the ways this Maryland town celebrates itself every September. poolesvilleday.com.

Virginia Scottish Games and Festival. Tartan as far as the eye can see during this celebration of all things Scottish. (703) 912-1943; vascottishgames.org.

october

Annual Blackwater Refuge Open House & National Wildlife Refuge Week. A host of free special programs, hikes, and activities, including tours of areas not normally open to the public, are offered to mark National Wildlife Week. friendsofblackwater.org.

Berkeley Springs Apple Butter Festival. Annual apple butter–making contest celebrated with a parade, sidewalk sales, music, and lots of other fun small-town activities including a board and mustache contest. (800) 447-8797; berkeleysprings.com/newtbs/apple-butter-festival.

Bowie International Festival. Art, food, song, and dance from around the globe, held the first Saturday of Oct at Allen Pond Park. cityofbowie.org.

Fell's Point Fun Festival. A more than four-decade-old outdoor festival held the first full weekend in Oct.; preservationsociety.com.

Leesburg Kiwanis Halloween Parade. Candy, kids, costumes, and fun. leesburgkiwanis.org/Page/15698.

Richmond Folk Festival. Riverfront celebration of the tapestry of American culture, complete with music, dance, crafts, storytelling, and food. (804) 788-6466; richmondfolkfestival.org.

Virginia Wine Month. A month devoted to Virginia's fruit of the vine. virginiawine.org/october-wine-month.

Waterford Homes Tour & Crafts Exhibit. A juried crafts show of artisans from across the country and tours of the historic homes not often open to the public. waterfordfoundation.org/fair.

november

Chestertown Book Festival. A celebration of the authors, books, and literary traditions of Maryland's Eastern Shore. chestertownbookfestival.org.

Richmond Zine Fest. Creators of 'zines get together to trade 'zines and meet others in the indie publishing world. Sometimes held earlier in the fall season. richmondzinefest.org.

Water Fowl Festival. waterfowlfestival.org. A highlight of the Eastern Shore's year.

december

Chesapeake Beach's Brightest Beacon on the Bay. Holiday lights decorate the bay at night. chesapeake-beach.md.us.

Christmas in Middleburg. The Middleburg Hunt trots down Washington Street on horseback with their hounds following them. Also a parade, crafts, shopping, and music.

First Night Talbot. Ring in the new year with this alcohol-free family-friendly celebration that culminates with the crab dropping. easternshore.com/firstnighttalbot.

First Night Warrenton. Music, magicians, and lots of other good, clean fun to start the year right. And a traditional Grand Illumination gathering on the Old Courthouse green at midnight.

Garden in Lights at Annmarie Garden Sculpture Park. Twinkling lights create glowing sculptures in the woods. (410) 326-4640; annmariegarden.org.

Garden of Lights, Brookside Gardens. Much-loved annual holiday lights display. (301) 962-1400; montgomeryparks.org/brookside/garden_lights.shtm.

Garden of Lights, Wheaton. Displays light up the garden during the holiday season. (301) 962-1453.

Miracle on 34th Street. The row houses in Baltimore's Hampden neighborhood deck the street with enough wattage to light a small nation. Lights stay on until 11 every night except Christmas Eve, when they shine all night long. christmasstreet.com.

National Harbor's Annual Outdoor Holiday Market. Stock up on holiday gifts and decorations at this yearly outdoor market overlooking the Potomac. NationalHarbor.com.

index

INSIDERS' GUIDE®

The acclaimed travel series that has sold more than 2 million copies!

Discover: Your Travel Destination.
Your Home. Your Home-to-Be.

**To order call 800-243-0495
or visit www.Insiders.com**